The Enigma of a Violent Woman

Karla Homolka has proven to be a figure of enduring interest to the public and media for the last 20 years. However, despite the widespread Canadian and international public commentary and media frenzy that has encircled this case, Homolka herself remains an enigma to most who write about her.

In contrast to much of the contemporary discussion on this case, this book offers a comprehensive and detailed examination of the legal, public, and media understandings and explanations of Homolka's criminality. Drawing from multiple fields of study and varied bodies of critical literature, the book uses Homolka as an object lesson to interrogate some of the narratives and conceptualizations of "violent women," the problematic normative constructions of womanhood and "acceptable femininity," leniency in sentencing, taboo and disgust, and questions of remorse. The authors address broad questions about how women convicted of violence are typically constructed across four sites: the courts; the academy; the mainstream media; and public discourse.

This unique text is extremely important for feminist criminology and socio-legal studies, offering the first comprehensive academic effort to engage in dialogue about this important and fascinating case.

Jennifer M. Kilty is Associate Professor in the Department of Criminology at the University of Ottawa. Her research primarily focuses on gender and different aspects of criminalization, including the social construction of dangerous girls and women, the medicalization/psychiatrization of criminalized women, self-harming behaviours, drug use, and more recently the criminalization of HIV nondisclosure. She recently edited two books, *Within the Confines: Women and the Law in Canada* and *Demarginalizing Voices: Commitment, Emotion and Action in Qualitative Research*, both published in 2014.

Sylvie Frigon is Professor in the Department of Criminology at the University of Ottawa, where she has been teaching since 1993. She is currently Joint Chair in Women's Studies at the University of Ottawa and Carleton University and Senior Research Associate at Peterhouse, University of Cambridge. Alongside academic publications, she has published two novels, *Écorchées* (2006) on the issue of women in prison, and *Ariane et son secret* (2010) on a little girl's quest for her imprisoned mother. She has also worked with Claire Jenny, choreographer and director of the Parisian dance company Point Virgule, with whom she published a book on dance in prison (2009). She is currently working on her third novel funded by the Ontario Arts Council and works in partnership with Le Grands Ballets Canadiens of Montreal's Centre for Dance Therapy.

"The spectre of Karla Homolka has invaded our understandings of criminalized women. By turning the gaze away from Homolka to interrogate our cultural fixation with her, Kilty and Frigon adeptly reveal the factors that coalesced to produce this enigmatic figure, enjoining us to rethink her as the paradigmatic Criminalized Woman."

Elizabeth Comack, *University of Manitoba, Canada*

"Exploring narratives of violence, remorse, and ideal victims/offenders, Kilty and Frigon deconstruct notions of femininity, whiteness, class, and taboo in relation to the cultural preoccupation with Karla Homolka. This courageous feminist examination shifts the gaze to deliver a nuanced understanding of Homolka as enigmatic subject who both disgusts and fascinates."

Sheri Fabian, *Simon Fraser University, Canada*

"This book offers a commanding contribution to feminist, criminological and media studies and brings a much needed alternative and more holistic reading to the exceptional case of Karla Homolka. By offering an innovative and impressively thorough account of media, judicial, and legal depictions of Canada's most notorious criminalized woman, Kilty and Frigon offer an eye-opening and thought-provoking analysis of the more significant intersections of race, class, hetero-patriarchal culture, broken taboos, and issues of remorse which have conjoined to shed, on Karla Homolka, a quasi-permanent evil aura. The book's rigorous academic undertaking will go far in changing traditional criminological, judicial, and media interpretations of women who commit acts of violence. This important book is a valuable and most welcome addition to criminological and gender studies."

Joane Martel, *Laval University, Canada*

The Enigma of a Violent Woman

A Critical Examination of the Case of Karla Homolka

Jennifer M. Kilty and Sylvie Frigon

Routledge
Taylor & Francis Group
LONDON AND NEW YORK

First published 2016
by Routledge
2 Park Square, Milton Park, Abingdon, Oxon OX14 4RN

and by Routledge
711 Third Avenue, New York, NY 10017

Routledge is an imprint of the Taylor and Francis Group, an informa business

British Library Cataloguing in Publication Data
A catalogue record for this book is available from the British Library

Library of Congress Cataloging-in-Publication Data
Names: Kilty, Jennifer M., 1978– author. | Frigon, Sylvie, author.
Title: The enigma of a violent woman : a critical examination of the case of Karla Homolka / by Jennifer M. Kilty and Sylvie Frigon.
Description: Farnham, Surrey, UK ; Burlington, VT : Ashgate, [2016] | Includes bibliographical references and index.
Identifiers: LCCN 2015038017 | ISBN 9781472471956 (hardback : alk. paper) | ISBN 9781472471963 (ebook) | ISBN 9781472471970 (epub)
Subjects: LCSH: Homolka, Karla. | Women serial murderers—Canada—Case studies. | Violence in women—Canada—Case studies. | Murder—Canada—Case studies.
Classification: LCC HV6517 K56 2016 | DDC 364.152/32092—dc23
LC record available at http://lccn.loc.gov/2015038017

ISBN: 978-1-4724-7195-6 (hbk)
ISBN: 978-1-315-61612-4 (ebk)

Typeset in Bembo
by Apex CoVantage, LLC

MIX
Paper from responsible sources
FSC
www.fsc.org
FSC® C013985

Printed in the United Kingdom
by Henry Ling Limited

Contents

Illustrations

Figures

Tables

Preface

More than 20 years have passed since the image of Karla Homolka's bruised "raccoon eyes" appeared on the cover page of *The Ottawa Sun* (1993). The famous photograph was taken by the St Catharines General Hospital in December of 1992 and was released to the public prior to Homolka's 1993 trial. The photograph shows long, dark bruises under her eyes, the result of a severe head injury, called a contra-coup, which results when a moving object impacts the head in a stationary position. In Homolka's case, the injury was due to then husband Paul Bernardo beating her on the back of the head with a police style metal flashlight. Initially, the forensic evidence clearly marked and positioned Ms Homolka as a victim of serious intimate partner violence. However, the more shocking revelations came when it was established that not only was Ms Homolka victimized by Mr Bernardo, but that she had also participated in his efforts to sexually victimize and kill other young women. It is at this juncture of victim/victimizer that the collective sense of unease with Ms Homolka's character was sown; this apparent crisis in her identity is also the epicentre of our interest in critically analysing the emerging and shifting socio-legal and media narratives about her character or personhood, as well as the different social reactions to those narratives.

Rather than posting her as either singularly victim or victimizer, we conceptualize Homolka as simultaneously *in danger* and *dangerous*, character constructions that are inexorably linked rather than mutually exclusive. Much of the media coverage and the sparse extant academic literature emphasize Homolka's *dangerousness* with little consideration for the ways in which her victimhood is inherently connected to her acts of violence. This is where we modestly hope to provide a more complex, nuanced, and critical reading of different aspects of Homolka's role in this case. Our intent is not to question her guilt or responsibility; it is, rather, to contextualize her actions – a controversial journey we embarked upon delicately, slowly, and cautiously. In order to undertake this task rigorously, we surrounded ourselves with fact-finding evidence strategies. We secured the court transcripts from Homolka's 1993 plea and sentencing hearing and from her 17-day testimony and cross-examination as the Crown counsel's star witness in Paul Bernardo's 1995 trial and conducted a systematic review of every news media article published in the Canadian Newsstand database that referenced Homolka in some way.

The original impetus to conduct a case study of Karla Homolka emerged from the first author's Master of Arts thesis, which was supervised by the second author. Our joint interest in this case continued over the years, long after the completion of the thesis. For us, this book is the result of years of struggle and disquiet about a case that simultaneously captivated and repulsed the Canadian public. Despite the publication ban that prevented Canadian media coverage of the details of Ms Homolka's 1993 plea bargain, trial, and sentencing hearing, public knowledge of the case was informed by the American news media, which covered the case quite intensely (Crosbie 1997). As a popular trial, the case came to be recognized internationally and the shocking details created international reverberations that engendered fear about a new breed of violent woman (Barron and Lacombe 2005; Comack 2014; Comack and Brickey 2007; Pearson 1997). Closer to home, as Canadian authors, we struggled – and continue to struggle – with writing about a case that caused the families so much pain and feared that writing this book would add to their suffering, which we do not want to do. As feminist criminologists we were troubled by what we read and heard about the case and Ms Homolka specifically. For example, we have colleagues that conduct critical, progressive, and liberal-minded research on homicide, terrorism, and other acts of serious violence, whose reactions toward Ms Homolka oftentimes uncritically adopted media tropes that were especially condemning. This surprised us. We jointly and separately presented our work on this case at a number of different conferences – at the Canadian Social Sciences and Humanities Congress (2003), the Women's World Conference (2009), and at Simon Fraser University (2004), Duke University (September 2011), and the University of Cambridge (October 2011) – these experiences confirmed just how entrenched the media tropes are in our collective narrative about Homolka's character and participation in these crimes. These moments reinforced our unease but also the need to address this case in a critical fashion. It became clear that we needed to attend to the complexities of this case and how it continues to hold meaning that affects the ways in which we interpret and politically respond to women who commit violence. For an obvious political example, despite Homolka clearly presenting an exceptional case and notwithstanding the fact that she would likely never be granted a pardon given the seriousness and high-profile nature of her crimes, the federal conservative government used her as an example to justify making changes to the pardon process that make it much more costly and difficult to receive.

On a cultural level, it is worth mentioning that the Hollywood film *Karla* (2006), was withdrawn from the 2005 Montreal International film festival and there was a public outcry in Ontario to ban showing the film in regular theatres. In fact, then province of Ontario Premier, Dalton McGuinty, openly called for the public to boycott the film; in the end, theatres in the city of St Catharines, the site of the crimes, refused to show the film. In contrast, Charlize Theron won an Academy Award in 2003 for her nuanced portrayal of serial killer Aileen Wuornos in the film *Monster* as having murdered her victims out of self-defence following an initial experience of sexual assault. While Wuornos killed more people than Homolka and her victims were adult men who were buying her sexual services, Homolka's were white teenage girls. Moreover, the cases had very different outcomes; Homolka received a 12-year sentence while Wuornos was executed by the state of Florida. Our comparison here highlights the political nature of the efforts to ban *Karla* and the differential cultural responses to these two films. Part of our interest in examining Homolka resides in how and why this particular case hit such a nerve with the Canadian public and in the cultural and political responses we have witnessed in relation to Homolka and to this case. While Canadian media are often heralded as less sensational than that of our American counterpart (Taras 2001; Dowler et al. 2006), Karla Homolka's characterization in the relentless media coverage awarded to her contraindicates this. Even 7 years after her successful release from prison in July 2005, CTV journalist Paula Todd tracked Homolka down in Guadeloupe and produced an E-book entitled, *Finding Karla: How I Tracked Down an Elusive Serial Child Killer and Discovered a Mother of Three* (2012).

Although we spoke about it for years, we first began to conceptualize this book in 2008 after the first author completed her doctorate. Since that time, this book project has proved difficult to prioritize; we would often work on it enthusiastically for a few months, only to set it aside for lengthy periods of time. Nevertheless, while each of us allowed other endeavours to take priority, like so many journalists we always seemed to return to talking and thinking about Karla Homolka. Although fraught with potential pitfalls, somehow we were still determined to write this book. Time and hindsight, however, can be quite useful in academic work. It has been ten years since Karla Homolka was released from federal custody and despite the public and government's worst fears she has not been charged with any new offences and does not appear to pose the dangerous threats many believed she continued to pose. We felt uncomfortable with the most common explanations that offered simplistic narratives that emphasized her "violent nature" with little thought accorded to the context within which she participated in these acts of violence or to Paul Bernardo's main role in the crimes. It was as though it was more acceptable that he committed rape and murder because we expect men to be violent. Most often, women are victims and not perpetrators of violence, but Karla Homolka straddled the line between these two positions. Having said this, and while we do not wish to minimize Ms Homolka's participation in these heinous crimes, we also cannot turn a blind eye to the ways in which her experiences of victimization effectively fostered feelings of disempowerment that constrained her ability to resist her abusive husband's demands. Although we have addressed similar difficult issues in other publications (Kilty, 2010; Kilty and Frigon 2006; Frigon 2003, 2006), throughout our struggles to write this book we often paused to think about and reflect upon what each chapter could contribute to the extant literature on women and violence and why these discussions with respect to such a controversial figure are necessary. It is our hope that we are able to shed light on how certain criminal cases come to occupy such prominent spaces in media and broader culture and how one-dimensional and often sensational tropes come to narrate our interpretations of women who commit acts of violence.

Jennifer M. Kilty and Sylvie Frigon
December 2014

Acknowledgements

Writing this book has been a very long undertaking, largely because of our apprehension that the focus and content of the book could be upsetting to some; it is certainly not our intention to cause any further distress to the victims' families. It is our hope that the rigorous academic undertaking documented in this book helps to shed light on the problematic gendered characterizations of women who commit violence and the ways in which these historical tropes find their way not only into contemporary news media coverage but also into juridical narratives and discourses.

We would also like to express our thanks and gratitude to the four graduate students that assisted us on this project in a number of different ways over the years. Our sincerest thanks to Adina Ilea, Haley Crooks, Erin Dej, and Laura Shantz who helped us to collect and organize the news media data, conduct literature reviews, format the manuscript and to discuss different analytic constructs as we were applying and using them. You are each talented emerging scholars and your assistance has made our research and writing process much more enjoyable and certainly more manageable.

Finally, we want to offer our thanks to the Ashgate team for their support of what some publishers might consider a controversial text. You ensured us a smooth publishing process, for which we are very grateful.

1 Introduction

For more than 20 years Canadians have been fascinated with and often disgusted by the enigma that is Karla Homolka. Her infamy stems from her participation in the abduction, sexual assault, and murder of three young women, including the accidental death of her younger sister Tammy. There are many different accounts of the tragic story of Karla Homolka and Paul Bernardo, including those that are detailed in the criminal court transcripts, press archives, true crime novels, academic texts, a comic book (*Killer Karla*) a Hollywood major motion picture (*Karla*), and dramatic and infotainment television shows featuring episodes based on case details that were "ripped from the headlines." To varying degrees, all of these representations search for meaning in what can only be understood as meaningless violence through attempts to explain Homolka's and Bernardo's actions. Ultimately, these popular characterizations monsterize, psychologize, and infantilize Homolka (Morrissey 2003) and our inability to reach a plausible explanation for her participation in these acts of sexualized violence culminates in her construction as "morally vacuous" (McGillivray 1998) and what we identify as a lingering enigma. She is a shadow that we cannot pin down. It is important to note, however, that the gaze in all of these texts, narratives, and visual representations is unidirectional, primarily focused on Karla Homolka and her torrid but volatile relationship with Paul Bernardo, while Bernardo is rarely at the centre of the gaze. As but another violent man, Bernardo is less fascinating, less atypical; this is partly due to the fact that he received a life sentence and was declared a dangerous offender, which the media interpreted as a more just sentence than Homolka's plea agreement. While Homolka remains central to our analyses, in this book we attempt to turn our analytic gaze outward and back onto the media, the courts, and the public in order to examine the intense cultural fascination with this case and with her. In this way, we somewhat decentre Homolka from our gaze. Rather than trying to explain the inexplicability of her participation in a series of horrific sexual assaults and homicides, we instead situate Homolka as an object lesson in order to examine the prolonged and intense social interest with her role in this crime drama.

For those readers who are unfamiliar with this case, we begin by providing an overview of the main facts and details before engaging in a brief discussion of agency, which is a central concern to those authors, both scholarly and journalist, who have written about Homolka and her involvement in this case. To better contextualize the analyses found in the proceeding chapters, we then consider the importance of the visual (via a discussion of the videotape evidence) in fixing the public's gaze concretely on Homolka.

The Facts of the Case

Those around her described Karla Homolka as "a regular kid" (Appleby 1993, A1) who displayed "nothing outstanding" (Brazao 1993, B2) before the details of her crimes came to light. She met Paul Bernardo while attending a veterinary conference in Scarborough, Ontario, a suburb of Toronto, in October 1987. Homolka was only 17 at the time; she lived with her parents and two sisters in St Catharines, Ontario, while attending high school and working part-time at a pet store. Bernardo was 23 and working as a book-keeper having just graduated with a degree in accounting from the University of Toronto. Unbeknownst to Homolka, Bernardo had already perpetrated a series of sexual assaults and attempted sexual assaults in Scarborough that led to his dubbing as "The Scarborough Rapist." Between 1987–90 Bernardo raped or sexually assaulted upwards of 18 women and lingering speculation remains about whether there are other victims (Campbell 1996). The police first became aware of Bernardo as a potential suspect in these rape cases as early as June 1990 when they received two calls identifying him as the suspect in the widely publicized composite drawing generated from victim descriptions, including one call from the wife of Bernardo's close friend. Bernardo was interviewed by police in November 1990 and voluntarily gave samples for forensic testing, although because the authorities did not prioritize him as a suspect given his social characteristics (that is, educated, white, middle class) and confident congenial presentation of self, it took 26 months – during which time he and Homolka committed their crimes – before the Toronto police were informed that Bernardo's DNA matched that of the Scarborough Rapist and for him to be placed under 24-hour surveillance (Williams 2004).

The pair quickly formed an intimate relationship and Homolka was described as being "'wildly' in love with her Toronto beau" (Brazao 1993, B2); the two became engaged on 24 December 1989. Official medical and psychiatric reports presented during Homolka's sentencing hearing and throughout Bernardo's criminal trial documented that the power dynamics that structured the couple's relationship were unequal and marred by intimate partner violence. The couple's 6-year age difference contributed to their unequal power relations and to Bernardo's control of Homolka, and, over time, he increasingly exerted violent physical, sexual, and emotional abuse against her and sought to control her every action. The FBI would later suggest that Homolka was a compliant victim of Bernardo, who they characterized as a sexual sadist (Galligan 1996).

Over the course of their relationship, Bernardo also became obsessed with Karla's younger sister, Tammy. His desires extended well beyond mere interest; he spied on Tammy, masturbated in her room while she slept and asked Karla to assist him in sexually assaulting her. Homolka and Bernardo first attempted to sexually assault Tammy in July 1990 after feeding her spaghetti laced with Valium; however, Tammy began to regain consciousness during the assault and the couple aborted their plans. On 23 December 1990 following a family Christmas party at the Homolka family home, the couple drugged Tammy with the anaesthetic halothane that Karla had stolen from the veterinary clinic where she worked. Bernardo and Homolka filmed their sexual assault against Tammy until they realized she had aspirated and choked on her own vomit. Despite a large and very visible chemical burn on Tammy's cheek and the suspicious actions of both Karla and Paul, which included cleaning the basement and laundering the sheets on which Tammy had lain during the sexual assault while waiting for the ambulance to arrive, Tammy's death was ruled accidental.[1] Shortly after Tammy Homolka's death, Paul Bernardo and Karla Homolka rented a large cape cod style bungalow home in Port Dalhousie, an upscale suburb of St Catharines that rests on the shores of Lake Ontario.

In June 1991, Homolka brought home 15-year-old "Jane Doe" after spending the day with her; Homolka met Doe at the local pet store where she worked in 1989 and the two became friends. The couple gave Doe an alcoholic drink laced with the sedative Halcion, which Homolka stole from her employer at the veterinary clinic; after Doe lost consciousness they sexually assaulted her, again filming the attack. The next morning, Jane Doe awoke feeling nauseated and thought that she was suffering from a hangover; she had no memory of the sexual assault. Two months later, and in the same fashion, the couple perpetrated a second sexual assault against Doe.

Shortly after the first attack on Jane Doe, Bernardo kidnapped Leslie Mahaffy from her backyard on 15 June 1991. The couple kept Mahaffy alive for just over 24 hours, during which time they repeatedly sexually assaulted her, again recording the events with their home video camera. On 16 June Paul Bernardo strangled Leslie Mahaffy to death with a black electrical cord. The couple stored Mahaffy's body in the root cellar of their home in order to host the Homolka family for a father's day dinner on the evening of 16 June 1991. The following day, Paul Bernardo dismembered Mahaffy's body and encased her body parts in a series of concrete blocks. When Homolka returned home from work that day, she assisted Bernardo in disposing the concrete blocks and the tools he used to dismember Mahaffy's body in nearby Lake Gibson. In a strange twist of fate, Paul Bernardo and Karla Homolka were married on the day that Mahaffy's body was discovered. While Bernardo abducted Mahaffy on his own, Homolka assisted him in kidnapping Kristen French from a church parking lot on 16 April 1992. The couple posed as tourists asking for directions in order to get French to approach their car. As with Mahaffy, the couple took the girl back to their home and proceeded to sexually assault her while filming the events. Bernardo strangled Kristen French to death with the same black electrical cord he used to kill Leslie Mahaffy after holding her captive for 3 days so that the couple could attend Easter dinner with Homolka's family.

Following the discovery of Kristen French's body less than a kilometre from Leslie Mahaffy's gravesite, the Niagara and Halton Regional Police Forces created the Green Ribbon Task Force (GRTF) in a collaborative effort to find the killer. Despite the joint cooperation of these two regional police forces, "the communication between GRT[F] and the Metro [Toronto] Service [who were investigating Bernardo for his potential involvement in the Scarborough rapes], about Bernardo was inadequate. There was no case management information system to ensure the effective communication of suspect information" (Campbell 1996, 161). In addition to the lack of open communication and information sharing, the information management systems that were available at the time were inadequate in terms of managing the volume of public response and investigatory information uncovered, meaning there was no way of assembling the information pertaining to a potential suspect. In his formal review of the Bernardo Investigation, Justice Archie Campbell (1996, 161) concluded that "Metro and the GRT[F] might as well have been working in different countries so far as Bernardo was concerned, and Bernardo slipped through the net."

On 27 December 1992, Paul Bernardo severely beat Karla Homolka with a large metal flashlight. She was hospitalized because of her injuries, which at the time she claimed were the result of an auto accident. Upon returning to work in January 1993, Homolka's co-workers alerted her family to her condition and her parents insisted she leave Bernardo. When she was collecting her belongings Homolka unsuccessfully searched for the videotapes of the sexual assaults, which she knew Bernardo moved between different secret caches around the house. Homolka left her husband and following her parents' advice went to stay with her aunt and uncle in Brampton, Ontario, in order to create geographic distance between she and Bernardo. This coincided with the police learning of Bernardo's forensic match to the Scarborough rapes 1 month later.

On 11 February 1993 Homolka retained a lawyer and began the process of making a deal to share information about Bernardo with the police, including disclosure about the existence and content of the videotaped evidence, in exchange for a plea agreement and lesser sentence. The police arrested Bernardo in his home on 17 February 1993. Because the videotapes of the crimes were not recovered during the lengthy police search of the couple's home, the police and Crown had a weak forensic case against Bernardo and needed Homolka's testimony to ensure a conviction. While Crown counsel rejected awarding Homolka full immunity for her role in the crimes in exchange for her testimony against Bernardo, eventually they struck a plea agreement. Plea-bargaining is widely practiced in Canada and is a form of negotiation between a person charged with an offence and a crown prosecutor. It most often takes place before the trial, may take several forms and serves two purposes. First, it increases the certainty of the outcome via a guilty plea. Second, plea-bargaining also saves valuable court time, expense and the inconvenience of a criminal trial. Crown prosecutors felt they needed Karla Homolka to testify against Paul Bernardo in order to secure a conviction against him and agreed to exchange her testimony and cooperation with the police for a 12-year sentence. When this "deal" was made public it sparked media and public uproar. Although she had disclosed the existence of the videotapes of the sexual assaults, the police did not find them in their searches of the home; after the police search of the home ended, Bernardo instructed his then lawyer, Ken Murray, to secure them. Murray retrieved the videotapes, which were hidden in the bathroom ceiling behind the light fixture, and withheld them for 17 months during which time Homolka's plea bargain was finalized. When Murray finally turned the videotapes over to the police, many questioned the soundness of Homolka's "sweetheart deal" and the Ontario provincial government ordered a formal inquiry to investigate the validity of the plea agreement, which was conducted by the Honourable Justice P. Galligan (1996). While Galligan concluded that at the time it was made the plea agreement was necessary to ensure a conviction against Bernardo, had Ken Murray not withheld the videotapes there would have been no need to make the deal. Homolka disclosed the details of her involvement in the sexual assaults and homicides and gave testimony as a witness for the Crown at Paul Bernardo's trial in exchange for pleading guilty to the two murders. She received a reduced sentence controversially described as 5 years for each Mahaffy and French and 2 years for her sister Tammy Homolka, for a total of 12 years. Once the deal was formalized, a preliminary hearing was ordered at which time Homolka pled guilty.

In June 1993, Karla Homolka pleaded guilty to two counts of manslaughter for the deaths of Leslie Mahaffy and Kristen French. Her confession and the details of the case were presented at this time, but a strict publication ban was enacted to ensure that Bernardo would receive a fair trial. Subsequently, while unofficial news and rumours began to circulate about the case,[2] few of the details could legally be reported, which led to a furor among the press who felt that the 2-year wait until Bernardo's trial was too long for such revelations to remain secret. Homolka was sentenced to 12 years in prison and was transferred to the Kingston Prison for Women to begin serving her time. She would spend 2 years in prison before being called to testify at Bernardo's trial.

Paul Bernardo's trial began in the summer of 1995 in the metro Toronto courthouse. The trial lasted nearly 4 months and drew mass interest from both Canadian and American media; there were daily queues for seats in the courtroom, as well as an unprecedented interest in the case by journalists, evidenced by the deluge of reporting produced throughout the duration of the trial. Once the trial began, the publication ban on Homolka's preliminary hearing was lifted. While Crown counsel and police investigators constructed Homolka as a victim early on, the videotapes of the crimes and her courtroom performance drastically changed Homolka's public image, leading many to argue that she was at least as equally guilty as Bernardo and some reporters went so far as to suggest that she was the mastermind behind the crimes. On 1 September 1995 Paul Bernardo was convicted of two counts of first-degree murder and two counts of aggravated sexual assault. He was sentenced to life imprisonment and was later declared a dangerous offender, meaning the Correctional Service Canada can imprison him for an indeterminate period of time.

Although both Homolka and Bernardo were convicted in the early to mid-1990s, media interest in the couple and in the case continues to this day. Over the years, details of Homolka's time in prison were routinely featured in news stories accompanied by photographs showing her in her cell, blowing out candles on a birthday cake and spending time with fellow prisoners. On 4 July 2005, Karla Homolka was released from prison, having served her 12-year sentence to warrant expiry – a rarity in Canadian corrections, where most prisoners are released on parole at two-thirds of their sentence. Initially, the provincial governments of Quebec (where she was incarcerated) and Ontario (where the crimes took place and she was tried and convicted) sought to impose a section s. 810.2 order of the *Canadian Criminal Code*, which allows the court to impose restrictions on a warrant expiry offender still considered to be a potential danger to the public. While the order was initially granted, it was overturned on appeal shortly after her release.

After the section 810.2 order was rescinded, Karla Homolka slowly faded from media headlines. Reporters continued to attempt to track her whereabouts and notify the public of her presence; however, these reports grew less frequent in the intervening years. The most recent reports indicate that Homolka remarried and changed her name, gave birth to and became the mother to three children, and moved to Guadeloupe with her family (Todd 2012).

Questions of Agency

In her text, *When Women Kill: Questions of Agency and Subjectivity*, Belinda Morrissey (2003) examines Karla Homolka's multiple and at times contradictory subjectivities as exemplified in her own narratives and performatives, as well as those proposed about her by mainstream and feminist legal and media institutional discourses. Morrissey (2003) focuses the thrust of her argument on Homolka's agency and responsibility in perpetrating sexual violence against four young women; her aim being to problematize the reliance on victimism discourses to explain women's violence at the expense of retaining a sense of agency for women who act violently. While her argument that we must avoid denying that women can willingly and with purpose and intent act violently is important, at times her position may also be read as contributing to the negation of the impact that victimization can have on the decisions women living in abusive relationships make – including their participation in perpetrating violence against others.

While she does not deny that Homolka experienced abuse, she does appear to question the duration and extent to which Bernardo beat Homolka – namely whether the abuse was ongoing throughout the duration of the relationship or if it came only at the end and therefore after they had committed the sexual assaults and murders and when Homolka finally left her husband. Despite physical and psychiatric forensic evidence supporting Homolka's claims of ongoing abuse over a long period of time (R. v. K. Bernardo 1993; R. v. P. Bernardo 1995), Morrissey's minimization of the effects of victimization on Homolka situates her analytic point of entry as beginning from the position that Homolka lied about or exaggerated the abuse she experienced in order to cast doubt on her agency and responsibility. This position effectively constructs Homolka as always already manipulative, which is a typical stock narrative about women who commit violence. It also denies the value in narrative standpointism that feminists have argued is central to understanding women's experiential and material realties (Harding 1986, 2004). While Morrissey (2003) provides evidence for her interpretation, namely the videotapes of the sexual assaults and of the couple's private sex life – in particular the tape the media dubbed the "fireside chat"[3] – and the multiple love letters Homolka wrote to Bernardo throughout their relationship, she also acknowledges that hers is but one reading of Homolka's multiple subjectivities. We suggest that this same evidence can be read differently. We will return to this point and to a more detailed discussion of the videotapes shortly.

In this vein, Morrissey allies herself with the narratives offered by more conservative journalists and suggests that Homolka exaggerated her victimhood and even "*managed to convince* no fewer than three court-appointed psychiatrists that she had been regularly and severely beaten, although they were unable to agree on whether she had developed BWS"[4] (Morrissey 2003, 150) [our emphasis]. Here we sense Morrissey's disbelief in Homolka's performative of the battered wife at the same time that we are able to sense her belief that Homolka is both cunning and highly manipulative – to the point that she would be able to con three independent psychiatrists. Inherent in Morrissey's position is the argument that because of the societal inability to believe that women can be intentionally violent, even psy-experts are likely to lend their views in favour of an explanation of Homolka's involvement that is rooted in her victimization. We suggest that this conceptualization is too extreme in that it posts agency and victimism as polar opposites, effectively creating a strict dichotomy of either having full agency and control or being without. Instead, we argue that it is a more nuanced approach to conceptualize agency as existing along a continuum that recognizes the potentiality for multiple sites of both constraint and enablement.

In her efforts to stress the inherent problems associated with resorting to a victim discourse to explain women's involvement in perpetrating violence, Morrissey, to our detriment, focuses her analysis exclusively on Homolka despite the fact that Homolka acted in partnership with her abusive husband, Paul Bernardo. To examine Homolka's participation in the sexual assaults and homicides without contextualizing her life at that time and the victimization she experienced at Bernardo's hand overemphasizes her agency, dangerousness and Otherness. For example, Morrissey describes Homolka as completely denying her agency and thus responsibility for her role in the crimes; she effectively characterizes Homolka not only as a sadist, but also as the catalyst for Bernardo's own sadism:

> Karla's complete inability to take responsibility for *any* of her actions during the entire five-year period of her relationship with Paul Bernardo was the sticking point for many watching proceedings. For Karla denied her agency for every act she undertook; ranging from the innocuous, such as her

> decision to send her partner hundreds of sexy cards and letters throughout this time, to the sinister, for example her theft from her workplace of the drugs necessary for the rapes of her sister and her sister's friend,[5] and her determination not to free Kristen French or to help Leslie Mahaffy when she had the chance (150–1). . . .Without a submissive woman, as the argument also ran in Homolka's case, a sadistic man would never act, but together the two may become a lethal pair.
>
> (152)

Morrissey draws on Freud's discussion of the beating fantasy to further her argument that Homolka is in fact, and equal to Bernardo, a sadist. In doing so, Morrissey contends that the relationship was not one of master and slave as Homolka would have us believe, but the "the union of two sadists, driving each other on, searching for the same unfullfillable desire" (152):

> To act in concert so effectively, as both these couples did, insists upon mutual need. For, other than following slavishly the wishes of the beloved, what are the pleasures for the masochist in aiding their partners to destroy young girls they, themselves, have also raped and violated? Could not the pleasure be more sadistic in origin, based on *both* partners' desire to dominate, to violate and, finally to possess utterly?[6]
>
> (Morrissey 2003, 152)

This interpretation contributes to the production of Homolka as a mythical figure of evil and to the process of monsterization Morrissey claims is uncritical and problematic for our cultural understanding of Homolka and other women who commit similar acts of violence. By stressing only Homolka's agency (something we do not deny), she actually reconstructs Bernardo and Homolka as equally sadistic, equally agentic and thus equally responsible for the sexual assaults and murders. The implications of this position are more far reaching than designating Homolka to be a sadist; Freud's beating fantasy, which suggests a characteristic or personality transformation that results from looking on while others are harmed to enjoying the pain and suffering to which others are subject at your hand. If we are to accept this position, we must also reject Homolka's narrative of victimization as little more than a callous attempt to recuperate her soiled legal and public image. This argument, in effect, fully rejects Homolka's standpoint, narrative and experiences as nothing but performances in the dramaturgical or theatrical sense. Consequently, Homolka as a subject is rendered unknowable – an elusive enigma; she is recast here as hyper-fluid in her construction and presentation of self, "as a truly blank canvass, a tabula rasa waiting to be written into being by her next lover" (Morrissey 2003, 151).

While Morrissey works to disrupt the effects of both mainstream and feminist legal and media discourses, which she argues are built on stock stories about the nature of women and women's criminality under hetero-patriarchy (for example evil witch, man-hating lesbian, black widow, femme fatale and so on), her characterization of Homolka casts her as the fully agentic sadist who would otherwise remain an unknowable enigmatic subject. We suggest that this characterization functions as a stock story in and of itself. We accept Morrissey's (2003) argument that our readings of the legal, media and other cultural conceptualizations of Homolka are interpretations of the multiple subjectivities she expressed. However, the goal of this book is not to provide an alternative reading of Homolka *per se*, and the different readings offered in this text do not attempt to "explain" Homolka's actions, or necessarily to draw conclusions about why she participated in these acts of sexual violence. Rather, this book attempts to shed light on why we as a culture remain so incredibly fascinated by Karla Homolka. The object of our analysis is therefore the series of characterizations of Homolka offered in newspaper reporting, court transcripts and judicial decisions. What is it about these characterizations of Homolka that the public is captivated and even "obsessed" enough to readily consume every detail, story and sound bite that is published about her?

Turning the analytic gaze outward makes us (rather than Homolka alone) the object of critical analysis and interpretation. To help set the stage for the discussions offered in the following chapters, in the next two sections we discuss the now infamous videotape evidence and the role of voyeurism in Homolka's cultural casting as an enigmatic character. We suggest that the videotape evidence of the sexual assaults and of Bernardo and Homolka's personal sex life was the lynchpin that began to unravel acceptance of Homolka's narrative of victimization and that fixed our gaze on Homolka (and away from Bernardo) as always already duplicitous.

Sedimenting our Gaze: The Videotape Evidence

> And they all have the same complaint: They cannot draw Karla. Intent on capturing not just the physiological, but some suggestion of character, they valiantly put pen or pencil or chalk to blank sheet of paper, each day hoping to convey the essence of the person in the witness stand. But she eludes them. There are no distinguishing qualities, they say, no shadings of personality etched on her delicate, symmetrical features, no detail of emotional permutation, no hint of the internal life on the external countenance. It is as if Karla Homolka is beyond definition or description or the one-dimensional depiction of an illustrator. If not for the infamous videotapes and the dozens of photographs already submitted into evidence, one might actually suspect that Homolka – like the poltergeists who spook haunted houses – cannot be arrested on film. Most significantly, this convicted killer, this self-admitted sexual predator – a woman who assaulted not just strangers but her own youngest sister – does not wear her crimes like a stigmata. Her transgressions do not stain her skin, like the ugly markings on Tammy Homolka's slack, dead face. She speaks, in places, of her shame and her regret over the deaths of Tammy, Leslie Mahaffy, Kristen French. Just as she did again yesterday, when revisiting the scheming and plotting which led to the sexual assault on Tammy.
>
> (Di Manno 6 July 1995, A9)

This quote illustrates our cultural reliance on the visual to make sense of crime and the criminal subject, as well as how that subject is perceived to be feeling; for example, it makes reference to the difficulty photographers and court-room artists had in depicting "shadings of [Homolka's] personality" and her expressions of shame and regret. Our primary reliance on the visual as a way to orient us in the social world is also demonstrated by the growth in surveillance studies. In fact, Foucault's (1977) early conceptualization of the prison as a panoptic structure spurred an entire field of critical surveillance, security, prison and governance studies. His work redefined spaces as being "impregnated with disciplinary practices" and as being "shaped and changed by social power relationships" (Koskela 2000, 251). Moreover, risk society theorists suggest that our ability to survey others and thus to engage in a kind of voyeurism has become a key component of neoliberal citizenship (Frosh 2001). While the purpose of surveillance cameras in public spaces is to exercise the power of the gaze so as to monitor and control behaviour and to secure the space, Bernardo and Homolka used video cameras to document their sexual assaults on their four victims as well as their own sex life. At first glance, the difference between these two uses of video imagery, and thus of the gaze, appears obvious – one uses the gaze to try to govern and protect its object (the public citizenry); the other uses the gaze to pornographize sexual violence against its object. However, both imply that the power relationships that shape video imagery in particular spaces reduce social communication to the visual (Koskela 2000, 254).

Surveillance is thought to protect the public who remain the object of the camera's gaze, which Koskela (2000, 243) describes as "a gaze without eyes" because unless someone (that is, security or police personnel) is monitoring that camera as a crime takes place it is unlikely to act as a preventative security measure. For Bernardo and Homolka the camera's gaze always had eyes as Bernardo not only staged and directed the assaults, but also repeatedly watched the video footage. Similar to private and state/public surveillance, Bernardo and Homolka's use of video cameras to record the sexual assaults demonstrates the politics of seeing and of being seen – of "who has the right to look and whom will be looked at" (Koskela 2000, 251). What is particularly relevant for the present discussion is how the visibility produced by the power to see, gaze or survey "overpowers the other senses" to the degree to which "there is nothing more than that which meets the eye" (Koskela 2000, 254). Combining this interpretation of gaze theory with Frosh's (2001) examination of photography as a performance of power and Butler's (1999) notion of sedimentation enables us to provide an alternative reading of the videotaped evidence of Homolka's involvement in the sexual assaults.

Frosh (2001, 43) outlines how photography has both representational and spectacular power. Photography's representational power comes from its ability to tell a particular story through pictographic narrative; at the same time, representational power "ignores the 'knowledge' of that power among photographers, viewers and the photographed themselves" (Frosh 2001, 44). Frosh is arguing that in order to fully understand the nature, meaning, and genesis of the photograph, we must understand the social context within which the image was created (acknowledging the roles of both the photographer/subject and the photographed/object) and within which it is viewed (acknowledging the audience and the politics of who has the power to see). Photography's spectacular power comes from "being put on display" (Frosh 2001, 44). The photographer has the power to make certain people visible and to choose how and when to put them on display as a spectacle, endowing them with the ability to affect public observation, and to control "the production, distribution and iconography of the images" which suggests a "degree of power over those they photograph" (Frosh 2001, 46–7).

Certainly Paul Bernardo and Karla Homolka maintained power over their victims and over the images they took of them. The videotapes of the sexual assaults are frequently referenced as evidence of Homolka's duplicitous nature, notably that she was more than the victim and unwilling participant that she claimed to be. Prior to their discovery there was some institutional and public acceptance of Homolka's victim narrative but this was shattered in the courtroom when the image of a smiling Homolka was seen to wilfully participate in the sexual assaults (Galligan 1996). Homolka maintained that she only "acted happy" for the camera because she was terrified of her husband and was in fact ashamed and repulsed by her actions. Few believed this assertion; however, it was established during Bernardo's 1995 trial that at different points in time both Leslie Mahaffy and Kristen French were also found to smile, wave, and act happy for the camera's gaze – instructed to do so by Bernardo under threats of violence. For example, the following is a courtroom exchange between Karla Homolka and Crown prosecutor Ray Houlahan during Paul Bernardo's trial:

Houlahan: Can you comment on what just happened? In other words, why is Kristen smiling and waving at the camera?

Homolka: Because by now she knew that she had to make a good video for Paul.

Houlahan: How did she know that?

Homolka: Because of things that he had told her throughout the period of her confinement. I don't think, I don't think he told her to smile and wave at the camera, but she, she tried to do everything she could to make herself seem, to make him, to make it look like she was enjoying herself.

(R. v. P. Bernardo 1995, 815)

In a discursive move that angered and disgusted journalists and the public, Homolka likened her own onscreen performance to that of her victims – claiming that Bernardo constantly reminded and beat her for having ruined his only videotape of Tammy:

> So whenever he made other videotapes in the future I smiled and acted happy so I wouldn't ruin another videotape and give him another excuse to beat me. This [the tape of the assault on Tammy] is the only tape that is in existence that shows my true feelings.
>
> (R.v. P. Bernardo 1995, 185–6)

Frosh (2001, 49) argues that there is an assumption that people want to look at the gazed object (a common effect of a panoptic society); this assumption is made plain when, and reflecting Homolka's narrative, both the subject and object of the gaze are "in the know" and perform accordingly. The spectacular power of photography in this case may have initially rested with Karla Homolka and to an even greater extent Paul Bernardo, but following Homolka's confession and the eventual discovery of the videotapes, that spectacular power shifted from the couple producing the films to the public that devoured every reported detail of the case and voyeuristically surveyed Homolka's every move. In this sense, the media and the public reversed Bernardo's and Homolka's predatory private gaze so as to create a public or synoptic (Mathiesen 1997) and socially regulating gaze. Frosh writes:

> Hence, the conjunction between the public realm of visibility and the material viewer raises voyeurism to the level of social regulation: visibility as public social power depends for its force on the secure invisibility of the desiring viewer entrenched within the private domain. By making the gaze of the private viewer integral to public visibility, the concept of voyeurism undoes the reification of public and private as two static domains and re-establishes them as the terms of a dynamic separation, as social correlates of the spatial distinction between inside and outside, of the psychic constructions of self and other, and of the epistemological categories of fantasy and reality. Indeed, voyeurism can be seen as that moment when the public/private boundary is instituted within the construction of subjective experience, creating across the visual field the separate identities of public citizen and private person, a process whose precariousness requires its regular reiteration.
>
> (Frosh 2001, 49)

Voyeurism is a useful concept in helping to explain the sensationalism attributed to Karla Homolka. The videotapes of the sexual assaults demonstrate the blurring of the public/private that Frosh discusses as well as the role of voyeurism in this case. The tapes are voyeuristic in nature, showing images made in private space but against the will of the subject's object. These private images were then subject to the collective gaze of the public through the performative of the courtroom drama. While there is no debating that the tapes represent sexual violence, they also demonstrate the power of photography to create images that do not wholly represent the context within which they were made. It is at this juncture that the representational and spectacular power of photography and our conceptualization of the cultural voyeurism that propelled this case to become a national spectacle find a theoretical connection to Butler's (1990) notion of sedimentation.

Butler uses the term "sedimentation" to describe how gender norms produce the idea of a natural sex or a real woman, noting that this process occurs over time and through the acts of reiteration and citation (Butler 1990; Jagger

2008). Using the geological process[7] as a metaphor, Butler uses the term to emphasize how gender norms become so entrenched that they seem innately natural rather than orchestrated. Sedimentation, therefore, both enables and constrains gender performances; as such, while they are open to (re)interpretation, the reified nature of these norms entrenches them as the status quo. When individuals perform outside these norms, these new or alternative performatives, to borrow a metaphor from Foucault (cf. 1972, 1994), mark "points of rupture" in an individual's life. Such massive ruptures often reflect identity transformations that are infrequent but highly significant. Performing in the videotapes of the sexual assaults marks a point of rupture for Homolka and evidences her transgression of the bonds of sisterhood, norms of womanhood and femininity, and a series of sexual and death taboos, which we discuss in detail in chapter 4. In short, the videotapes reflect her criminal capacity and thus her potential dangerousness.

In her efforts to explain the videotapes as points of rupture while testifying against her ex-husband, Karla Homolka wove together a narrative that situated her participation in the crimes as emerging as a result of her victimization – a narrative that she maintained throughout the 12 years of her incarceration and following her 2005 release (Kilty and Frigon 2006; Morrissey 2003; R. v. P. Bernardo 1995). Homolka's steadfastness that she is not what she appeared to be on film demonstrates her "loss of control over 'representation' by the photographed" (Frosh 2001, 55). Frosh draws on Freud's notion of the uncanny and the fear of the "double" to help explain the photographer/videographer's power, noting how threatening it can be to one's sense of self to encounter "one's double as an unfamiliar version of oneself" (2001, 55). Using this idea of fear of the double helps us to explain why Homolka's narrative and performative appear to contradict one another; with two polar opposite characterizations (victim/woman in danger and victimizer/dangerous woman) which should we believe?

Undeterred by Homolka's challenges to the verisimilitude of the videotapes, many different actors (that is, journalists, lawyers that worked on the trials, socio-legal scholars and the public) interpreted the videotapes as direct and unencumbered evidence of Homolka's duplicity and dangerousness, and thus as eviscerating the believability of her victim narrative (for example see: Denov 2004; Galligan 1996; McGillivray 1998; Morrissey 2003; Pearson 1998). By essentializing the videotapes as unadulterated truth, Homolka's victim narrative is easier to reject. The result is that Homolka is perversely memorialized, and in Morrissey's (2003) words monsterized, as an enigma – as a predominantly *dangerous* woman whose narrative is incongruous with her onscreen performance because she fails to take responsibility for her actions. While we do not wish to deny the horrific violence the videotapes depict or the fact that Homolka participated, we must remember that they reflect a moment in time that may be discontinuous with the present or with Homolka's broader character. Therefore the videotapes, the media portrayals of her identity, the crimes and her release, and the trial records provide insight into the varying characterizations of who she is, or perhaps more accurately of whom she is perceived to be. It is our goal to examine the various layers of representation of Homolka that are offered by these different texts and to think through the connection these representations have with our own cultural fascination with her as an iconic and enigmatic criminal figure.

While Morrissey (2003) more readily accepts the videotape performative as truth, we draw on Frosh's (2001, 52) description of the photograph as "characterized by stasis" and on Butler's notion of sedimentation to challenge this. Photographs remain frozen in time and as a form of evidence they are "discontinuous with the present" (Frosh 2001, 52). Partially due to the acceptance of the videotapes as truth, the public view of Homolka is frozen in time – she is only what we see on the tape – which we suggest can be seen as an "other-constructed performative" given that she, like her victims, performed *for* Paul Bernardo. Once an individual commits a crime, particularly if that crime is of a violent nature, they are stigmatized and forever identified *as* that crime – as though the crime itself becomes their master status and master identity (Goffman 1963; Weisman 2009). Homolka is identified as a sexually violent woman in a society where it is an anomaly to be a female predator (Denov 2004); but if we were to situate her participation in the crimes as a point of rupture in her life, we may then characterize her participation as an aberration rather than the primary feature of her identity. However, due to the extraordinary tragedies of this case the public's gaze remains fixated upon the "morally vacuous" (McGillivray 1998) woman we cannot explain. In the next section we outline our goal of (re)turning the gaze in order to examine the roots of our cultural fascination with and repulsion by Karla Homolka.

Returning the Gaze: Voyeurism and the Cultural Casting of Homolka as an Enigma

Morrissey's focus on Homolka reifies her as the centre of the case and pushes her abusive husband Paul Bernardo to the margins of our collective thought and analysis. While we agree with Morrissey that mainstream legal and media discourses did not deny Bernardo's subject status, it is not as though his agency was never questioned; in fact, legal, media and scholarly narratives placed Homolka at the centre of the crimes and as the formidable catalyst to Bernardo's sexual and violent aggressions, thus partially limiting his agency while steadfastly maintaining hers. Problematically then, but akin to mainstream legal and media narratives, Morrissey's gaze remains uniformly on Homolka, which she does in order to provide a critical reading where other feminist scholars have remained silent. We too examine Homolka rather than Bernardo; however, instead of trying to explain who Homolka is in terms her identity(ies) and subjectivity(ies) we turn our gaze outward and back onto the audiences that are attempting to make sense of Homolka's participation in these crimes. Why is it that *we* are so fascinated with, fixated upon, and even obsessed with Karla Homolka?

Clearly, her anomaly as one of very few women convicted of sexual violence marks her as unique. As Canadian legal scholar Anne McGillivray (1998, 256–7) writes:

> There was widespread belief that she had known where the videotapes were hidden, that she willfully concealed the Jane Doe incidents and, most centrally, that her claims of being under Bernardo's control – a central tenet of the plea bargain – were spurious. Speculation was fed by a publicity ban on the plea bargain which stood until Bernardo's trial. Print and website sources imaged demonic duos, vampirism, Barbie and Ken perfect-couple perfect-murderers, sexy "Killer Karla," the comic "Karla's Web" featuring Homolka's psy confessions. *The gaze centres, always, on Homolka.* [Our emphasis]

Characterizations of Homolka as a hyper-dangerous and eroticized cultural aberration to an essentialist version of femininity and womanhood were prolific in media narratives. As noted in the introduction, there have been multiple retellings of this case in different cinematic and textual formats: fiction and non-fiction books (Burnside and Cairns (1995) *Deadly Innocence*; Crosbie (1997) *Paul's Case*; DeAngelo (2011) *the Twisted Relationship of Paul Bernardo and Karla Homolka*; Pron (1995) *Lethal Marriage*; Williams (1997) *Invisible Darkness* and (2004) *Karla: A Pact with the Devil*; Todd (2012) *Finding Karla: How I Tracked Down an Elusive Serial Child Killer and Discovered a Mother of Three*); a play (1997 *Famous*); a comic book (*Killer Karla*); episodes of popular television crime drama and infotainment shows (*Law and Order, Law and Order: Special Victims Unit, the Mentalist, Criminal Minds, MSNBC Investigates, Close to Home, CSI: Crime Scene Investigation, Wicked Attraction*, and *Inspector Lynley Mysteries*); and even a Hollywood major motion picture starring *That 70's Show* and *Orange is the New Black* actress Laura Prepon as Homolka (*Karla*).

Nearly 15 years ago – 5 years after Homolka's plea bargain in 1993 and 3 years following the conclusion of Paul Bernardo's trial in 1995 – Anne McGillivray (1998) described Homolka as a morally vacuous and enigmatic subject. It is this moral vacuity that we fear, which we have witnessed in other cases on much grander scales yet with much less fanfare. For example, the more recent case of Canadian serial killer and pig farmer Robert Pickton, who was found guilty of 6 murders with forensic evidence of at least 20 more,[8] generated less media coverage despite the obvious technological and Internet advancements between 1993, when Homolka was convicted, and 2007, when Pickton was convicted. We use this case as a comparative example because it has many similar elements: white perpetrator with female victims; certain "grisliness" to the details of the crimes (for example luring vulnerable victims, corpse dismemberment, and lurid mechanisms for body disposal);[9] victim drugging; sexual victimization; and even court-ordered publication bans in both cases. A quick search on the Canadian Newsstand database reveals the raw numbers.

Table 1.1 Descriptive statistics comparing volume of Canadian news coverage of Karla Homolka and Robert Pickton

Canadian Newstand Search Terms	*All Results (as of January 2014)*	*Results in Year of Apprehension/Homolka's Plea Bargain*	*Results in Year of Trial*
"Karla Homolka"	9,229	1993 – 598	1995 (Bernardo's trial and end of publication ban) – 1953
"Robert Pickton"	8,067	2002 – 630	2006 – 354 2007 – 1,330

What these numbers show is that despite the number of victims (4 versus 26 – and potentially upwards of 60) and there being a similar volume of news coverage for each case during the years that the accused were first identified and then tried, overall, there is more coverage of Karla Homolka than there is for Robert Pickton. A more general Internet Google search for these names shows 211,000 hits for "Karla Homolka" and only 96,000 results for "Robert Pickton". These brief descriptive statistics demonstrate that our gaze is riveted to the spectacle of Homolka; she is an enigma of our cultural imaginary. One of the primary goals for this book is to examine this gaze.

The power of "the gaze" comes from the power to look, which is a clear subject position and which exists in opposition to the object position of being looked at. Traditionally, men have occupied the subject position of looking at women, who become objects of the gaze in this relationship (Massey 1994; Mulvey 1975). This understanding of the gaze primarily emerges from feminist, psychoanalytic and cinema studies literature that examines how multiple oppressions (that is, gender, race, class and sexuality among other intersecting oppressions) affect subject/object positions in terms of who has the power to look – with women experiencing a kind of "to-be-looked-at-ness" (Mulvey 1975). There can be a voyeuristic fascination for those who have the power, ability, and facility "to look" – of being able to see others, while remaining hidden from a returned gaze or view.

In its strictest and most commonly understood sense, voyeurism is a sexual proclivity where the individual reaches sexual arousal and pleasure by watching people engaged in intimate or private behaviours, including but not limited to sex acts, and watching individuals undress, go to the washroom or bathe. Voyeurs often supplant their own engagement in a sex act with voyeuristic gazing upon others in these intimate or private moments. In a hetero-patriarchal culture, women, as opposed to men, are more likely to be the objects of the voyeuristic gaze, which increases their insecurity and as Brown states, their "exaggerated visibility" (Brown 1998, 218), which can marginalize women "by being at the centre (of the looks)" (cf. Rose 1993; Koskela 2000, 255). If men maintain the subject position of spectator holding the gaze, women not only become objects of that gaze, they become a spectacle at which to look. In this sense, women are hyper-visible, where,

> Visibility ensures normalization and control. It produces "purity" (Douglas 1966). Visibility is cleanliness: "light" equates with "soap". Surveillance has become a mechanism with the aims of guaranteeing purity and the exclusion of feared strangers: "the Other" in a literal as well as metaphorical sense.
>
> (Koskela 2000, 260)

The panoptic gaze of surveillance in late modern society is a method of trying to prevent victimization and thus of maintaining purity (Douglas 1966; Giddens 1991). Contemporary discussions of the surveillance society (Foucault 1977, 1980; Mathiesen 1997) where hyper/techno-visibility is thought to produce a mechanism of control, transparency, disciplined self-regulation, and thus safety amongst citizens (Koskela 2000), also provides insight into our cultural fixation with Karla Homolka. While Morrissey (2003) emphasized the power of Homolka's gaze upon her victims as evidence of her sadism, we examine the roots of our cultural fixation and rigid gaze on Homolka. To do so, in the proceeding chapters we engage in discussions of Homolka's dual construction as both a woman in danger and a dangerous woman (chapter 2); the way that Homolka's similarity to dominant members of Canadian society and to her victims elicited greater public shock and outrage at her involvement in these crimes (chapter 3); the role that Homolka's violation of different sexual and death taboos played in generating widespread and collectively felt disgust (chapter 4); and how interpretations of Homolka's remorse influenced the attention paid to this case (chapter 5).

Notes

1 It is important to note that Tammy Homolka's death was considered an aggravating factor in Homolka's 12-year sentence, which was described as 5 years for Leslie Mahaffy, 5 years for Kristen and 2 years for Tammy Homolka (R. v. Karla Bernardo 1993).

2 As the publication ban could only be enforced in Canada, the rumours were very much fuelled by American media, and later, Internet discussion groups, the Internet being a new limited technology at the time.

3 This is a reference to a videotaped conversation between Homolka and Bernardo, filmed in her sister Tammy's bedroom, where she plays for the camera and claims to have enjoyed it when he sexually assaulted Tammy. In an effort to appease Bernardo, she also dressed in her deceased sister's clothing and recited a monologue about wanting to sexually assault other young girls. During her testimony and cross-examination at Paul Bernardo's trial, Homolka stated that this conversation was a show for Bernardo who was angry that she had "ruined" the videotape of the sexual assault against Tammy – a point that we discuss further below.

4 BWS is the acronym for Lenore Walker's conceptualization of Battered Woman's Syndrome. For more detailed examinations of the use of the battered woman's syndrome as expert testimony in Canada, see Frigon 2003; Sheehy 2014; and Sheehy et al. 2012a,b.

5 Morrissey's quote is mistaken on this fact – as Jane Doe (a fourth rape victim) was not a friend of Tammy Homolka's, but rather a young woman Homolka came to know as a result of their mutual interest in animals.
6 In this quote Morrissey refers to two different cases each involving a couple that together sexually assaulted and murdered a young girl/s – Canadians Paul Bernardo and Karla Homolka and Australians Barrie Watts and Valmae Beck. See her book for more comparative analysis.
7 The sedimentation process involves particulate matter being carried by water or wind, deposited on the surface of the land or seabed and consolidating into rock over lengthy periods of time.
8 The trial judge decided to divide the murders into two groups – trying Pickton for 6 homicides, while staying charges of 20 others – in order to minimize the length of the trial and of jury responsibility so as to avoid the potentiality of a mistrial. Given that Pickton was convicted and sentenced to life imprisonment, the Crown decided not to spend more taxpayer dollars on a second trial for the remaining 20 cases. It is also of note that the scope of this case in terms of body count exceeds that of the Bernardo-Homolka case to an even greater degree, as upwards of 60 women went missing from the downtown eastside of Vancouver during the years that Pickton was actively killing women from this area. So while there is forensic evidence of his involvement in 26 of these cases, many believe him to have committed several other murders. The erosion of forensic evidence over time is a common problem in forensic examinations.
9 Bernardo dismembered Leslie Mahaffy and encased her body in different concrete encasings so that he and Homolka could more easily dispose of the parts into Lake Gibson. Pickton fed his victims to the pigs on his farm.

2 Dissecting the Gaze

The Contradictory Constructions of Karla Homolka as *in Danger* and *Dangerous*

The photograph depicts a tall blonde man looking dapper in a tuxedo and staring confidently into the lens of the camera. The glimmer in his piercing baby-blue gaze is matched by the serene smile of his beautiful and petite blonde bride who is wearing a luxurious white wedding dress and veil. The lush green summer foliage shimmers in the sun behind the couple, coding a new beginning into the image. This attractive wedding picture was taken at St Luke's Anglican church in Niagara-on-the-Lake on 29 June 1991, during a lavish wedding complete with horse-drawn carriage, champagne, and a roast pheasant dinner (Williams 2004). The glossy photograph can be read as a typical and otherwise normal visual display of contemporary wedding day bliss that exudes the promise of "the good life"[1] (Ahmed 2010; Berlant 2011), namely the upwardly mobile suburban happiness marketed by the wedding industry. This picture is a mere snapshot in time, but one that marks an important life event – the wedding day of Paul Bernardo and Karla Homolka.

When considered amongst the bank of visual imagery and visual representations of Karla Homolka that we have witnessed over the years and the broader media tropes and discourses about the "violent woman," the contradictions that make up the genealogy of Homolka's perceived dangerousness come into sharp focus. By tracing constructions of Homolka that foreground and read her eyes, her smile, and her body as objective visual proof of alternately victimhood and absolute monstrosity, we get a clearer picture of the ways in which these embodied constructions are cemented in the collective consciousness. In this chapter, we examine the ways in which different cultural readings of Homolka's embodiment(s) are intimately connected to the ways in which her beauty is variously read as evidence of both her victimhood and her monstrousness, which created a kind of "representational meltdown" (Miller 2004) in media, juridical, and public discourses.

The Bernardo-Homolka case has captivated audiences and media attention for nearly 25 years. Partially because the most common explanations offered about Homolka's role in the crimes have been superficial and simplistic, for many her character has defied cultural comprehension. While the image of Paul Bernardo faded from the limelight, the media have consistently maintained their gaze on Karla Homolka (McGillivray 1998, 255), a gaze that remains preoccupied with her appearance, body, physicality, and sexuality. As our gaze fades away from Paul

Figure 2.1 Paul Bernardo and Karla Homolka wedding photograph
Source: © Sun Media

Bernardo, our attention supplanted by other violent men like Robert Pickton and Colonel Russell Williams, the ever-present focus on Homolka remains intact. She is often constructed as an enigma and the duality of her persona continues to perplex those who attempt to gain an understanding of her behaviour and her controversial courtroom testimonies. This chapter uses the *body* as a lens to produce a genealogy of Homolka's dangerousness. Genealogy does not entail a search for a singular point of origin and is rarely a linear development. Foucault (1980) describes genealogy as a method that aims to trace the varied and contradictory ways that a particular discursive "truth" is presented to reveal the influence that differential and intersectional power-relations have on the production and maintenance of that truth. It was Foucault's position that there can never be one singular truth, but rather many, because truths are typically supported by and thus come to uphold the power of particular interest groups, discourses, and institutions. For Foucault, all truths are questionable.

In this chapter, we examine the discourses that were used to evidence Homolka's construction as a *dangerous* woman and a woman *in danger* (Frigon 1996) as different truths during different moments in time. We suggest that these representations are in line with traditional depictions of the violent woman whose physicality and sexuality foreclose more nuanced readings of "the specific contextual materiality of the body" (Price and Shildrick 1999, 5); for Homolka these representations exist along a continuum of victimization and violence. We adopt a feminist position that is guided by standpoint epistemology, which Harding (1993, 2004) identifies as privileging the perspectives of marginalized individuals or segments of the population. As standpoint feminism posits that knowledge is situated and subjective, using it as our epistemological frame allowed us to lend weight to Homolka's voice and narrative in order to reclaim what Cain describes as a fractured site of knowledge:

> What is important is to reflect upon a uniquely fractured site, reclaim it as a standpoint for knowledge production and political work and use this theoretical reflection to understand the relationships with others sites and standpoints. . . . Moreover, because standpoints are relational as well as theoretically reflective, we can understand that the sites and standpoints of both individuals and groups change as people go their own ways or work together.
>
> (Cain 1990, 135)

Unpacking Homolka's dual construction as both the devil and the damsel in distress reveals the extent to which constructions of her character are written, in great part, at the level of the body. Since the 1990s, a growing number of feminist scholars (Haraway 1991; Butler 1990, 1993; Bordo 1993) have built on the work of Simone de Beauvoir who argued that women's bodies must be understood as lived in specific contexts. From girlhood, women are socialized to live and experience their bodies as objects for another's gaze, a state that is not biologically given but results from "education and surroundings" (de Beauvoir 1953, 307). Feminists working in this vein interrogate the notion of a natural body and place the body back into their work as a central locus of inquiry, suggesting that "subjectivity and identity cannot be separated from specific forms of embodiment" (Ahmed 2000a, 88). Many contemporary feminist theorists, including those working in the disciplines of law and criminology, anchor their work in readings of the body, the discourses that circulate around it, and constructions of the body as a text (Ahmed 2010; Alcoff 2005; Frigon 1996, 2006; Grosz 2008; Schildrick 2002; Sobchack 2004; Young 2005). Doing so enabled us to problematize the normative and thus dominant productions of truth about Homolka's character as read through legal and media narratives that rely on and are rooted in particular constructions of her body.

Using a standpoint perspective allows us to question the intimate relationship between Homolka and Bernardo and to investigate the power-relations that impacted her choice and agency with respect to her crimes.[2] Feminism advocates for a focus on women's victimization in order to render the personal political, although it is often critiqued for constructing women as without agency (Faith 2001, 294); instead, we attempt to situate Homolka's choice within the constraints she experienced. Using the theoretical underpinnings associated with the concepts of being *in danger* and *dangerous*, we aim to present a more nuanced depiction of Homolka as a woman, a victim, and a victimizing agent in order to more accurately portray her personhood. In this sense, we situate her actions as constrained and thus not as freely chosen and completely voluntary. Examining Homolka will aid future analyses of other women convicted of violent or sexual crimes, especially those that are sensationalized, by unravelling the longstanding tropes and stereotypes that essentialize women's violence as the result of a deviant sexual body or diseased mind without consideration of the patriarchal power-relations that contribute to their violence (Comack and Brickey 2007).

Contextualizing Women's Violence and Victimization

Historically, criminological literature has typically ignored women as a unique analytic subject group, promoted stereotypical constructions of women's character and motivations and offered problematic gendered explanations of crime committed by women. By abstracting women from their analyses, criminologists have for the most part resorted to applying results obtained by studying men to women (Smart 1976). Feminist criminologists refer to this tradition as "malestream" research (Daly and Chesney-Lind 1988), which tends to adopt a supposedly gender-neutral approach, but characterizes the norm and standard as inherently male. Malestream research can be detrimental to our understandings and explanations of women who commit violent crimes, which are often constructed in an extreme and sensationalistic fashion that reinforces stereotypes and myths about the inherently violent nature of women criminals (Comack 2014; Dell 1999; Gilbert 2002; Seal 2009; Sjoberg and Gentry 2008). Women who commit violent crimes are thus viewed as violating or perhaps rebelling against traditional feminine roles (Bertrand 1979; Faith 1993; Gilbert 2002; Schur 1983; Seal 2009; Sjoberg and Gentry 2008; Smart 1976). The anxiety caused by the violent woman who troubles the two sex/two gender paradigm by transgressing boundaries of traditional femininity is evidenced by the press and public fixation on the iconography of Karla Homolka's white, upwardly mobile, suburban life. Homolka's enigma lies in the inability to reconcile her material experiences of battery, constrained choice, self-preservation, and violence.

It is important to realize that while women make up 6 percent of the total federally sentenced prison population in Canada (Mahony 2011); they are charged with 20 percent of all violent crimes (Kong and AuCoin 2008). Shaw (1995a) contextualizes this point by highlighting that of the 85 women convicted of murder or manslaughter, there were a variety of mitigating factors to be considered: Several women killed their abusive partners and their crimes were impacted by drugs or alcohol; several women had killed "johns" or drug dealers for money; and four women were involved in a homicide that occurred during a robbery although none of these women actually did the killing. Attesting to their endangerment, the Task Force on Federally Sentenced Women (1990) contended that 80 percent of women serving federal sentences were victimized before their incarceration. Shaw (1995a, 115) suggests that focusing on women as victims of crime replaces one inaccurate label with another – "the fallen woman becomes the helpless victim with low self-esteem" (also see Pollack 2000, 2006; Pollack and Kendall 2005).

Although it is over-simplistic to see all criminalized women primarily as victims, which may be read as a denial that women make choices to be violent (Denov 2004; Shaw 1992), this divisive hybridity between victimization and victimizing others has become entrenched in contemporary discussions of violence (especially violence committed by women) and is thus important to examine. Critics suggest that feminists neglect analysing women convicted of violent crimes in an attempt to maintain a focus on the violence that many women continue to experience in private (Comack 2014; Comack and Brickey 2007; Faith 1993; Morrissey 2003; Shaw 1995b). Certainly if we fail to acknowledge that women can be violent, we run the risk of rendering all women harmless (Allen 1987; White and Kowalski 1994). As Allen writes:

> Against the bald facts of the criminal allegation or conviction, these reports counter-pose a subtler and more compromising version of the case, which systematically neutralises the assertion of the woman's guilt, responsibility and dangerousness, and thus undercuts any demand for punitive or custodial sanctions.
>
> (Allen 1987, 55)

Allen is somewhat extreme in her assertion that recognizing the relationship between a woman's victimization and her acts of violence will "neutralise" her guilt and "undercut *any* demand for punitive or custodial sanctions" [our emphasis], yet this trope remains in the ongoing legal debates about the veracity of the battered woman syndrome defence in cases where a woman is accused of killing her abusive partner (Sheehy 2014). Both Denov (2004) and Allen (1987) suggest that the recognition of women's victimization has led professionals, such as the police, psychiatrists and judges, to infantilize women who perpetrate violent and sexual crimes:

> However, by *over* emphasizing women as victims, there is the risk of depriving women of their moral agency. By realigning the offender's behaviour within the margins of victimhood, whether a victim of circumstance or a victim of a male partner, the female sex offender and her offence were more easily placed in accordance with traditional scripts regarding gender and sexuality.
>
> (Denov 2004, 121)

The fear is that the rare woman who commits an act of violence but who claims she did so as a result of her victimization will "get away with it." However, at the same time that it rankles cultural and legal sensibilities to think that a woman's violence will go unpunished to the full extent of the law, there is rarely a simultaneous counter-discussion of how the men who beat their partners routinely go unprosecuted for their actions. While Denov focuses exclusively on the dangers of overemphasizing women's sexual victimization out of concern that it will nullify their agency, it is our position that ignoring the abuse a woman experiences only results in *over*emphasizing the heinousness of her crimes. We do not seek to minimize Homolka's role as perpetrator, there is no question that she participated in these assaults and should have gone to the police to try to prevent them; rather we aim to present a more nuanced and balanced analysis of her role in these crimes. Contextualizing Homolka's actions as occurring within a climate of violence does not "neutralise" her involvement or render her harmless; rather, it moves us away from seeing her *only* as a criminal monster to be feared and allows us to generate a more holistic understanding of this case and her personhood.

We suggest that Homolka's case presents a challenge to the literature on the social construction of violent women. In fact, Morrissey (2003) specifically described Homolka as presenting a kind of "limit case" for feminist scholars who for the most part avoid writing about her because her actions were so severe and the harm she participated in causing was toward innocent girls rather than her abuser. This suggests that feminist criminologists may have, consciously or unconsciously, eschewed commenting on Homolka because they feared she threatened the political momentum in combating violence against women, which has been a staple of feminist social organizing for the last four decades. Comack (2014, 36) similarly describes Homolka's involvement in these crimes as a "decisive event" that contributed to shifting interpretations of women's violence toward explanations that proclaimed that not only are women violent, but that "women's violence is quantitatively and qualitatively equal to that of men's" (37). Homolka's social construction is much more complex than simple categorizations as *either* dangerous or in danger; rather she occupies the unique position of reflecting both characterizations at the same time. While we contend that the abuse Homolka endured impacted her agency and constrained her choice, her victimization does not excuse or neutralize her criminality, it does, however, provide context.

We adopt the notion of the victimization-criminalization continuum (Comack 2014; Comack and Brickey 2007) to better situate women's acts of violence as it "draws insights from intersectionality theory to showcase how systemic factors (relating to patriarchy, poverty, and colonialism [to name but a few]) contribute to women's vulnerability to victimization, thereby restricting their agency or capacity to make choices" (Comack 2014, 42). While critics might question this continuum as applied to Homolka, who was white and middle class and living with her parents when she first met Bernardo, there is evidence of Bernardo grooming her sexually and isolating her from friends and family over time. The 6-year age difference between the couple is also significant as it highlights her youth (she was 17 when she began dating the 23-year-old Bernardo), naivety and immaturity – factors that enabled Bernardo to groom her so effectively. However, by situating Homolka's violence within the context of her victimization we must be careful to acknowledge that there are degrees of victimization that differentially mark and separate her from her victims – no matter Homolka's desire to showcase the likeness between them. Homolka's ability to cross such clear moral boundaries and disgust thresholds by harming innocent others rather than her abuser degrades her victim narrative and forces us to question her moral turpitude.

When Karla Homolka entered into a plea agreement with the province of Ontario she pled guilty to two counts of manslaughter, and symptoms of the battered woman syndrome were raised as mitigating factors to her involvement in the crimes. The battered woman syndrome was first successfully raised in a Canadian court during the fall of 1990 in R. v. Lavallée (Comack 1993; Frigon 2003). Since the Lavallée[3] case, the court's acceptance of the battered woman syndrome has been limited (Frigon 2001; Shaffer 1997; Sheehy 2014; Sheehy et al. 2012a, b). While Homolka discursively constituted her crimes as resulting from her endangerment, which suggests that her actions functioned as a battery prevention technique, this position differs greatly from those women who act violently toward their abuser in order to ward off and end the violence to which they are subject. Some literature suggests that the expert evidence on the battered woman syndrome mitigates women's responsibility for their violence (Frigon 1996, 2001; Sheehy 2014) although there is concern that syndromizing women's actions may strengthen the power of psychiatric diagnoses that explain women's behaviour as disorderly rather than reasonable (Comack 1993; Hatty and Hatty 1999; White and Kowalski 1994). By contrast, Homolka's actions were not reasonable. Nor does she fit the strict criteria necessary for using expert evidence of the battered woman syndrome; the most blatant discrepancy being that she did not kill her abuser, but rather assisted him to rape and kill teen girls.

Sensational readings of Homolka's sexuality, criminality, and victimhood were invoked in media and juridical discourses that starkly narrated her identity as *either* a dangerous woman or a woman in danger. This paradox of dangerousness created a problematic understanding of Homolka's personhood as these constructions represent two polar opposite and seemingly mutually exclusive categorizations, which resulted in social and legal confusion about her character and motivations for her crimes. Homolka is difficult to comprehend precisely because she does not fit neatly into a good versus evil typology. How does one woman embody two dialectically opposed extremes? Is it possible to accept her narrative of victimhood while also realizing her potential dangerousness? In the next section we problematize the dichotomous narrative of victimization/dangerousness by examining the inexorable link between Homolka's endangerment and her criminal actions.

Victim and/or Villain

Narrating Homolka's Victimization

When Homolka first came forward to the local police in early 1993, she confessed not only to her involvement in the crimes and the existence of the videotape evidence, but also to her victimhood. She and her lawyer, George Walker, narrated a horrific tale that emphasized her role as a battered woman. By presenting herself first and foremost as a battered woman, they were able to successfully suggest that her participation in the sexually motivated homicides was forced rather than voluntary. With medical and psychiatric evidence to support her claims of abuse, Homolka, Walker, and Crown counsel during Bernardo's trial, Ray Houlahan, were able to call greater attention to her persona as a victim who had little other choice than to participate in the homicides engineered by her abusive spouse than to her persona as a violent woman. At the onset of her trial in 1993, Homolka's image as a battered woman was featured prominently in much of the media coverage of the case. Given the extensive degree of media sensationalism that followed this case from its inception, the court ordered a publication ban of Homolka's plea and sentencing hearing to better preserve public neutrality prior to Bernardo's trial, which would take place 2 years later. Then lawyer for Bernardo, Timothy Breen, problematized the publication ban as having the exact opposite effect – that it would foster a one-sided characterization of Homolka as a victim:

> Timothy Breen, acting for co-accused Paul Teale (Bernardo), said a publication ban sought by the Crown in the trial of Karla Homolka (Teale) would leave the public with a misleading impression about her. "The public impression of her is as a victim of my client," Mr Breen said of Ms Homolka, 23. "If there is a ban on publication, that impression will not be dispelled, but fostered. . . . The effect of the publicity is to insulate Karla Bernardo from the truth."
>
> (Appleby and Abbate 29 June 1993, A1)

The publicity of which Breen speaks includes a full-sized front page photograph of Homolka with blackened eyes, shown in Figure 2.2 below, that initially appeared in the *Toronto Sun* and was reprinted many times in newspapers across the country. This image provided visual verification to Homolka's claims of being a victim of domestic battery and is linked to the delay in her arrest after she came forward to the authorities and to her "soft" handling by the police. Breen's warning that the public impression of Homolka as Bernardo's victim would strengthen as a result of the ban was accurate, but only to a point – which we discuss further below. Moreover, his claim that the publicity the photo generated would "insulate [her] from the truth" suggests that she was not a "true" victim. As Foucault asserts, genealogical analysis uncovers universalisms that are held up as truths; the debate over whether or

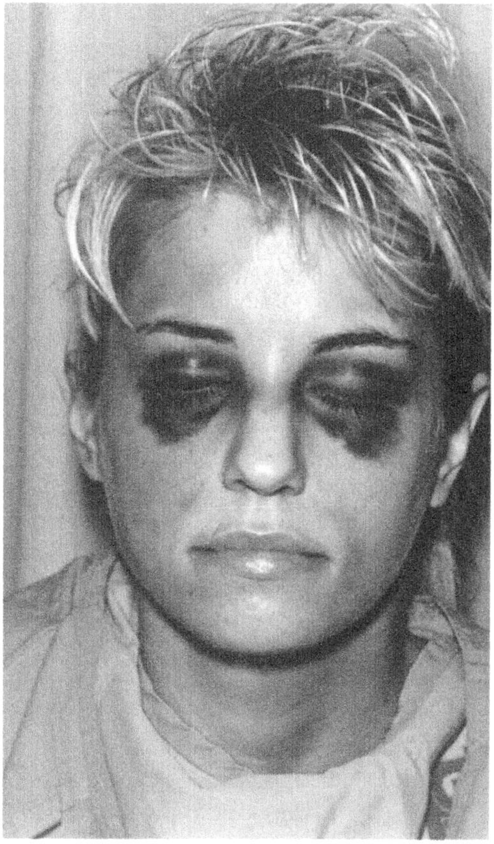

Figure 2.2 A battered Homolka with "raccoon eyes"
Source: © Sun Media

not Homolka was a victim or villain is a debate about the truth of her character – as though there is but one truth.

Homolka's discourse of abuse, learned helplessness and involuntary participation in the sexually motivated homicides was woven throughout her submissions for the plea bargain and her testimony at Paul Bernardo's trial. Figure 2.2 shows the widely circulated and reprinted photograph of Homolka in a blue hospital garment, her eyes practically invisible behind deep and dark purple bruises. The bruises were the result of a severe beating in which Bernardo repeatedly hit her about the head with a metal flashlight that caused her brain to slam against the front of her skull. While this photograph was accepted early on as visual evidence of her victim status, it was later passed over in favour of photographs that revealed her open eyes, images that were instead used to depict Homolka as a cold-blooded killer.

The attending physicians that drafted the first expert record of the domestic violence Homolka experienced took the photograph shown in Figure 2.2 at the St Catharines General Hospital in early 1993. This record marks the first time that Homolka sought medical treatment for the abuse Bernardo inflicted upon her, having done so at the request of her parents. The photograph offers definitive forensic and visual evidence that Bernardo physically abused Homolka. Justice Kovacs referred to the different psychiatric reports that documented her victimization to support the logic behind his sentencing:

> From about six months after their meeting, Paul Bernardo commenced a systematic, physical, and psychological abuse of the accused according to the report of Dr Arndt. The beatings escalated. He strangled her, threw knives at her, hit her with firewood, hit her with his shoes, and finally with a flashlight. He stabbed her with a screwdriver, pulled out handfuls of hair from her head, punched her, kicked her, and raped her. He pushed her down stairs. On one occasion her foot was punctured when he pushed her onto a board with a rusty nail. He systematically made her feel unworthy and cut the contact with her family down.
>
> (R. v. Bernardo 1993, 97)

> She knew what was happening but she felt totally helpless and unable to act in her own defence or in anyone else's defence. She was in my opinion, paralysed with fear and in that state of she became obedient and self serving. . . . Karla is not a dangerous person. In my opinion, Karla has a good prognosis, but she will require much assistance. . . . I had no doubt that Karla was a passive, non-violent person. . . . Even in her extremity she was unable to attack Paul in a final attempt to protect herself from what seemed certain death.
>
> (R. v. K. Bernardo 1993, 98–100)

Initially, the police, news reporters, and journalists accepted Homolka's discourse of abuse and torture at the hands of Paul Bernardo. The early psychiatric evidence clearly states that Homoka is not a threat or an inherently dangerous person, even going so far as to call her passive and non-violent. This framing does not neutralize Homolka's actions or deny her responsibility for them; rather, it speaks to her broader non-violent character and by rooting of her violence in her relationship with Paul Bernardo it suggests that she does not pose a continued threat to the public. While Breen's earlier comments foreshadow the public's changing perception of Homolka, his role as Bernardo's defence counsel clearly biases his position. Similarly, given the plea agreement already in effect, Justice Kovacs could not reject the victim narrative without the risk of throwing the criminal justice system into disrepute. While media and public views of Homolka shifted over time, there were some commentators that preserved Homolka's status as victim whilst recognizing her involvement in the crimes. For example, long after all of the grisly case details were made public at Bernardo's 1995 trial, Justice Galligan (1996, 42) quotes heavily from the expert medical and psychiatric evaluations that reference Figure 2.2's photo in his report:

> On examination today, Karla is in distress, quite anxious and understandably so. Her eyes reveal raccoon's eyes, bruising all around the orbits, a large contusion to her head with what feels almost like a depressed fracture, although x-rays have ruled this out. She has a subconjunctival haemorrage in the left eye, which was seen by Dr Marriott, and she was re-assured. She has several bruises down the left side of her neck, along her arms, with a very large bruise in the upper right arm which is about three centimetres by three. About 75% of her legs from mid-thigh down are bruised, quite dramatically and swollen to the touch. She cannot move them due to pain. On the right thigh, about 3 cm. above the right knee, there is a puncture wound which she says was caused by Paul Bernardo when he punctured her with a screwdriver. On the left leg, there is a large isolated contusion about 6 inches by 3 inches, quite warm and tender.

The photograph of Homolka's battered face complete with "raccoon eyes" provided a visual image to the police, the courts, the media, and the public that could not be easily discounted or dismissed. The way in which the photographs were initially accepted as visual proof of Homolka's victimization point to the significance that visual representations of the body took on at different stages throughout the unfolding of this complex case. Visual evidence of Homolka's marked and battered body led the press to initially paint her not as a social actor but rather a helpless victim, an animal lover whose every move was controlled by a sadistic Bernardo, an image she corroborated during her testimony. As Butler argues, "[the body] bears on language all the time being 'simply linguistic stuff', for it cannot be understood or spoken of outside of signification" (Butler 1993, 68). Given Bernardo's identity as a serial rapist, early constructions easily juxtaposed his violent character against the visible bruises that lined Homolka's eyes and the puffy contusions that marred the skin of her thighs and lower legs that visually narrated her character in alignment with traditional tropes of female victimhood.

Legal affirmation of Homolka's identity as a battered woman resulted from its acceptance as a mitigating factor in her sentencing and was later corroborated in the Galligan Report. This construction follows traditional gendered discourses that align violence with the masculine hard body and victimization with the feminine soft body (Jeffords 1994; Neroni 2005). This trope sheds light on why the female body is often read as Other, even monstrous, when it is found engaging in violent acts. While it is essential to lend weight to Homolka's narrative of victimization, we must also realize that law and the courtroom setting in which she testified confined and contained her discourse, just as it would for the other legal actors involved (Harding 1986; Smart 1989). Legal logic dictates that Homolka would want to absolve herself of some degree of responsibility for her role in the crimes in order to make her character look less damaged, but in doing so she relinquished agency (McGillivray 1998). On the contrary, she may have wanted to vilify Bernardo in order to secure his conviction, for fear of his violent reaction toward her were he to be released. George Walker included in his submissions the following explanation for his client's participation in the crimes:

> It moves on to the occasional violent, physical assault, the promises of not doing it again and it continues on a gradual scale, and ultimately in my submission, it would have followed that my client would not have escaped Mr Bernardo. It was only a matter of time. She does not seek to minimize her involvement, it is right there. Mr Segal has read the facts in. She does not take exception to the facts. She was there. She was there when both Kristen French and Leslie Mahaffy died and she was there when her own sister died. But, once the sister died, Paul Bernardo had her. But from that point on, as the doctor said, indicated, there was very little that she could do in her own mind.
>
> (R. v. K. Bernardo 1993, 78–9)

Walker's narrative clearly positions Homolka as at risk of becoming Bernardo's "fourth victim." By associating her identity as a victim with her identity as a victimizing agent, Walker inexorably links the two constructs along a continuum of dangerousness. While not negating her involvement, this move positions her victimhood as the epicentre of her actions and implies that they were not freely chosen. If her victimhood intersects her criminality and the two are not mutually exclusive categories, it is logical to presume that Homolka's ability to make unconstrained decisions was ultimately confined by her relationship with Bernardo and her fears of what he would do to her and her family. Rather than constructing Homolka as hapless and "doing it for love," one must consider that her choice was restricted not only by her increasing involvement in the crimes, but also not only by her increasing fear of Bernardo.

Narrating Homolka's Villainy within the Context of Victimhood

Karlene Faith (1993, 259) writes of the varied ways in which longstanding stereotypes about female criminality are exaggerated and overemphasized in the media to the point of becoming stock narratives that the wider public can easily identify. She suggests that "the monsters serve as the sick/bad backdrop for potential normalcy" which sets up a stark and unhelpful dichotomy between righteous and dangerous women that Carol Smart describes in her discussion of the ways in which women's bodies are essentialized as unruly:

> Legal, medical and early social scientific discourses intertwine to produce woman who is fundamentally a problematic and unruly body; whose sexual and reproductive capacities need constant surveillance and regulation because of the threat that this supposedly "natural" woman would otherwise pose to the moral and social order.
>
> (Smart 1992, 8)

Smart describes how women's bodies are constituted as a threat in need of surveillance and regulation – a form of protectionism that often takes shape in the form of legal paternalism. When a woman is involved in a violent crime, mass media depictions often reify the helpless victim/demonic monster binary that aligns the female criminal with existing misogynistic representations that equate femaleness with being innately nurturing and helpless and, at the same time, with the potentiality for unpredictable violence. That the psychic and political investment in the figure of the violent woman serves to shore up status quo patriarchal power-relations and gendered social roles and norms is well documented in the literature (Comack and Brickey 2007; Howarth 2002; Robert et al. 2007; Kamir 2006; Kilty 2010; Naaman 2006, 2007; Neroni 2005; O'Shea 2006; Robertson 1996). Women who transgress different boundaries have long been constructed as deviant and disorderly and are frequently positioned as the social scapegoats that preserve the gendered power-relations that oppress women as a group (Frigon 1996; Gilbert 2002; Seal 2009; Sjoberg and Gentry 2008).

The paradox of dangerousness was obviously approached differently by Crown and defence counsels at Paul Bernardo's trial as a result of their different goals regarding the couple's fate. John Rosen, Bernardo's defence counsel, attempted to mitigate the extent of Homolka's abuse in order to reconstruct her as dishonest and manipulative so as to threaten her credibility as the star witness testifying against his client. As Bernardo's entire defence relied upon Rosen's ability to discredit Homolka's testimony, he attempted to recreate her as overtly dangerous. He did this in two primary ways – first, by questioning the severity of the abuse Homolka claimed to have suffered and second, by suggesting that she was sexually deviant and enjoyed the couple's sexual exploits – a point that we examine further in chapter 4.

Rosen: Yeah. You had professionals to deal with, you had parents to rely on, you had all your support system that was with you in St Catharines, right?

Homolka: Yes.

Rosen: Okay. And the person who you say was being abusive and pushing you around was the one who lived in Toronto, an hour and a half away, right?

Homolka: Yes.

Rosen: He's the one who had no connection to St Catharines, did he?

Homolka: Yes.

Rosen: He's the stranger in that group? It isn't like he lifted you out of your support system and isolated you in a strange city, among strange people, and no support system? He didn't do that, did he?

Homolka: You don't have to be physically isolated to feel emotionally isolated.

(R. v. P. Bernardo 1995, 1323)

Homolka's final response is especially important as it demonstrates her recognition of the effects of the abuse she endured for over 6 years. Her response is both accurate and timely, as it speaks to the reality of living with an abusive partner while also attempting to prevent Rosen from harming her reputation as a credible witness. Rosen's attempt to discredit Homolka is not simply damaging to her believability, it is damaging to our comprehension of other battered women. His failure to recognize the process and cyclicity of abusive relationships is detrimental to women suffering violence from their partners for it suggests a degree of certainty as to a universal pattern of abuse.

When asked about why she performed sex acts on their victims, Homolka composed a discourse that intertwined her victimhood with her criminality:

Houlahan: And why did you perform these sex acts and allow them to be performed on you?

Homolka: Because I was told by Paul, and I knew from past experience that if I didn't do what he told me to do I would get beaten and have to do it anyway. It wasn't a case of saying "no" and just taking a beating, it was a case of saying "no" and being beaten until I did it.

(R. v. P. Bernardo 1995, 661)

This is a particularly powerful statement. Homolka suggests that she contemplated refusing to participate in the sexual assaults, but was unable to because of Bernardo's systematic abuse. By accepting her discourse as reminiscent of other battered women we are confronted by her humanity and are more compelled to accept her claims of victimhood. However, when contextualizing her story, her victimhood becomes partially negated by, while at the same time partially mitigating, her criminality. Is her self-preservation a negative form and site of resistance, whereby her agency is developed and choice present? While commentators suggested that Homolka either failed to exercise her agency, by failing to go to the police or by freeing their victims, or exercised it through wilful participation, we should consider that while her thought processes were constrained, she did have the ability to make decisions that would have changed the outcome of events (Chandler 1999, 178). Suggesting that she had agency free from domination neglects the abuse she experienced; at the same time, Homolka's most problematic decision was to sacrifice others in order to save herself.

While Homolka's victimhood was evidenced by medical and psychiatric evidence, her discourse of involuntary participation in the crimes was confused by her testimonies regarding why she smiled and seemed in high spirits during the filming of the sexual assaults. Homolka testified that during the sexual assault against her younger sister Tammy, Bernardo asked her if she was enjoying herself; when she responded that it was "fucking disgusting," Bernardo shut the video camera off and beat her about the head (Galligan 1996, 80). Homolka claimed that it was this incident that caused her to act as though she was enjoying herself while on camera in future; that acting happy was a battery prevention technique.

She then identifies the similarities between her onscreen performance and those of her victims:

Houlahan: And what else happened because of your response of him asking you that and what happened in the future in that regard?

Homolka: He never let me forget that I had ruined his only videotape of Tammy and he constantly beat me for it right up until the very time I left him. So whenever he made other videotapes in the future I smiled and acted happy so I wouldn't ruin another videotape and give him another excuse to beat me. This is the only tape in existence that shows my true feelings.

(R. v. P. Bernardo 1995, 185–6)

Houlahan: Can you comment on what just happened? In other words, why is Kristen smiling and waving at the camera?

Homolka: Because by now she knew that she had to make a good video for Paul.

Houlahan: How did she know that?

Homolka: Because of things that he had told her throughout the period of her confinement. I don't think that he told her to smile and wave at the camera, but she, she tried to do everything she could to make herself seem, to make him, to make it look like she was enjoying herself.

(R. v. P. Bernardo 1995, 815)

In this testimony, Homolka carefully positions her own victimhood in close proximity to Kristen French's, a discourse that suggests both she and French believed that Bernardo would kill them. By linking her behaviour to French's, Homolka argues that what could be criticized as calculated and dangerous was actually her attempt at self-preservation. While Homolka likens herself to French and Mahaffy in order to similarly construct herself as one of Bernardo's victims and to downplay her moral agency and role as a victimizer, the public read this discursive move as trivializing the suffering of the "true" victims of this case. By suggesting that she and French reacted in the same way to Bernardo's abuse, Homolka attempted to justify what appears on the video recordings to be her enjoyment in sexually assaulting their victims by positioning the videos as an act. The counter-side to this discursive move is that it also showcases her skill at performance, which was read by many as evidence of her ability to con everyone around her and served to further anger an already indignant public. Miller (2004) argues that "indignation forces disgust to aid in the cause of justice by motivating action against the offender; without indignation disgust too often withdraws or averts the gaze" (196). Our collective indignation that Homolka would attempt to ally her character with that of her victims drew our disgusted gaze back in, made it impossible to look away, and fuelled public resentment toward her that continues to this day.

Photographic documentation has long been instrumental in forming our cultural language and signs; for many, cameras were meant to "mitigate . . . the imperfections of memory" (Freud 1930 [2000]) and perception. Understood in this way, photographic evidence is not only considered objective, but also a corrective to the fallible naked eye. The fact that the videos reveal Homolka to be a smiling participant in the sexual assaults was taken by most as evidence of her monstrousness and resulted in explosive media vilification of her deviant sexuality. Rather than considering the context of abuse to which Homolka was subject and the similarity of the performances that Mahaffy and French also displayed on film, legal and media discourses unequivocally mobilized the videotapes as proof positive of Homolka's dangerousness.

A common stereotype about violent women (Gilbert 2002; Seal 2009; Sjoberg and Gentry 2008), accusations of Homolka's lesbianism and/or bisexuality reveal the extent to which her sexuality and sexual body were utilized to cement her construction as dangerous, which is particularly salient given that her victims were constructed as having innocent and pre-sexual bodies worth mourning.[4] Homolka's relationship with a woman during her incarceration was also central to media constructions of her as hypersexual and sexually deviant. As Millbank writes: "when lesbians are killers, or killers are presumed to be lesbian . . . their sexuality is always central to the tale" (cited in Kamir 2006, 262). This narrative is easily located within historical characterizations of violent women as lesbian or as exhibiting a deviant sexuality (Faith 1993; Gilbert 2002; Seal 2009; Sjoberg and Gentry 2008) such as is fetishized on the impossibly addictive Netflix television show *Orange is the New Black*, ironically also starring Laura Prepon who played Homolka in the film *Karla*. Homolka vehemently and repeatedly denied that she enjoyed participating in the sexual assaults. However, the discovery of the videotapes shifted interpretations of Homolka's victim narrative, personhood and criminality. No longer was she the battered wife of a sexual sadist who was party to Bernardo's ultimate dangerousness, she was the sexually deviant woman that engaged in "sex role-playing [and] pretended to be slain schoolgirls to try to please her husband" (Pron and Rankin 1995). Acceptance of Homolka's discourse of forced participation dissipated over time as her reconstruction as sexually deviant, dangerous, and narcissistic ensued:

> The woman who says she was too weak to say no to Bernardo was quick with denials and corrections during the interrogation. "That is a lie," she kept saying. . . . But she stuck to her tale of being terrorized into helping Bernardo in the sex slayings. People anxious to see her turned the front of the downtown Toronto courthouse into a campground each night. In the courthouse hallways, spectators debated the credibility of Homolka's story and compared it with Rosen's scenario. They left divided on whether Homolka was more victim than villain.
>
> (Lawton 13 July 1995, A4)

Her credibility in jeopardy, Homolka was steadfast in her courtroom testimony that she was a victim, but this placed her in an uncomfortable liminal space. While she could claim space as a victim with expert documentation to support that narrative, the videotapes also revealed her potentiality for violence. The videotapes thus worked both for and against her case; it documented the abuse and depravity to which the victims (and, by extension, Homolka herself) were subject, but they also show Homolka as an active participant in the crimes thus making her assertions of victimhood appear disingenuous. Before the videotapes were recovered, Homolka's confessions were the primary source of information about the abductions, sexual assaults, and murders. With their discovery, the police and the courts now had a startling visual image of Homolka appearing to enjoy her role in the sexual assaults. This visual, while not disclosing any new evidence, provided the authorities with a graphic image that came to define Homolka's dangerousness by unravelling her self-narrative as a battered woman. Kirk Makin, one of the journalists who covered the trial in its entirety, describes the sea change in feelings felt by members of the press as the case progressed:

> Central to the trial, of course, was the plaguing question of domestic abuse. Was Karla Homolka a victim? This question ultimately transformed the proceeding into the trial she never had. After watching every second of testimony, it seemed evident to me that she was beaten at various times in her marriage, though not to the extent she claimed. In her looking-glass world, Ms Homolka would have us believe a battered, terrified woman was involuntarily sending those pathetic mash notes asking her assailant to abuse her more. Sorry, can't buy it. In fact, about the only part of her testimony I found easy to accept was her account of how her husband killed Leslie and Kristen. Even then, the point was surely not whether she fully enjoyed it, half enjoyed it or derived only minimal kicks. . . . The female journalists were onto Ms Homolka first, almost as though they instinctively smelled on her the telltale odour of fraudulent teen angel from their own youths. Women covering the trial were at first perplexed, then impatient, with the male journalists who for a time gave Ms Homolka the benefit of the doubt.
>
> (Makin 2 September 1995, D1)

Makin captures what was for many citizens the heart of the case, the question that plagued legal actors, journalists and the public with each passing day that Homolka sat on the witness stand. Was she a victim, or only a villain? While he accepts that Bernardo beat her, Makin minimizes the extent to which she experienced emotional, physical, and sexual abuse, which is unfortunately common amongst detractors of the battered woman syndrome. What he fails "to buy" is that her actions, both minor (for example obsessively writing love notes to her abuser) and major (for example participating in the sexual assaults), could be attributable to her fear of Bernardo. Most intriguingly, Makin submits that female journalists read Homolka's "tells" more quickly – even instinctively – than did male journalists, which underscores the aged trope that criminalized women use their meekness, their role as victims, their beauty, and their sexuality to manipulate men (Comack and Brickey 2007; Faith 1993; Frigon 2003; Kilty 2010; Naylor 1995).

Homolka tried to earn sympathy by not relinquishing her victimhood, continuing to associate her plight with that of her victims, and explaining her own criminality by way of her endangerment. While this battery prevention technique resulted in what can only be viewed as a cold and detached attitude, it does not deny her involvement in the crimes. Consequently, Homolka's discourse forces an acknowledgment of the extenuating circumstances surrounding her crimes. While careful not to dismiss her criminality, we can see how her victimhood partially aids in explaining it. In the next section we examine Homolka's construction as a selfish and narcissistic woman due to her willingness to place her own welfare and that of her abuser ahead of the safety of their victims.

Compliant Victim of a Sexual Sadist or Selfish and Narcissistic Woman?

The contradictory constructions of Homolka as both *dangerous* and *in danger* were further complicated by FBI profiler Roy Hazelwood's assertions in his paper on the compliant victim of a sexual sadist.[5]

> Having met, seduced, and transformed a "nice" woman into a sexually compliant and totally dependent individual the sadist has validated his theory of women. The woman is now a subservient, inferior being who has "allowed" herself to be re-created sexually and has participated in sexual acts that no "decent" woman would engage in, thereby confirming that she is a "bitch" and deserving of punishment.
>
> (Hazelwood et al. 1993, 477)

Hazelwood proposed that although rare, Homolka's compliance with Bernardo's wishes as a self-defence technique is not the first case of its kind. He contends that the compliant victim of a sexual sadist's ability to harm others at the request or demand of their abusive partner is a form of self-preservation, for which a criminal defence may be raised akin to cases where the battered woman syndrome is recognized as evidence supporting the claim of self-defence when a woman murders her abuser. However, Hazelwood positions the compliant victim defence as only diminishing responsibility for criminal activity, not as that which should engender a full acquittal.

Justice Galligan accepted Hazelwood et al.'s (1993) theory and recognized the abuse that Homolka endured at the hands of a sadistic man as the impetus for her criminality:

> Karla was subjected to repeated sadistic sexual attacks. She was humiliated, beaten, tied up, and raped over a period of years. She was manipulated into being a participant in what eventuated in the death of a much-loved sister. She was advised on her wedding night that her new husband was a rapist.

> She was told that if she ever tried to leave her husband he would track her down and kill her. Or else, he would kill her remaining sister and her parents. She was living with a sexual sadist and she was convinced that from this bewildering fate there was no escape.
>
> (Galligan 1996, 80)

Acknowledging Homolka as the victim of a sexual sadist might add an explanatory layer but it did not lend greater clarity to interpretations of her character. Because we cannot position Homolka solely as a victim, what appear to be mutually exclusive categories are fused, her status as dangerous forever emphasizing her body in danger; her bruises and scars evidence not only of her victimhood, but also her potentiality for violence – her endangerment becoming the very root cause of her dangerousness. In his second book on the case, Stephen Williams (2004) included a photo Bernardo took of Homolka bound in handcuffs and gagged during one of their sexual encounters that evidences elements of sadism in the couple's sexual life, although this photo was also alternately read as confirmation of Homolka's sexual deviancy. While this particular photo did not emerge until years after the peak of media sensationalism, another photo was reprinted many times in newspapers across the country and became the pre-eminent visual image of Karla Homolka.

The photograph shown in Figure 2.3 depicts Homolka with a heavily lidded gaze, which news coverage frequently described as "sinister," "dead eyed," or as

Figure 2.3 The gaze to be feared

Source: © The Canadian Press

a "dead blue stare." However, her narrowed gaze could also be read as evidence of negative emotions, such as distrust, distaste, anger, fear, or the skepticism that commonly accompanies steeling oneself to endure something difficult. Given that this photo was taken during her time on the witness stand, as she is en route to court, this seems a logical reading. Like the multi-varied readings of Leonardo da Vinci's famous painting of the Mona Lisa, Homolka's half-smile may be read as both inviting and guardedly knowing. While Homolka may have been judicially accepted as a compliant victim of a sexual sadist, following the disclosure and public knowledge of the contents of the videotapes, media coverage constituted her more as a narcissistic and even psychopathic female predator.[6] This photo came to symbolize and signify her dangerousness and evil character and was published with texts that detailed the nature of Homolka's daily attire, cosmetics application and coiffure. While reporters obsessed over Homolka's beauty, petite stature, blond hair, and sexual allure, they used such descriptions to identify her as a narcissist who aided her sadistic husband to sexually assault and murder young women in order to secure her delusional fantasy of idealized nuptial bliss.

Narcissism is a personality disorder characterized by symptoms such as a need for admiration, fantasies regarding success and love, a lack of empathy, a grandiose sense of importance and the ability to be interpersonally exploitative (American Psychiatric Association 2013). Constructing Homolka as a narcissist reifies her narration as dangerous. For example, during his final submissions Justice Kovacs stated:

> The accused placed her own interest and that of Paul Bernardo Teale ahead of the interests of the victims. That is the greatest crime against charity. Throughout all these events and over a considerable period of time afterwards the accused continued to carry on her normal activities, apparently unconcerned for other potential victims. She came forward only when her own life was in danger.
>
> (R. v. K. Bernardo 1993, 106)

In this narrative, Homolka's selfishness is characterized as a symptom of her narcissism. Justice Kovacs constructs Homolka as a narcissist with agency who only left her abusive partner and disclosed her story to the police when she felt as though her own life was in danger. This reading implies that she had the ability to exert power within this violent relationship and that she was psychologically capable of putting her own interests ahead of others. Crown counsel Houlahan hints at this strategy when questioning Homolka about why she assisted in procuring a young woman for Bernardo's infidelities:

Homolka: Because I was afraid of him, and because this would make him happy. And I was a lot better off with him being happy than him being angry with me.

Houlahan: Didn't you care, him having a relationship with another woman?

Homolka: Basically, I wanted him to find somebody else to leave me alone, to let me go.

(R. v. P. Bernardo 1995, 463–4)

Homolka's reasoning demonstrates her lack of empathy and her ability to exploit another young woman in order to save herself. Clearly demonstrative of her capacity for dangerousness, her ability to resist Bernardo came from her complacency in putting other young women in harm's way. Homolka not only participated in the sexual assaults, she also failed to help the girls to escape. This is of particular importance because on two separate occasions, Homolka was alone in the house with Kristen French. Homolka admitted that while she contemplated releasing French, she ultimately decided against it:

> Because, first of all, I was scared because I was so involved in it. And, second of all, all I could picture was the two of us walking down the stairs and Paul coming in and freaking and killing.
>
> (R. v. P. Bernardo 1995, 669)

While acknowledging that she had the opportunity to free French, Homolka testified that she felt as though she was unable to do so because of her fear of being caught and killed by Bernardo. Homolka's fear was not that Bernardo would harm French, as she knew at the time of the abduction that French would be killed; rather she feared for her own life, believing that Bernardo would kill her for releasing their victim. Homolka's focus on her own life reveals certain narcissism and her inability to balance the consequences of her actions against her fears demonstrates her potentiality for violence.

John Rosen made a more damning attempt to construct Homolka as narcissistic in order to discredit her testimony and possibly earn a reduced sentence for his client:

Rosen: It wasn't until you were guaranteed a deal that you could live with to look after yourself, Karla Homolka, that you ever spoke to the authorities about this murder?

Homolka: I followed my lawyer's advice.

Rosen: That may be, but it took him 3 months to negotiate that deal, and in that time, especially the 6 months from January of '93, 5 months, to May of '93, you held your silence until you were looked after, right?

Homolka: I followed Mr Walker's advice.

Rosen: Isn't that really what this is all about, is that, is that your whole demeanour from the time you left your husband until today, even when you gave your evidence was to say: "Not me. I didn't do it. I was forced to do it. Everybody believe me. I'm looking after Karla, right?"

(R. v. P. Bernardo 1995, 1050)

Rosen directly attacks the sincerity of Homolka's testimony, contending that she was not the victim of an abusive and controlling husband, but rather a willing participant and thus a self-serving and manipulative woman. He questions the truthfulness of her evidence, implying that she invented a victimized caricature to downplay her role in the crimes and to secure a plea agreement. This commentary upholds the stark and problematic dichotomy between victimhood and offending behaviour that is so prevalent in legal and correctional discourses that it borders on sociological cliché. Given that this divisive trope is so common in the criminological imaginary, it is seductively easy to accept Homolka's construction as only narcissistic and dangerous, rather than to also accept her as a victim. Unfortunately, this explanation does a disservice to women who are experiencing violence at the hands of a sadistic intimate partner and does little to aid in generating a more nuanced and complex reading of Karla Homolka. In the final section of this chapter, we examine the controversial issue of Homolka's plea bargain, which journalists dubbed both the "sweetheart deal" and the "pact with the devil."

The Sweetheart Deal, aka, the Pact with the Devil

The plea agreement that the Crown and George Walker negotiated for Homolka was predominantly described in both media and juridical discourses alternately as a "sweetheart deal" and "a pact with the devil," which was also the title of Stephen Williams's 2004 book. While the process of negotiating a plea agreement in exchange for information and testimony has been a legally accepted practice for well over a century in Canadian and British criminal law, the fact that Homolka received one disturbed many Canadians. Justice Galligan (1996, 89) related the Crown's position regarding the plea agreement:

> Moreover, everyone involved in the process disliked the deal and disliked the result. They have confirmed to me that Murray Segal would not have made the agreement if the circumstances had not demanded that he do so. All of the persons who were involved told me that if the videotapes had been available at the time, Karla Homolka would have found herself in the prisoner's box beside Paul Bernardo.

While Homolka's narrative of abuse was legally accepted as a mitigating factor in her sentencing, it is clear that Crown counsel and the police did not believe she should receive a reduced sentence. Despite the fact that there was physical and psychiatric evidence to support her claims of battery, the Crown felt that the abuse did not justifiably mitigate her actions. The Crown's desire to see Homolka sentenced at least equally severely as Bernardo undermines their stated acceptance of the evidence. This was a plea agreement of evidentiary necessity that sat uncomfortably with all those involved.

Homolka not only confessed to her involvement in the deaths of Leslie Mahaffy and Kristen French, but also to her role in the death of her sister.

Confessing to a crime the police were unaware of demonstrates her willingness not only to cooperate with the authorities but also to ensure that the degree of her criminality be known. It also establishes her desire to disclose incriminatory information despite personal costs to her and her family. It can be argued that Homolka's willingness to come forward with this information indicates a certain degree of honesty within her testimony.[7] While not excusing her involvement in the crimes, we contend that it is crucial to recognize her role as secondary and that treating Homolka and Bernardo equally indicates a failure to recognize the fundamental differences between the two. On this point of evidentiary necessity, Justice Galligan (1996, 215) writes:

> This sentiment is expressed in different forms. It can be summarized in 2 contentions: that Karla Homolka got a "sweetheart deal" and that she was given "preferential treatment". The first decision, to agree to a twelve-year sentence, was driven by sheer necessity and not by a desire to treat Karla Homolka differently than any other criminal. I have no doubt that the Crown would have preferred that Karla Homolka appear in the prisoner's dock with Paul Bernardo facing first degree murder charges. However, without her evidence, at the time the decision was made, the police did not have the evidence to charge Paul Bernardo with the offences arising out of the deaths of Leslie Mahaffy and Kristen French, much less convict him of them.

While acknowledging that it is false to suggest that Homolka received preferential treatment, Justice Galligan contradictorily suggests that the 12-year sentence was only given because of practical necessity. The Crown would have preferred to charge and convict Homolka of first-degree murder. We suggest that this position represents a failure, possibly due to political and emotional influences, to accept that Homolka's involvement was coerced or partially forced, that she does not represent the same danger as Bernardo and thus does not warrant the same sentence.

We contend that Homolka's everydayness – her whiteness, middle-class upbringing, education, and familial support – situated her as an accepted member of the community, and that this membership contributed to the collective shock felt when she transgressed the most serious socio-cultural boundaries of community membership (a point we explore in depth in the next chapter). Not only did the public not expect this behaviour from one of its most beautiful members, it did not know how to process or make sense of the conflicting narratives she herself, media reporters, and the different legal actors and experts spun about her. Commentators frequently juxtaposed the public's shock and anger at the crimes against Karla's "ordinary" life and upbringing:

> Outside the courthouse here the watchers hissed at her, this pretty young woman. Mothers, their babies in strollers, cast loathing looks at Karla Homolka as she arrived each day of the five-day trial in a gray Dodge

> Caravan chauffeured by plainclothes Niagara Region police. Many called her "tramp" and one wished she'd "rot in hell." . . . Homolka was by most accounts a dutiful daughter – protected and loved by her parents, who sat at her right side throughout the hearings. She's an animal lover, gentle and caring; a nurse to sick cats and dogs. She commands loyalty from her many friends. To shield her from media cameras, some held a flattened cardboard refrigerator box in front of her as she lounged recently by her parent's back-yard swimming pool. On its surface, Karla Homolka's very middle-class life has seemed to ride on still waters, with barely a ripple. But beneath ran an undercurrent of horror.
>
> (Hall 7 July 1993, A18)

While Homolka had the privileges of a safe and happy middle class upbringing, most criminalized women do not. Rather, it is typical for women in conflict with the law to experience poverty, precarious housing, homelessness, neglect or abuse as a child, trauma and victimization as an adult, addiction and mental health complications (Comack 2014; Comack and Brickey 2007; Faith 1993). For many women, these experiences coalesce into a cycle of victimization and criminalization that is aggravated for women of colour, especially Aboriginal women (Balfour and Comack 2006). By contrast, Homolka did not experience violence nor was she involved with the criminal justice system prior to her relationship with Bernardo. Homolka is an oddity in criminal law; she is demographically different than most criminalized women, including those that commit acts of violence or who are legally designated dangerous offenders, she also served her sentence to warrant expiry rather than receiving parole at two-thirds of her sentence – the norm in Canada.

The collective cultural shock that flowed from her involvement in these crimes generated a moral panic around women's violence (Kilty and Fabian 2010) that made us question: how are we supposed to differentiate between good and bad, between safe and dangerous and ultimately between those we can trust and those we should fear? Homolka's monsterization as an aberration of femininity and womanhood reveals an exaggerated emphasis on her capacity for dangerousness. To categorize an individual as a monster serves to separate them from the rest of the community; in this case, it also allowed us to separate Homolka's participation in the crimes from the context of the prolonged physical, sexual, and emotional battery to which she was subject. Rather than recognizing her role as a reticent accomplice, her construction as the violent woman of our nightmares reified the figurative subject of the moral panic as a new breed of criminal woman, one who is able to commit egregious harm and to manipulate the criminal justice system in order to receive an unjust sweetheart deal.

There is one image that illustrates Homolka's narcissism particularly well and it is the cartoon graphic designed by celebrated Canadian artist Anita Kunz that was originally used for the cover page of the now defunct *Saturday Night* magazine issue that published Patricia Pearson's essay *Behind Every Successful Psychopath: Why Karla Homolka was the Perfect Match for Paul Bernardo.*[8] Kunz's cartoon image of Homolka is a caricature of the wedding photo shown above in Figure 2.1 and it depicts that same heavily lidded gaze in the photo presented in Figure 2.3. Here, cartoon Homolka's gaze is fixated on the over-sized diamond engagement ring on her right hand, which gives off the only light in the otherwise dark graphic, and depicts what was described as her obsessive desire to marry Bernardo even after learning of his violent nature and sadistic sexual tendencies; as though the perfect wedding was the light that disturbingly attracted her like a moth to a flame. The illustration goes so far as to parody the woman who earned the "sweetheart deal" by portraying her in a wedding dress with a sweetheart neckline. The image accentuates her flowing blond hair and voluptuous body that were described in detail throughout the newsprint coverage. Homolka's iconography as the alluring woman whose actions we could not understand upholds traditional narratives about women using their femininity to commit violence as exceptionally cunning and supported claims that she deceived the court to receive a lenient sentence. Because she did not receive a life sentence like Bernardo, Homolka was easily cast as the cleverest of the pair, intelligence that the media identified as evidence of her duplicitousness and ability to mislead the court.

At the time, Homolka's cooperation with the authorities was essential to convict the more dangerous Paul Bernardo. Had the police located the videotapes earlier, Homolka's confessions would have been rendered superfluous and she would have been charged alongside her husband. The plea agreement angered Canadians, many of who were willing to allow the criminal justice system to fall into disrepute in order to appeal her sentence. Well-known Canadian legal scholar and practicing lawyer Alan Young wrote to the Attorney General with the hope that he would do just that; his letter was included as an appendix to the Galligan Report:

> Most people have little interest in the trial of the accused, Paul Bernardo, as they seem to assume that justice will be served at the end of his trial. Nevertheless, there has been, and will continue to be, a public outcry regarding the lenient sentence awarded to Ms Homolka in exchange for her testimony. It is not an overstatement to suggest that her twelve year sentence is a travesty of justice. . . . I have studied the terms of her plea negotiation agreement and I have concluded that re-prosecuting her is fraught with procedural and evidentiary obstacles which may prove to be insurmountable. However, I am of the opinion that seeking leave to appeal her sentence is legally and morally sound, and that such a course of action would be politically wise. . . .The Crown did what it had to do at the time in order to bring Mr Bernardo to justice. However, I also believe that Ms Homolka manipulated and misled the Ministry of the Attorney General and was therefore able to secure a sentence which did not take into account her full involvement regarding the deaths of T. Homolka, L. Mahaffy and K. French. In addition, there were other sexual assaults committed by Ms Homolka which were not disclosed prior to her being sentenced in July 1993.

Young's text exhibits our point well. While Bernardo was largely understood as the more dangerous of the two, the gaze remained fixated on Homolka because the public felt robbed of justice knowing that she would not spend life in prison, which Young describes as "a travesty of justice." Young is careful not to accuse the Crown of having being duped, instead citing the temporal necessity of securing Homolka as the star witness before the discovery of the videotapes. Court transcripts and the Galligan Report reveal that Homolka did disclose the content of her participation in the sexual assaults, however she entrenched her involvement firmly in a narrative of coercion, force, and victimization that painted an image of a fearful woman participating under duress. To the contrary, the videotapes revealed her smiling on camera – a seemingly willing partner.

Moreover, it was Homolka who made the videotapes known to police in the first place, revealing their existence and content during her interrogation. While there was much public, media, and legal backlash toward Homolka's failure to disclose the sexual assault on Jane Doe, there was virtually no recognition of her forthrightness about the existence and content of the videotapes. Despite the fact that after the official conclusion to the police search of the couple's home Bernardo instructed his then lawyer, Ken Murray, to remove the videotapes, which he had hidden in the ceiling behind the light fixture in the bathroom, the gaze remained on Homolka as the deceptive and manipulative actor. Murray planned to use the videotapes to show Homolka as a willing participant and liar in open court and subsequently kept the tapes for over 17 months, during which time the plea agreement was formalized. He was later found not guilty of obstructing justice and was not disciplined by the Law Society of Upper Canada.

To characterize Homolka's plea agreement as a sweetheart deal reflects gendered rhetoric that relies on and upholds historic tropes that narrate criminalized women as using their femininity to manipulate legal actors (traditionally men) in order to receive judicial leniency or what Pearson (1998) describes as "chivalry" in sentencing. Similarly, describing the plea agreement as "a pact with the devil" sustains her monsterization as evil incarnate. Both descriptions are problematically shallow and do not reflect the sincere complexity of this case or the complicated effects of Homolka's relationship with Bernardo.

Conclusion

Homolka's simultaneous construction as a *dangerous woman* and a *woman in danger* of a sadistic and abusive husband is demonstrated throughout the newsprint coverage, the court transcripts and the Galligan Report. This dichotomous construction only bolstered Homolka's characterization as a rare and sensational figure of female dangerousness and angered and incited fear amongst the public. As time passed and the case evolved there was a clear shift in how Homolka was discursively constructed. While key media and legal actors initially accepted her narrative of victimhood, they eventually abandoned that belief and steadfastly focused on her dangerousness. Throughout the evolution of this sensational and emotionally driven case, Karla Homolka has straddled characterizations of these two elusive categories of womanhood.

Homolka's initial self-construction as a battered woman, who participated in sexually violent crimes to appease her sadistic husband, played on the historic characterization of criminalized women as established victims. This discourse bordered on constructing her criminality as falling under duress. Following the recovery of the videotaped evidence of the sexual assaults, acceptance of Homolka's victim narrative was replaced by her social construction as an overtly and uniquely dangerous woman. Given that the plea bargain was formalized by the time the videotapes were uncovered, the court was compelled to accept Homolka's victim narrative and secondary involvement so she could continue as the Crown's star witness in Paul Bernardo's trial; her testimony secured Bernardo's conviction, the party deemed to be the more dangerous of the two. The graphic visual images of a smiling Karla Homolka on the videotapes were permanently damaging to her self-construction as a victim, which led most journalists and reporters to question her narrative of abuse as little more than hyperbole. Over time, Homolka's beauty and charm came to be seen not as evidence of her passive femininity and potentiality for victimhood, but as weapons she narcissistically used to manipulate and endanger others. The videos provided an explicit and voyeuristic look inside the couple's sex life that left little to the imagination – or perhaps more aptly, caused our imaginations to run wild. More than that, however, they cemented the cultural view of Homolka as deceitful, sexually deviant and dangerous while exculpating belief in her victim narrative.

Through her participation in the sexual assaults and homicides, Karla Homolka not only transgressed the social norms of accepted femininity, she violated the law and the moral values of the community. Homolka seemingly represents the two opposing ends of the victimization-criminalization continuum where her endangerment came to define her dangerousness. But violence casts a long shadow and considering its effects does not neutralize her responsibility, it adds important explanatory context. The paradox of dangerousness generated in this case helped to crystallize a broader moral panic surrounding a new category of criminal woman (Comack 2014; Comack and Brickey 2007; Kilty and Fabian 2010), the sexually violent female predator, and reified Homolka as an iconic figure of dangerousness. Women who participate in violent crimes are negatively typified in part because they are so far removed from the gendered expectations of hetero-normative femininity[9] (Faith 1993; Kilty 2010; Kilty and Fabian 2010; Naylor 1995; Snider 2004). While not excusing Homolka's criminality, her involvement is more complex than was established in media accounts. Our genealogy of her dangerousness unfolds how the social construction of Karla Homolka's body, sexuality, femininity, criminality and personhood shifted and transgressed. Over 20 years have elapsed since she was sentenced, but Homolka's image and persona continue to haunt our social and cultural imaginary. In the next chapter we unpack Homolka's everydayness via explorations of hegemonic femininity, whiteness, and classed and spatial inclusions in order to contextualize why she remained at the centre of the media and juridical gazes.

Notes

1 Affect theorists Sara Ahmed and Lauren Berlant carried out an in-depth analysis of the cultural politics of emotion and the ways in which objects (here the wedding photo) accumulate "positive affective value as social goods" (Ahmed 2010, 21). These objects are, of course, embedded within gendered assumptions about femininity, behaviour, and social relations.

2 Chandler describes "choice rhetoric as emphasizing women's ability to choose different directions. Choice feminists are in fact susceptible to critique in that they ignore the reality, or 'truth,' of the constraints of violence imposed upon women's ability to make choices" (1999, 143).

3 In 1990, Angelique Lyn Lavallée was acquitted of murdering her common law husband, Kevin Rust, based on evidence supporting her claims of suffering from the Battered Woman Syndrome. The Crown appealed the acquittal to the Manitoba Court of Appeal, which overturned the original verdict and ordered a new trial. Lavallée appealed against the Manitoba Court of Appeal's decision to the Supreme Court of Canada, who in 1990 allowed her appeal and upheld her acquittal.

4 We examine the tropes of ideal victimhood and inconsistent offenders in detail in chapter 3 and sexual taboos and Homolka's construction as sexually deviant in chapter 4.

5 An RCMP protégé of Hazelwood's provided the Green Ribbon Task Force with Hazelwood et al.'s paper in 1993 as a theoretical forensic explanation for Homolka's behaviour; this paper was used as the basis for Homolka's defence and as justification for the plea negotiation. The paper was included both as evidence at Homolka's 1993 plea and sentencing hearing and in the appendices of Justice Galligan's report. Hazelwood would eventually travel to Kingston, ON to interview Homolka at the Prison for Women in 1996.

6 We examine Homolka's characterization as psychopathic in relation to interpretations of her as a remorseful or remorseless subject in chapter 5.

7 Critics argue that she was not forthcoming or honest in her disclosure of events because she did not reveal the sexual assault on Jane Doe until after she signed the plea agreement. Homolka contended that she did not remember the assault at the time and that she began to have memories of it in dreams while incarcerated in the Kingston Prison for Women. Her position was supported by psychiatric evaluation.

8 Pearson published this essay in Kindle format in 2012 via Canadian Writers Group and kept the image as the cover design for the ebook. We were unable to secure copyright permission to reprint the image, which may be accessed online. Retrieved from: http://www.canadianwritersgroup.com/index.php/e-books/successful-psychopath/

9 Hetero-normativity entails the reproduction of heterosexual relations as the norm and dominant side of the sexuality hierarchy. Used in conjunction with femininity it emphasizes relations of ruling based on the traditional nuclear family structure and women's role in the domestic sphere.

3 Ideal Victims and Inconsistent Offenders

Notes on the Effects of Whiteness, Gender, Space, and Class on the Cultural Fixation on Karla Homolka

Much feminist criminological literature has endeavoured to deconstruct archetypal characterizations of women as either passive victims or monstrous Others (Balfour and Comack 2006; Boyd 1999, 2004, 2008; Jiwani 2006; Kilty and Frigon 2006). Despite these advancements, critical race scholars have documented the failure of second and third wave feminism to incorporate race into their analyses (Collins 2000) and critical whiteness scholars point to the maintenance of a pervasive ideology of colour-blindness that permeates institutional discourses (that is, media, legal, political, and academic) and the everyday narratives of citizens in western cultures (Frankenberg 1993, 1997; Garner 2007, 2012). While criminologists have studied how race contributes to the social construction of dangerous groups of persons of colour, for example, imagery of the "young black mugger" (Doran 2002), "crack mom" (Boyd 2004, 2006, 2008) or "gangster/gang-banger" (Fontaine 2006), all of which conjure a heightened public fear of specific racialized groups, there are fewer examinations of how whiteness affects our understanding of violence, victimhood, and justice.

As racialized minorities are disproportionately over-represented at all levels of the criminal justice system (Comack and Balfour 2004), discussions of institutionally entrenched racism and ethnocentrism have predominantly attempted to document differences across race in policing, arrest, and charging and sentencing (Dell 2002). While this is obviously important, few scholars have examined the role whiteness plays in our interpretation of violence and victimization. This lack of critical engagement positions whiteness as normative and raceless (Frankenberg 1993, 1997; Garner 2007, 2012), implying that it has little effect upon our understanding or (re)presentation of criminal cases. Yet it is often only when a white victim is harmed by a person of colour that race is considered an aggravating factor in the crime itself (Hewitt 2005); as Elizabeth Comack and Gillian Balfour write, "the worst thing you can do is kill a white woman" (2004, 88). Building on this line of thought, critical race scholars argue that the criminal justice system effectively privileges a kind of white innocence in cases involving white offenders and racial minority victims (Jiwani 2006, 2010; Razack 2000).

Nils Christie's (1986) conceptualization of ideal victimhood is useful here. Christie identified a binary categorization of deserving and undeserving victimhood that "illustrates the construction of a kind of disposable victimhood that is based on physical, racialized, classist, sexualised, and gendered notions of what it means to be a victim and to experience victimisation" (Kilty and Fabian 2010, 132):

> By "ideal victim" I have instead in mind a person or a category of individuals who – when hit by crime – most readily are given complete and legitimate status of being a victim. The ideal victim is, in my use of the term, a sort of public status of the same type and level of abstraction as that for example of a "hero" or a "traitor". It is so by at least five attributes: (1) the victim is weak. Sick, old or very young people are particularly well suited as ideal victims. (2) The victim was carrying out a respectable project. (3) She was where she could not possibly be blamed for being – in the street during the daytime. (4) The offender was big and bad. (5) The offender was unknown and in no personal relationship to her.
>
> (Christie 1986, 18–19)

Christie acknowledges that this is not an exhaustive list of possible attributes that may contribute to the production of ideal victimhood; for example, he does not mention race or whiteness, nor does he explicitly discuss class or femininity/masculinity. In this chapter we expand upon Christie's conceptualization by examining the effects of these oppressions on the cultural fascination with this case and with Homolka specifically. Not surprisingly, given that both the offenders and the victims in this case were white, there has been a lack of critical attention paid to the ways in which race contributed to our cultural interpretation and consumption of media coverage of the case and its actors. However, critical scholars argue that we must study the salience of whiteness, how it is performed, the ways in which it is masqueraded as universal and legitimized as normative and thus how it affects institutional explanations of violence and victimization such as those advanced in the media and the courts (Frankenberg 1993, 1997; Headley 2004; Yancy 2004). Examining whiteness forces us to confront how white privilege is structurally embedded and might therefore affect police and media attention toward certain cases rather than to others.

In this chapter, we conceptualize the degree of media coverage as indicative of the intense cultural preoccupation with Karla Homolka, which we suggest is borne from the intersection of considerations of whiteness, hegemonic femininity, space and class, and the similarity between the mainstream public, the victims and the offenders (Gilchrist 2010; Jiwani 2006; Jiwani and Young 2006; Razack 2000). We examine these particular attributes as sources of socio-cultural and political privilege that intersected and supported the construction of the young girls in this case as ideal victims. As institutional discourses emphasized Homolka's similarity to her victims, they cultivated an image of a woman who could blend in with and thus go undetected in the community; in other words, she was constituted as a predator hidden in plain sight. Lending to the shock Homolka's participation in these crimes elicited, this image runs counter to Christie's explanation that for the victim to be awarded complete and legitimate status, the offender must be "big and bad." Together, these constructions of Homolka and her victims help to better contextualize the media frenzy that surrounded this case and the subsequent cultural fixation on Homolka as an "inconsistent offender" and enigmatic subject.

The Ideology of Colour-blindness and the Effects of Whiteness on Newsworthiness

Critical race and whiteness scholars problematize the ideology of colour-blindness that permeates western societal discourses and associated practices. These scholars identify colour-blindness as entrenching racist beliefs and narratives within law, policy and other institutional discourses that effectively marginalize non-white individuals (Brown et al. 2003; Frankenberg 1993, 1997; Garner 2007, 2012; Headley 2004; Yancy 2004). Whiteness can play a key role in drawing legal, media and thus public attention to certain cases and actors rather than to others – attention that subsequently bolsters the widespread cultural preoccupation with certain victims and offenders. In her explanation of colour-blindness, critical whiteness scholar Ruth Frankenberg discusses the implications of colonial discourses, such as those that shape Canada's socio-political history:

> One effect of colonial discourse is the production of an unmarked, apparently autonomous white/Western self, in contrast with the marked Other racial and cultural categories with which the racially and culturally dominant category is co-constructed. In this context it has also for the most part been Other, marked subjects rather than white/Western, unmarked subjects whose racial and cultural identities have been the focus of study. Within this framework for thinking about self and other, the white Western self as a racial being has for the most part remained unexamined and unnamed.
>
> (Frankenberg 1993, 17)

Frankenberg argues that colour-blindness (or in her words, colour-evasion) discursively produces the unmarked white body as normative and posits whiteness as racelessness.[1] One dangerous consequence of coding whiteness as raceless is that it "leaves in place whiteness as defining a set of normative cultural practices against which all others are measured and into which all are expected to fit" (Frankenberg 1993, 204). In this way, whiteness lends itself to the production of ideal victimhood, as it is the cultural norm that allows white victims to experience a more complete and legitimate victim status than non-white victims.

In terms of the volume of local and national media coverage, there is no question that certain cases are awarded more in-depth and prolonged attention than others. Media studies have taught us that there are a number of key factors that determine the newsworthiness[2] of a story, which Jiwani (2006, 38) defines as "what makes a story worth telling"; these factors include, but are not limited to: the placement of the article; the sensationalism of the headline grabbers; the tone, emotion and themes elicited in the text; the size, colour, and placement of photographs; the length or word count of the article; and the ability to create a continuing and prolonged news item or theme (Gilchrist 2008, 2010; Jewkes 2011a,b; Jiwani 2006; Surette 2007; Wardle 2007). In conjunction with a "when it bleeds it leads" approach to journalism that preys upon fear of crime, it is common for cases involving extraordinary acts of violence, especially those that include sexual violence, to be heavily reported upon so as to capture and maintain public and cultural interest (Jiwani 2006; Surette 2007; Kilty 2010).

There are barriers, however, that can prevent such extensive coverage – even in cases involving violence, multiple disappearances, and sexual crimes. For example, when sex workers are victimized it is often seen as a risk associated with their work rather than a culturally produced (and often racialized) act of violence that posits certain groups and individuals as in some way blameworthy for their own victimization (Gilchrist 2008, 2010; Kilty and Fabian 2010; Jiwani 2006; Razack 2000). Framing violence as resulting from some characteristic or action taken or not taken by the victim creates a binary between deserving and undeserving victims (Christie 1986; Gilchrist 2008, 2010; Kilty and Fabian 2010) and can hamper media reporting that tends to focus only on "the extreme" – namely, those details of events that are most shocking, often exaggerated and sensational – in order to sell copies of the paper, get viewers to tune in, or instigate discussion (Jewkes 2011a,b; Surette 2007). As Comack and Balfour (2004, 89) explain, race is a key factor in both legal and news media attention and the discursive framing of violence and victimization:

> If the victim happens to be Aboriginal, the lawyer suggests, although admittedly it is still a "serious crime," "You do not have to worry about the aggravating factor of your client having killed someone particularly deserving of protection by society." Defending a client charged with killing an Aboriginal person becomes easier by virtue of the racist perspective that the deceased deserved to die. The death is less of a concern to white middle-class people who do not view Aboriginal peoples as deserving of protection.

Comack and Balfour identify race and whiteness as a key value structure that modulates our understanding of acceptable victimhood. The authors clearly draw on Nils Christie's (1986) notion of the ideal victim, incorporating Aboriginality to exemplify how, in Canada, an ethnocentric court and public more readily sympathize and empathize with white victims; a fact that is exacerbated when the victim is white and the offender is a racialized minority. Scholars that examine racial disparities in media coverage and content of certain victims or offenders have afforded emphasis to identifying the ways in which racial minority victims are overlooked in comparison to white victims and to the variations in coverage and trial outcome when white offenders rape and murder victims who are visible racial minorities (Gilchrist 2008, 2010; Jiwani 2006; Jiwani and Young 2006; Razack 2000).

These studies show that in order to be constituted as an ideal victim one must be seen and cast as wholly innocent and "pure", which are also conventional discursive descriptors of whiteness. As innocence is essential to constituting ideal victimhood, it follows that the individual be either young or old and thus weak and vulnerable (Christie 1986). Only when the victim is understood to be innocent will the case solicit sensational and prolonged media coverage and attention. The four victims in this case were all young white girls, easily cast as children or adolescents and thus as weak or especially vulnerable. Less the rape victim identified only as Jane Doe,[3] Canadian newspapers frequently displayed the images of Leslie Mahaffy, Kristen French, and to a lesser extent Tammy Homolka on the front page – a technique Wardle (2007) claims helps to humanize the victim and elicit compassion in the audience. More costly, but also more effective in this effort, the newspapers also frequently used colour photographs, many of which were school photos that served to emphasize their youth and thus their vulnerability, weakness, purity, and innocence.

The whiteness or non-whiteness of the offender can also influence the degree of media coverage and thus public attention to a given case. In terms of news communications framing, the media coverage of the Bernardo and Homolka case largely endorsed a grand narrative that at once completely neglected race, which was not surprising given that both the victims and the offenders were white, and at the same time reinforced the victims' and offenders' likeness to mainstream (white) Canadian society. Here, whiteness is an absent presence, indicating its status as the raceless standard and norm that signals the unnamed and unmarked white bodies of both the victims and offenders in this case as legitimate members of the community and broader culture. The likeness between Homolka, her victims and the mainstream public was not only fostered based on their shared whiteness, but also on similarities related to space, class, and gender – points that are further elaborated upon below.

To readily showcase her everydayness and similarity to white middle-class Canadians, photographs of Homolka were also commonly found on the front page of local and national newspapers, especially in the early years of coverage leading up to the conclusion of Bernardo's sentencing hearing. Just as photographs of victims elicit empathy in the audience, photographs of Homolka provoked outrage that such an inconspicuous member of the community could participate in these crimes. For example, news headlines read: "Don't be fooled by Karla Homolka's Acting Job," "Homolka case suggests some women can choose to be monsters" and "At least we know the evil that is Karla Homolka." Photographs of Homolka attempted to make her look more sinister, the most famous being one where she is shown with a "heavily lidded eye" so as to give the image a more lurid appeal (shown in Chapter 2, Figure 2.3 of this book). Wardle (2007) also found that photos of accused persons and offenders often capture them staring blankly at the camera or being escorted in handcuffs by the police to encourage belief in their guilt. Such imagery of Homolka was common, for example photos of her being escorted from her parents' home in a prisoner transfer van to go to court. These photographs contributed to the media frenzy Homolka enthused. In fact, photographers were so zealous in their desire to capture images of Homolka upon her formal release from Joliette prison in 2005, that she was forced to lie down underneath a blanket in the back of a van in order to escape the gaze of their telephoto lenses.

Without considering the inclusionary effects of whiteness on our cultural interpretation of Homolka and the extensive press this case has received, one would be tempted to accept that there was no racial element to the case. In contrast, cases involving black on black violence are almost instantly read as "gang related," which problematically affixes Blackness as a cultural signifier of gang involvement and violence (Doran 2002; Peffley et al. 1996). Examinations of race or whiteness in cases involving white victims and white offenders are virtually non-existent, largely because of the absence of racialized differences between the actors involved in the crime. However, Stuart Hall directs us to make sense of those narratives and discourses that are absent so as to examine how a text, discourse, or representation is framed not only by what is explicit but also by what is implicit. In an important interview, Hall (1984) stated:

> It is not what an ideology says, which is what we usually think; it's in the things that ideology always takes for granted [such as whiteness], and the things it can't say – the things it systematically blips out on. That represents exactly the point of its selectivity, and that's how (if you take another ideological position) you see where the absences and silences are, and you can begin to interrogate the seamless web of that particular story from the viewpoint of another story as it were.

By re-centring discourses of whiteness as an absent presence and using it as an analytic construct, we argue that this likeness between the dominant culture, the victims and the offenders involved in this case contributed to fostering the shock, fear, and culturally embedded moral outrage that surrounded it and contributed to the broader cultural fascination with Homolka in particular. It was a common theme within newspaper coverage to describe Homolka's likeness to her victims and to the community at large, a factor that aided in the generation of greater media hype and cultural discussion about Homolka as an inscrutable character in this tragic drama. This sameness is primarily rooted in her whiteness, which is never explicitly named. Resistance or failure to name race is now a common feature of contemporary racialized discourse (Jiwani 2006; Razack 2003). We use italics in the following quote, from *The Ottawa Citizen* feature editor Janice Kennedy, to better emphasize the kinds of racialized discourses that were common in media reports:

> There is a young woman, only 23 even now with a lifetime of the indescribable already behind her, who loved animals and was, apparently, every acquaintance's typically "nice girl." There is *a face that you see every day* in your workplace, in your neighbourhood, perhaps in your home. Adolph Eichmann, balding and bespectacled, looked like the shopkeeper down the street and was an unremarkable personality. They say Jeffrey Dahmer,

> the Milwaukee cannibal, is quiet and boring. Karla Homolka Teale, by all accounts, has so far passed her short life *no differently on the surface than the mass of average young Canadian women.* Which may account for the public anger that boiled over this past week, the outrage that continues to seethe in the wake of her sentencing. It is less about publication bans and light sentences and useless calls for the return of the death penalty than it is about betrayal and fear. The outrage is code for the betrayal felt *in a world where nothing is as it seems. Barbie and Ken* have been on a murderous rampage, and the *natural order is turned upside down.* The outrage is code for fear. Karla Homolka Teale reminds us that evil is not in a distant and avoidable place, not necessarily among the *people of the night or the leather-jacketed punks on street corners.* It is among us. And it has *a face that resembles the comforting banality of our everyday world.*
>
> (Kennedy 11 July 1993, B2)

In a number of different turns of phrase throughout this excerpt Kennedy implicitly references the ordinariness of whiteness by highlighting Homolka's supposed everydayness. For example, she describes Homolka's as "a face that you see every day" that is similar to "the mass of average young Canadian women" and Homolka and Bernardo as "Barbie and Ken," one of the popular monikers with which the couple were dubbed by early 1993. These phrases are used to signify the alarming disjuncture between Homolka's image and the crimes she participated in. Kennedy designates this schism as "a world where nothing is as it seems" that turned "the natural order [] upside down." The author further contrasts Homolka's "banality" with implicitly racialized and classed archetypes of violence that she signifies with the phrases "people of the night" and "leather-jacketed punks on street corners." The hyper-visibility of these characters exemplifies the ways in which racialized discourses now materialize and function without having to overtly mention or name race, which Razack describes as a component of contemporary forms of culturalized violence (2003).

Having shattered the illusion that whiteness and being middle-class and female inherently affords a safe identity and thus person, this case forced white segments of Canadian society to reflect upon the fact that such exceptional instances of sexualized violence could be committed by individuals who were members of their own cultural group and communities, rather than by visible outsiders and members of marginalized and racialized groups. One result of this existential confrontation was the extensive volume of media coverage and the continued, and for a number of years, uninterrupted public consumption of the details of the case in the hopes of understanding how and why such tragedies could have occurred. This search for meaning cemented into a cultural fascination and even fixation upon Homolka as the "one that got away." Homolka's whiteness is signified through her supposed averageness, ordinariness, everydayness, or "banality" which led her to be seen as an inconsistent offender who was then recast as the epitome of evil – a point which Kennedy references in the above quote by her comparison of Homolka to Nazi Lieutenant Colonel, Adolph Eichmann.[4]

In the next section we outline how both Homolka and her victims were constructed in the news media as possessors of hegemonic femininity, an inherently white construct, and how this construction positions them as symbols of cultural value that, like whiteness, affects the perceived newsworthiness of this case.

Hegemonic Femininity

In their reformulation of the concept of hegemonic masculinity, Connell and Messerschmidt (2005) address the gender hegemony and hierarchy that maintains the subordination of women in the larger gender project. Hegemonic masculinity and hegemonic femininity were originally conceptualized as parallel constructs that documented the degree of relational power across different variations of how men and women perform the two. While Connell (1987) very briefly described the notion of "emphasized femininity" in *Gender and Power*, together the authors later revised the concept to argue that patriarchal power relations continue to disadvantage women in favour of men (Connell and Messerschmidt 2005, 848). Mimi Schippers problematized this reformulation, writing, "masculinity and femininity are hegemonic precisely in the ideological work they do to legitimate and organize what men actually do to dominate women individually or as a group" (2007, 93). While the feminine remains the denigrated side in this binary, Schippers rejects the idea that femininity cannot be hegemonic, suggesting that it is the quality content of the described femininity that signals whether it is hegemonic, subordinate or pariah in form (Schippers uses this term to designate a trait or characterization of the quality content that is contaminating to the relationship between masculinity and femininity – a point we return to shortly); she further notes that all three forms reproduce, legitimate and maintain masculine superiority and gender hegemony. For this inquiry, we adopt Schippers' conceptualization of hegemonic femininity:

> Hegemonic femininity consists of the characteristics defined as womanly that establish and legitimate a hierarchical and complementary relationship to hegemonic masculinity and that, by doing so, guarantee the dominant position of men and the subordination of women.
>
> (Schippers 2007, 94)

The intersectional effects of race and whiteness, class, sexuality, able-bodiedness, and spatial and geographic differences also influence and shape performances of (hegemonic) femininity. While these and other oppressions shape masculinities and femininities, it is important to remember that the two are eternally relational and do not operate in separate or distinct "spheres" (Connell and Messerschmidt 2005, 836; Schippers 2007). Masculinities are by and large defined and constituted by that which they are not, namely, feminine. This does not mean that men cannot exhibit traditionally feminine attributes, but rather that the masculinity of those who do will be constructed as effeminate, which is awarded a lowered or subordinate, rather than hegemonic, status. The same can be said for women who exhibit traditionally masculine traits, for example the masculine attribute of facial hair (Kilty and Fabian 2010), or athletic prowess in contact sports such as wrestling or body-building (Sisjord and Kristiansen 2009). These attributes are cast within a hierarchy and reflect a derogated or lowered status to their hegemonic counterparts. Masculinities and femininities are configurations of different practices that are accomplished through social action, discourse and performance and therefore vary according to the hegemonic gender relations in a particular social setting, meaning they are intensely context dependent (Connell and Messerschmidt 2005; Schippers 2007).

Media and legal characterizations of both Homolka and her victims identify them as exhibiting hegemonic femininity. Throughout both the trial transcripts and the news media descriptions of Homolka one constant was the continued emphasis on her physical and aesthetic appearance. Rife throughout the newsprint coverage are references to Homolka's beauty, which was embedded in descriptions of her as "Barbie" (to Bernardo's "Ken"), "blonde," "pale," "blue eyed," "beautiful," "beautifully/exquisitely coiffed hair," "perfectly tinted/coloured hair," "manicured nails," "pretty," "youthful/young," "petite," "thin," "vivacious," "a looker," "sexy," "seductive/seductress," "great figure," and "fit/toned/hard body." Her victims were described in a parallel way, less the references to their sexuality, which would have been uncouth to say the least given that they were underage youths who were sexually tortured. However, similar references to Mahaffy's and Tammy Homolka's blondeness, paleness, and blue eye colour and to Kristen French's beauty and "lush brown mane of hair" are implicit references to whiteness, a component of hegemonic femininity (Schippers 2007; Kilty and Fabian 2010). The victims were also typically described as "schoolgirls" and Homolka and Bernardo as "the schoolgirl killers" – another moniker that gained much traction in media coverage – so as to emphasize the girls' youth and vulnerability as ideal victims. The regular use of a picture of Kristen French in her Catholic school uniform, a common trope in hegemonic masculine sexual fantasizing (Jensen 2010), also served to highlight her weakness and defencelessness as a young girl and contributed to her constitution as an ideal victim who personified hegemonic femininity.

While these aesthetic likenesses between Homolka and her victims were made evident in news coverage and throughout courtroom proceedings, they alone did not constitute the totality of ways that Homolka was said to exhibit hegemonic femininity. Given that to be considered hegemonic the composition of femininity must support masculine supremacy in gender relations (Schippers 2007), we must consider other factors. For example, the much discussed comments Homolka published in her high-school yearbook that referenced her belonging to the "Diamond Club," a euphemism she and her group of friends used to describe their desire to marry young and to have a rich older man take care of them. Her self-construction as a would be wife and mother above all else, including sacrificing her acceptance to attend the University of Toronto in order to get married and work as a veterinary assistant, illustrates her adherence to traditional western conceptualizations of woman's deferential place at her man's side. What eventuated into an extraordinarily lavish wedding with guests who dined on pheasant, and the couple's arrival at the reception in a horse-drawn carriage was seen to signify her desire to live out an epic fairy-tale romance that is characteristic of hegemonic femininity.

Institutional discourses also questioned Homolka's excessive love-letter writing to Bernardo, which forensic evidence numbered in the hundreds. The sometimes-daily card and note writing reiterated her love for and worship of Bernardo, who demanded that she address him as "the King" (R. v. Bernardo 1995). Demonstrative of her subservience to the man that was physically, sexually and emotionally abusing her, Homolka testified that she wrote these letters, cards and notes as a way to appease Bernardo and thus as a kind of battery prevention technique. These examples illustrate how Homolka firmly entrenched her social actions, discourses, and performances in the production of hegemonic femininity that maintained and supported Bernardo's production of the more dominant hegemonic masculinity.

Homolka's subservience to Bernardo extended far beyond writing him love letters and addressing him with servile sobriquets. Much of her 17-day testimony and cross-examination at Bernardo's trial detailed the couple's sexual life and Homolka's sexual submissiveness, a key feature of hegemonic femininity. Homolka described how their sex life became one sided as,

> He stopped caring about what I wanted, and how I felt and what I needed sexually, and it was all for him. We would do what he wanted, when he wanted it, how he wanted it.
>
> (R. v. P. Bernardo 1995, 31)

Several days later, in a telling exchange with Paul Bernardo's defence attorney, John Rosen, Homolka explained that she had no control over if, when, where or how she and Bernardo engaged in sex, stating "I never denied Paul. I was his property." (R. v. P. Bernardo, 1995, 1498). Rosen and several journalists dismissed Homolka's claims, arguing that she was a willing participant in the couple's "kinky" and sadomasochistic (S/M) sex (Pearson 1997; Williams 2004) – a point we examine more closely in chapter 4. For the purposes of the current discussion, it is of note that Homolka consistently maintained a discourse of sexual submissiveness that was clinically accepted by correctional psychologists and psychiatrists (Galligan 1996). Scholars distinguish pathological submissiveness from consensual S/M relationships that are built on trust (Newmahr 2011). Given that Homolka's submissiveness was only witnessed in her relationship with Bernardo, her courtroom performative demonstrating her ability to resist aggressive defence counsel attacks against her character, this fact lends credibility to her narration as a compliant victim of a sexual sadist rather than either a sadist or masochist.

There is one final point related to hegemonic femininity that we wish to discuss. Underscoring the connection to motherhood, one of the most commonly described attributes of hegemonic femininity is that the woman be nurturing

(Kilty and Dej 2012; Schippers 2007). In her court testimony Homolka referenced two incidents to demarcate herself as a nurturing woman even in the midst of her participation in the sexual abuse of her victims. First, in response to Bernardo's pronouncement that he would rape her younger sister Tammy with or without her assistance, Homolka obtained the anaesthetic Halothane and sedative Halcion from the veterinary clinic where she worked as a way to prevent Tammy from remembering what she believed was an inevitable assault and to prevent Bernardo from hurting her family, which he had threatened to do if she failed to assist him.[5] Second, she claimed to have tried to comfort Leslie Mahaffy by offering one of her favourite stuffed animals to hold onto and by requesting that Bernardo sedate Mahaffy with sleeping pills before strangling her (R. v. P. Bernardo 1995). These are inconsequential details when considering the gravity of her crimes, but they illustrate that the same woman who could participate in the sexual assault and murder of young girls also attempted to provide some small degree of comfort to them. However, while showing care and nurturance are typically said to exemplify hegemonic femininity, Homolka's acts of kindness are forever tainted by the tragic context within which they occurred. We suggest that Homolka's hegemonic feminine status was also tainted and that she instead came to be seen as straddling the line between hegemonic and what Schippers (2007) calls pariah femininities.

Schippers (2007, 95) contends that aggressiveness, promiscuity and the sexual desire of other women are "practices and characteristics that are stigmatized and sanctioned if embodied by women" because they "constitute a refusal to complement hegemonic masculinity in a relation of subordination and therefore are threatening to male dominance." Like those who disbelieved Homolka's contention of sexual submissiveness and who argued that she was actually a promiscuous sexual deviant (Pearson 1997; Pron 1995; R. v. P. Bernardo 1995; Williams 2004), it was a common media trope to suggest that Homolka used her beauty and victim narrative to manipulate different institutional authorities, including police, lawyers, judges, correctional officials, social workers, psychologists, and psychiatrists. For example, over the years, Canadian journalist Christie Blatchford has written extensively about Homolka's character. Given her expansive coverage of the case it is worth quoting Blatchford at length:

> No sooner had Ms Homolka stood up to whisper in her best little-girl voice, "Oui," in answer to the formal reading of her name, than her lawyer Sylvie Bordelais was asking if the cuffs could be removed. Judge Jean Beaulieu agreed, and one of the two court security lads undid them, fumbling a bit as he drew close to her and took in that cloud of pale champagne-coloured hair and the heavy-lidded dark gaze and the frosty lipstick on that full mouth. At 35, she's still a looker. A dozen years in Canadian prisons is apparently a good thing, as the felon Martha Stewart would say, for womanly maintenance. Ms Homolka had easily the best hair in the room – layered, beautifully coloured, not a root to be seen and with a long side bang, this was no ordinary joint job – though it must be pointed out her competition came

> in the main from the wretches of the press. In a black sweater and caramel pantsuit, she was among the best-dressed and put-together. Forget rehabilitation; the Correctional Service of Canada is into the makeover. She's still got the old mojo working too. When the poor fellow struggling with the handcuffs – when Ms Homolka was young and in her prime, she had her a set of her own, so it may be she was amused at his awkwardness – succeeded, she favoured him with a breathy "Merci!" and I swear a faint blush rose to his cheeks. And damned if, by the time she was led in the courtroom a second time after the morning break, the shackles were nowhere to be seen.
>
> (Blatchford 3 June 2005, A1)

Blatchford styles Homolka's femininity as a calculated veil donned to charm those around her and to foster empathy amongst those guarding or evaluating her in some way. Blatchford's account documents how Homolka's hegemonic femininity morphed into pariah femininity when used as a tool, a carefully planned assemblage and performance to manipulate the men around her – a clear threat to male dominance. While it is considered courteous and is common to appear well groomed for court, the author painstakingly details aspects of Homolka's hegemonic beauty, through which she subtly references her whiteness ("cloud of pale champagne-coloured hair"), to underscore that she is not what she seems. Describing the eternality of her beauty ("heavy-lidded dark gaze and the frosty lipstick on that full mouth. At 35, she's still a looker") aids Blatchford's construction of Homolka as an inconsistent offender. In appearance, Homolka is "one of us" – a member of the dominant culture – a beautiful woman who could be "our" daughter, sister, friend, or mother. However, as media discourses mutated her hegemonic femininity into a kind of pariah femininity, journalists were able to constitute her as a kind of dark celebrity, a famous femme fatale.

In the next section we examine the classed and spatial inclusions that contributed to the perceived newsworthiness of this case, the construction of ideal victimhood and the construction of Homolka as an "inconsistent" offender.

Classed and Spatial Inclusions

The final point to consider for this reading of the extensive legal and media attention the Bernardo-Homolka case wrought centres on an examination of classed and spatial inclusion. Like the discussions of whiteness and hegemonic femininity, the everydayness of the locales in which these crimes were perpetrated contributed to the Canadian public's unease and astonishment at their having occurred at all. These crimes were not committed in a "dangerous" urban city, ghetto or slum, nor did they take place in an isolated and hard to find rural setting, which are the most common venues for media and filmic depictions of serious violent crime (Low 2001; Muzzio and Halper 2002; Pain 1997; Wallace 2008). Rather, the victims were abducted from middle-class, white, small town suburban surroundings, which are generally considered to be safe spaces occupied by a non-threatening homogeneous population (Banks 2005; Garner 2007; Muzzio and Halper 2002; Pain 1997; Wallace 2008).

It was a common theme throughout the extensive news coverage of this case to read descriptions of the settings involved as places and spaces where crimes of this nature do not occur; these sentiments "perform [] the obligatory function of restoring normative order to the violent disruption caused by the crime" (Wallace 2008, 399):

> Place descriptors help to set the scene for how we are to think of the place normally. In middle-class and affluent areas, crime stories generally cast the event as a disruption to an otherwise peaceful, happy, safe, or serene location. The socio-economic class of residents is a detail noted, often in an off-hand manner, in many crime stories.
>
> (Wallace 2008, 399)

Bernardo and Homolka rented a large, single-family, Cape-Cod-style home on a wide corner lot in the affluent St Catharines suburb of Port Dalhousie Ontario. It was located approximately one block from the south shore of Lake Ontario. Place descriptors commonly included references to the "well developed" and "lush green" scenery, "tree lined street/enclave," "seashell pink clapboard home," "perfectly manicured lawns/homes," "affluent/wealthy/well-to-do/upscale neighbourhood," "tight-knit community," "a community where everyone knows each other," and "peaceful/tranquil/quiet suburb/surroundings." These space and place descriptors suggest how affluence is thought of as an "inoculation" against violence (Wallace 2008, 404); it is of note that the couple rented their home and were struggling financially on Homolka's small salary as a veterinary assistant and what money Bernardo made smuggling cigarettes across the border. The couple used their home, similar to their lavish wedding, to generate an outward appearance of financial wealth and security to deflect attention from their criminal actions. The alarm evoked by the stark contrast between the violence and place and space in which it occurred lingered and has not waned with time. Subsequently, the house that the couple lived and committed the sexual assaults and murders in was easily cast as a permanently contaminated, stigmatized and disgraced space to the extent that the house was eventually torn down.[6] Take the following lengthy quote from a front-page feature article from the Regina *Leader-Post*; we use italics to highlight the place descriptors used:

> In the *quiet lakeside suburb* of Port Dalhousie, dormant recollections from a not-so-distant past are again beginning to stir. The *neighbourhood's gaze* is fixed on a house that now sits in a *long-vacant lot* on *tree-lined* Bayview Avenue, *steps from the southern shores of Lake Ontario.* Just months old, the *towering Victorian-style dwelling* is a curiosity for some, a welcome sight for others, and for still more a silent symbol of remembrance and regret. An oblivious eye might not give it a second look, despite the *crude wooden barricade blocking the*

> *front door*, a *glaring Private Property sign*, and the *absence of even a single blade of grass*. But even though its *pink clapboard* predecessor is long gone and secretly buried, everyone in town knows the dark secret of 57 Bayview Avenue, *the former lair* of Paul Bernardo and Karla Homolka. Susan Bull can barely stand to look at it. "I don't think a lot of people like having the house up," said the 25-year-old rape crisis counsellor said, stealing a furtive glance at its *darkened windows*. "I mean, how could anyone live there?" Four years after police *levelled the dilapidated house* where teenagers Leslie Mahaffy and Kristen French were brutally tortured, raped, and killed, no one is home to answer her question. But so far, the new house has been unable to extinguish the fear and guilt of a *tranquil community* that played unwitting host to Bernardo's and Homolka's reign of terror. "It's always in the back of my mind, all the time," said Bull, who shudders at the memory of walking past the Bernardo house every day for years as she made her way to school. The lesson, she said, is valuable, if bitter: what happened to a pair of southern Ontario schoolgirls in 1991 and 1992 could happen to anyone, any time, anywhere.
>
> (N.A. 25 March 2000, A1)

This quote speaks of an attempt to transform a contaminated and polluted (Douglas 1966) space that locals and journalists referred to as the "house of horrors" into one that is hopeful for the return to its essential nature as a "tranquil community." While the resident neighbour questions how anyone could want to live on the site, building a new home signifies the sanitization and reclamation of the space – an effort to move past the taint brought by the couple's "reign of terror" and to generate a clean slate for the typically unassuming Garden City, the official nickname for the city of St Catharines based on its 4 square kilometres of gardens, parks, and hiking and bike trails.

Christie (1986, 18–19) identified the importance of place, space, and activity in his description of the attributes that constitute ideal victimhood. Specifically, he suggests that to be considered ideal, the victim must have been "carrying out a respectable project" at the time of the offence. We qualify this assertion and suggest that it is not always temporally specific, but rather that to be seen as ideal the victim must never have engaged in a project that could be seen as disreputable or unrespectable. Christie also notes that the victim must be in a space and place that "she could not possibly be blamed for being – [such as] in the street during the daytime" (1986, 18–19). These attributes direct us to examine spatial inclusions and exclusions, which are inherently shaped by class and race/whiteness. In what follows, we outline the ways in which a hierarchy of ideal victimhood was established through references to safe suburban spaces and normative versus rebellious activities.

As we have demonstrated, the victims in this case possessed the social and cultural capital born from being white and middle-class, conveying hegemonic femininity and from their geographic location in small town suburbia. Despite the fact that all of the victims shared these attributes, the reporters and journalists created a hierarchy of victimhood amongst the girls, exemplifying how victims experience different degrees of blame for their victimhood. The couple drugged and raped the first victim, Homolka's younger sister Tammy, on Christmas Eve, 1990, when her parents agreed that she be permitted to have alcohol although underage in celebration of the holiday season.[7] Although Tammy was assaulted in her family home, not a space she could be blamed for being in, descriptions of her underage drinking hint of a less than respectable project. The fact that she was permitted alcohol under the supervision of her parents and siblings and in order to celebrate Christmas Eve discursively aided to redeem the respectability of an otherwise culturally prohibited activity. Also of note, there was significantly less news coverage and use of photos of Tammy Homolka than there was of Leslie Mahaffy or Kristen French, a fact that did not go unnoticed by the Homolka family:

> Dorothy Homolka says her family is once again bracing for the barrage of threats that come every time her daughter is in the news. "It's not that I want sympathy from people, just a recognition that Tammy was a victim. They talk about the two all the time and Tammy is left out".
>
> (Gillespie and Shephard 4 Nov. 1999, 1)

Supporting this claim, a general search in the Canadian Newsstand Major Dailies database revealed significant differences in the number of results generated. When searching anywhere in the text for the name "Tammy Homolka" there were 1,853 results; for "Leslie Mahaffy" 7,782 results; for "Kristen French" 9,415 results; and there were 10,202 results for the combined searches of "Karla Homolka" (9,229), "Karla Bernardo" (32), and "Karla Teale"[8] (941).

While the familial relation of Tammy and her assailants elicited a collective expression of disgust (a point we examine in greater depth in chapter 4), the fact she was the only victim who was not harmed by a stranger contributed to her victimhood being overshadowed by Leslie Mahaffy's and Kristen French's. In fact, there is evidence to suggest that of the three, it was Kristen French who was constituted as the archetypical ideal victim. Leslie Mahaffy was presented as a rebellious youth for breaking curfew, drinking with friends, and staying for extended periods of time at a friend's house when her relationship with her parents was troubled (Pron 1995). On the night of her abduction, Mahaffy was attending a party with a group of friends after returning from the funeral of a classmate who had died in a car accident. Despite the conflict it generated between she and her parents, Mahaffy broke curfew again that night and was locked out of her home as a result – her parents' attempt at shaming her and ensuring they knew when she returned home. It was by chance that Bernardo saw her return home; he then approached her and asked her to come to his car to share a cigarette. As Kirk Makin wrote in *The Globe and Mail* (21 May 2005, F1):

> In a tragically misbegotten bid to discipline a rebellious teen, Leslie Mahaffy's parents locked her out of the house. She approached a shadowy figure for a cigarette, and was plucked away.

From the beginning, the police characterized Mahaffy as a runaway and unlike French's disappearance there was no community-organized search when her parents reported her missing. Journalists did aim to foster sympathy and empathy in the audience by encouraging readers to consider the anguish Mahaffy's parents felt about their effort to teach their daughter a lesson, but this also re-emphasized Leslie as a rebellious teen who was not where she should have been that night, namely home in bed as per her parents curfew rules. For example, Jim Rankin of the *Toronto Star* wrote (29 Oct. 1995, E1):

> Tough love is a hard path for parents to take, and even tougher to talk about when it goes wrong. On June 14, 1991, Leslie had been out with friends mourning the loss of a good friend who had died in a car accident, along with three other teens. It was several hours past her 10:30 pm curfew when she walked to the side door of her home. It was locked, so was the front door. She didn't want to wake her parents. She called a friend from a payphone in a nearby plaza to see if she could stay over. She couldn't. The rest is history. Bernardo made it that way when he grabbed Leslie sometime after 2 am, raped her with the help of his then-wife, and strangled her.

While Mahaffy and her group of friends were consoling one another following the accidental death of a classmate – an understandable and "respectable project," they were also isolated from view in a wooded area where they were drinking underage. Moreover, Mahaffy did not return home until approximately 2:00 am, nearly 4 hours past her curfew. Given that Mahaffy was lured and abducted from a street in her white middle-class suburb, reporters and journalists jumped at the chance to use her story as a cautionary tale for children who fail to follow their parent's rules to the letter.

Although Paul Bernardo abducted Mahaffy on his own, Homolka participated in French's abduction. Bernardo and Homolka parked their car in a church parking lot on a very busy street near downtown St Catharines and feigned asking French for directions, who was walking home from school at the time. Having been abducted in broad daylight only added to the construction of French's ideal victimhood. She could not be blamed for participating in an activity she should not be engaging in (like both Tammy Homolka's and Leslie Mahaffy's underage drinking), for being in a space or place that she should not be in (like Mahaffy's partying in the woods) or for disobeying her parent's curfew rules. The media quickly latched onto the public fear associated with French's abduction as a way to warn parents that it was not just rebellious teens that were at risk, but that every child was at risk. If such a tragedy could happen to French, underscoring her ideal victim status, it could happen to any young girl.

Some reporter's, such as Jim Rankin from the *Toronto Star*, juxtaposed French's (ideal) victim status to Mahaffy's, noting the disparity in the tone of news coverage between the two:

> From the beginning, Kristen French was portrayed by the media as the "good" girl – defiant in the face of death. Leslie was the "bad" girl – the

> rebellious "runaway". That's the way Halton Region police initially treated Leslie's missing person report. And the runaway label stuck. She had gone away before, and investigators did little more than put her name in the police computer.
>
> (Rankin 29 Oct. 1995, E1)

Using Christie's conceptualization, French was the perfect or ideal victim. The gradation away from this status for the other two girls exemplifies how the attributes of whiteness, femininity, class, and space and place can come to affect coverage of certain cases and media constructions of both victims and offenders.

Unlike victims that fail to receive this degree of media attention and who are partially constituted as responsible for their victimization, all three victims in this case were missed and publically grieved by their communities and wider Canadian society. For example, hundreds of community members attended Kristen French's funeral, lining the downtown St. Catharines street where the church was located several persons deep and for several blocks as the funeral party left the church for the private burial. In cases where the victim is constructed as less than ideal there is less fanfare, less media coverage and less collective public mourning. Razack's (2000) detailed examination of the Pamela George[9] case and Gilchrist's (2010) comparative examination of the news coverage of three Aboriginal and three white homicide victims is a testament to this point. As Razack argues (2000, 93) "Pamela George was considered to belong to a space in which violence routinely occurs, and to have a body that is routinely violated, while her killers [two white male university students] were considered to be far removed from this zone." None of Homolka's victims were in spaces routinely subject to violence, nor did they inhabit bodies that are routinely violated; rather, their whiteness, hegemonic femininity and middle-class suburban life contributed to the heightened collective public shock and anger that was expressed in news media coverage of the case. Unlike Pamela George, Homolka's victims were *iconic.*

Conclusion

In this chapter we have endeavoured to demonstrate how whiteness, hegemonic femininity, and classed and spatial inclusions contributed to the media frenzy surrounding this case, the specific victims and Karla Homolka in particular. Homolka's exceptionality as an atypical woman offender certainly lent itself to heightened media attention, but emphasizing the similarities between Homolka and her young victims allowed journalists to cast an image of a predator lurking within the small town communities these girls were accustomed to safely moving in and through. Constituting the spaces and places where the crimes occurred as "idyllic small town Canada" brought home the unreality that such acts of sexual violence could occur without notice under the noses of the communities' residents. By situating the victim and offender as more alike than different, journalists were able to capitalize on the attention wrought by crafting a moral panic around women's violence (Barron and Lacombe 2005; Kilty and Fabian 2010).

As Sherene Razack (2003) has so adeptly argued, media accounts of violence are "culturalized" so as to typify that which occurs in white communities as exceptional and extraordinary, while that which occurs in indigenous, Black or other hyper-visible racialized communities as common and expected. Razack (2003) writes:

> When white men shoot their wives and children and set fire to the house, this is not seen as a violent practice typical of white culture (91). . . We are seldom asked to consider these as situations that have arisen from, or are sustained by, the tremendous misogyny of Western cultures and their emphasis on autonomous individuals who exist outside kin and community. (277)

Media and legal discourses situated Homolka's supposed everydayness and ordinariness as a white, middle-class woman living in an upscale suburb of a small Canadian city in stark contrast to her participation in these crimes. Homolka's whiteness stands her apart from the disproportionate numbers of the Black, Latina and Aboriginal women who fill North American prisons (Comack and Balfour 2006). While Homolka's victims exhibited Christie's attributes of ideal victimhood she does not fit his characterization of the ideal offender, a fact that reporters and journalists quickly and repeatedly pointed out. Homolka is not "big and bad" (Christie 1986, 19), she is petite, quiet spoken, well groomed, and beautiful. The fact that she knew two of her victims (her sister Tammy and Jane Doe, who was a social friend) also counters Christie's assertion that the ideal victim is likely to be victimized by an unknown offender. However, this correlates with the significantly fewer news articles that mentioned Tammy Homolka in comparison to Leslie Mahaffy or Kristen French. Despite the saturation of coverage and discussion of Homolka, she remains an enigmatic subject, which is what led to our impetus to examine the cultural fixation on her in this book. In the next chapter we again turn the gaze outward to study how disgust thresholds related to sex and death taboos contributed to the cultural fascination with Karla Homolka.

Notes

1 It is important to acknowledge the growing body of research on the hierarchy of whiteness that is largely affected by class positioning in capitalist democracies. This literature identifies, for example, that cultural productions of "white trash" exemplify the social distancing and lowering of certain white groups by affiliating them more closely with the cultural values of racial minority groups (Frankenberg 1993, 1997; Garner 2007, 2012; Hewitt 2005).

2 It is of note that what constitutes a sensational or newsworthy story is changing as a result of social media and online forums; research might now examine whether and the speed with which a story goes viral on the Internet, what hashtags are trending and how many "likes" a story receives online. However, given that this case began in the early 1990s, our research focuses on traditional news print journalism.

3 As she was underage at the time of her victimization, Jane Doe's identity and image were not legally permitted to be publicized. The fact that she was underage was emphasized

when she was mentioned in news accounts and during court proceedings; it was highlighted as demonstrative of her weakness and vulnerability and contributed to her constitution as an ideal victim.

4 The reference to Eichmann is extreme and shows Kennedy's stretched application of Hannah Arendt's classic examination of Eichmann and what she coined as "the banality of evil" to describe how the atrocities of the Holocaust were not executed by fanatics or sociopaths, but by ordinary citizens who participated because they were fulfilling their duty. While Eichmann hid behind the rhetoric of following military orders and law under the Nazi regime, Homolka's actions were of her and Bernardo's own making. Likening Homolka's narrative of domestic victimization as the cause of her participation in the crimes, which shifts some of her blame to the machinations of Paul Bernardo, to Eichmann's narrative of following orders is a leap of logic and scope that aids in the journalistic characterization of Homolka as the epitome of evil.

5 There was a similar case in Belgium where Michelle Martin initially refused then later accepted to participate in her husband Marc Dutroux's sexual assaults and murders of young women.

6 In chapter 4 we further examine this fact as an example of a cultural death taboo that was evoked by surpassing the community's collective disgust threshold.

7 It is of note that news coverage characterized Homolka's parents as somewhat lax for allowing their underage daughter to drink and for allowing the older boyfriend of their teenage daughter to spend weekends at their home.

8 Prior to their arrest, the couple applied to legally change their last name to Teale, reportedly because Paul Bernardo found his last name to sound too "ethnic". Although spelled differently, he chose the name from the serial killer played by Kevin Bacon in the 1989 film *Criminal Law*.

9 In 1995, Pamela George, who was an Aboriginal woman of the Salteaux First Nations, was raped, beaten, and left for dead by two white university students in Regina Saskatchewan. While charged with first-degree murder, Steven Kummerfield and Alex Ternowetsky were eventually convicted of manslaughter. Razack identifies how court and media discourses constructed George as a disposable victim as a result of her Aboriginality, gender, occasional participation in sex work, and presence in a poor region of Regina.

4 Breaking Boundaries

Notes on the Effects of Taboo and Disgust on the Cultural (Re)Presentations of Karla Homolka

> Something makes us look at the bloody auto accident, thrill to movies of horror, gore, and violence; something makes porn big business and still draws people to circus sideshows. Is there no moral offensiveness that doesn't by some dark process elicit fascination, if in no other way than in the horror, wonderment, and befuddlement such depravity evokes?
>
> (Miller 1997, 112)

In the above quote Miller describes how the raw and visceral felt moral emotion of disgust encourages us to gaze at and even fetishize the very horrors that cause us to feel disgust. Using Miller's work on disgust as the starting point and foundation for this chapter, we train our analytic gaze on legal and media discourses and onto the public as audience, to better examine the origins of the cultural obsession with Karla Homolka. In this chapter, we argue that the cultural fascination with Karla Homolka flows not only from discussions about her agency, responsibility or victimism as Morrissey (2003) and Pearson (1998) have suggested, but also from the sex and death taboos she violated with Paul Bernardo and the subsequent disgust these taboo violations elicited amongst a riveted public audience.

Disgust is the prevailing emotional response to actions that are considered taboo. We maintain that the collectively felt disgust at Homolka's participation in the sexual assaults (especially that against her younger sister Tammy) and murders of two adolescent girls contributed to the creation of the national media and legal spectacles and the long running cultural fascination with the woman we could not seem to understand and whose behaviours we could not explain beyond suggesting that she is exceptionally cunning, manipulative and ultimately "evil." In short, the public's disgust at Homolka's taboo violations helped to recreate her as the enigma we see characterized in media and legal accounts. To situate this discussion, we begin by outlining the connection between taboo and disgust.

Taboo and Disgust

> Some rules we just don't violate; nor would we get pleasure out of doing so. And what are those? The ones backed up by strong negative emotions of the most moral

> sort: guilt, shame, and, yes, disgust. Yet we remain intractably curious and fascinated by those who overcome such restraints. Those who violate the norms that hold us in their grips are objects of fear, loathing, awe – precisely the emotions that drive tragedy, horror, suspense, and some religious devotion.
>
> (Miller 1997, 114–15)

The notion of taboo has long been a source of intrigue for social scientists. First studied as an important socio-cultural organizational marker amongst "foreign" civilizations by white western anthropologists, taboos denote activities and behaviours that are viewed by the society or group as abhorrent and as violating the social norms and customs upheld by the wider group. Taboos are often, albeit not exclusively, constructed around beliefs about sexuality and sexual customs and death and mortality; they vary from culture to culture and, inevitably, shift and evolve over time (Webster 1973).

Mary Douglas' pioneering work on taboo in *Purity and Danger* (1966) pushed our use of the concept to consider notions of purity, danger, morality and, ultimately our understandings of order and disorder. While early anthropological writings suggest that "primitive" cultures believed that tabooed behaviours are sacrosanct and that their transgression permanently marks the individual transgressor and those s/he comes into contact with as impure, dangerous, tainted, soiled, and highly contagious, Douglas found that western societies actually use similar conceptualizations of dirt and impurity to describe risk and disorder, the two primary constructs that we use to organize and govern contemporary neoliberal societies. Late modernity is characterized by an ever-increasing drive to identify, name and categorize all manner of risks and threats in order to conquer uncertainty (Douglas 1966; 2001). Taboos endure as emotional stock narratives of unacceptable social behaviour that function as mechanisms to facilitate social and moral regulation by attempting to conquer risk and uncertainty.

Douglas argues that things that fail to fall in line with otherwise sharp conceptual distinctions are seen as polluting and thus as taboo. For example, some of the most taboo substances include those that exist both within and outside the body, including faeces, urine, pus, vomit, mucus, semen, and menstrual blood (Douglas 1966; Miller 1997). Miller's study of the anatomy of disgust illustrates the dynamic connection between emotions and taboo; he pushes Douglas' work beyond the structural reduction of taboos to things that do not fit existing classification systems and toward an understanding of an expansive conceptual grid that is hierarchically organized. Therefore, some things disgust more than others; for example, while faeces disgusts, we all must see, smell, and come into contact with it daily. The taboos that Homolka violated were much more serious in that they are generally considered threatening to the community and potentially to the moral fabric of society. Cultural feelings of disgust emerge from what we suspect the victim would experience, meaning that as spectators of this crime drama Canadian citizens became "guardians of propriety and purity" (Miller 1997, 198). The taboos Homolka participated in violating caused spectators to fear for their safety and for that of their loved ones, but also to feel disgust, an emotion that acts as a bond linking the public through their feelings of horror and disgust into a united, moral community.

Miller (1997) suggests that taboos generate a collective moral community largely because of the visceral emotions felt about the taboo substance or action. This association demonstrates that emotions are "richly social, cultural, and linguistic phenomena" that shape how we think about, react to and explain actions and behaviours (Miller 1997, 8; Ahmed 2004b). By merging Douglas' work on purity, danger, and taboo as risk and disorder with Miller's work on the anatomy of disgust, we may examine the connection between emotionality and our sedimented cultural gaze on Karla Homolka. Violating the boundaries set for us by taboos causes us to feel disgust. Disgust unnerves us, angers us, and makes us both fear and loathe that which we find disgusting. We work to avoid being contaminated by the disgusting object, substance, or person by removing it or ourselves from its presence (Ahmed 2004b; Miller 1997; Webster 1973). At this stage it is worth quoting Miller at length:

> Disgust is a feeling *about* something and in response to something not just raw unattached feeling . . . disgust necessarily involves particular thoughts, characteristically very intrusive and unriddable thoughts about the repugnance of that which is its object. Disgust must be accompanied by ideas of a particular kind of danger, the danger inherent in pollution and contamination, the danger of defilement, which ideas in turn will be associated with rather predictable cultural and social scenarios. . . . Disgust evaluates (negatively) what it touches, proclaims the meanness and inferiority of its object. And by so doing it presents a nervous claim of right to be free of the dangers imposed by the proximity of the inferior. It is thus an assertion of a claim to superiority that at the same time recognizes the vulnerability of that superiority to the defiling powers of the low. The world is a dangerous place in which the polluting powers of the low are usually stronger than the purifying powers of the high.
>
> (8–9)

Taboo things shock, sicken, and disgust us but they also entertain and captivate us. And when we come into contact, even visually, with something that disgusts us we often hasten to purify ourselves (Ahmed 2004b; Miller 1997; Webster 1973). Processes of purification may vary temporally and by culture, but typically include either the destruction or removal of the disgusting object/person so as to prevent contamination, pollution, or defilement (Ahmed 2004b; Douglas 1966; Miller 1997; Webster 1973). In this sense, disgust is culture constraining but also culturally constrained (Miller 1997, 26). When disgust is imbued with fear, such as in this case, we experience feelings of horror, which limits and at times denies options for purification because we feel we cannot escape, forget, or extricate ourselves from the horror itself. Part of our inability to purify post-Homolka is due to our continued horror at the sexually violent crimes; but in a hetero-patriarchal society it is also due to the horror and disgust that a woman would assist her sadistic partner to abuse other young girls – which is, in short, the cultural reaction to her having violated taboos related to sex, death, womanhood, and even feminism.

Our cultural gaze remains focused on Homolka's role in the crimes and many critics take the position that our ability to purify was damaged by the plea bargain reporters and journalists dubbed "the sweetheart deal" and the "pact with the devil" (Williams 2004), suggesting that purification could only be conceived of if she were imprisoned for life – the same as Paul Bernardo. These monikers, reiterated time and again in the news coverage, contribute to the sedimentation of Homolka's character in the eyes of the public largely because they maintain our gaze on the taboos she broke over 20 years ago as the "true" representation of her character. We do not question the material reality and disturbing nature of Homolka's participation in these crimes; rather, our interest was to examine the connection between three overarching taboo violations observed in this case, the disgust each violation elicited and how this emotional reaction to such taboo violations is linked to the cultural preoccupation with Homolka as a media subject and with the sedimented view we maintain of her.

Feminist Taboo: Breaking the Bonds of Sisterhood

> Karla Homolka, over and over again – and often at opportunities patently provided by Crown Attorney Ray Houlahan – depicts herself as a victim of Bernardo's brutality. It is *as if she equates her victimhood* with that of Tammy Homolka, Leslie Mahaffy and Kristen French. *As if she were part of that sisterhood of the dead.* [our emphasis] (DiManno 23 June 1995, A10)

One of the primary taboos Homolka violated, what we are calling "the bonds of sisterhood," partially emerges as a result of the second wave feminist claim about a unified bond of sisterhood amongst all women. Sisterhood was a term used to unite and empower women; feminists have long used it to demonstrate that women should seek strength in numbers by collectivizing in support of one another. The benefits that flow from this position clearly include a more unified challenge to misogyny and patriarchy and greater support for the rights of all women; however, this framing also sets up an inherently more derogatory characterization of those women who fail to unite or who threaten the bond. This case affords an extreme example. By prioritizing the satiation of Bernardo's sadistic sexual desires and her own life and safety above that of innocent others, by participating in the sexual assault of young women, by passively allowing her husband to murder those victims and helping to dispose of their bodies to "save herself," Homolka's self-narrative contributed to her construction as a cultural monster. In this chapter, we contend that Homolka was analytically dissected in the media and arguably constituted as more monstrous than Bernardo not only because a woman violated a number of cultural sex and death taboos, but also because she acted in ways that violate the key tenet of sisterhood that is common in feminist thought.

Karla Homolka was tirelessly characterized in media and legal discourses as lacking sisterly qualities (Morrissey 2003, 146). As the above quote from *Toronto Star* journalist Rosie DiManno elucidates, Homolka's victim discourse was read by many as a manipulative attempt to position herself "As if she were part of that sisterhood of the dead," more alike to her victims than different. This discursive move was described at the very least as morally questionable, and more commonly as a disturbing attempt to garner legal, media, and public sympathy. The news reporting of her testimony and cross-examination during Bernardo's 1995 trial in particular contained a number of comparative statements about the couple that emphasized the heinousness of Homolka's rather than Bernardo's actions. For one of the most overt examples, Canadian journalist Christie Blatchford wrote, "the betrayal was Homolka's, and this was made worse by her gender, as what gives both deeds ringing cruelty is the fact that Homolka is a woman" (1995). Participating in the sexual assault and death of three young girls, including her younger sister Tammy, and the sexual assault of a fourth victim known only as Jane Doe certainly posts Homolka as an archetypal anti-feminist figure. However, at the same time, this emphasis constructs Paul Bernardo as:

> A regular guy, at least in the minds of some . . . his indictment for twenty-eight rapes, performed during the early years of his relationship with Homolka, and his acknowledged sexual sadism in the rapes and murders of Tammy Homolka, Leslie Mahaffy, and Kristen French, were not sufficient to dislodge his claim to humanity.
>
> (Morrissey 2003, 148)

The cultural acceptance of Bernardo as a "regular guy" reifies male violence against women as customary and even as an expected part of patriarchal gender relations. Homolka, however, was monsterized for assisting him while subject to emotional, sexual and physical violence at his hands. As Crown counsel Murray Segal stated during Homolka's arraignment:

> What Your Honour has before you in my respectful submission, is conduct that represents the depths of human behaviour. Three young innocent lives have been ended in a shocking fashion. It is submitted that you have before you an entire breakdown in the basic moral code by which society operates. What sort of person would agree to placing her sibling's life at risk? The cumulative destruction is unprecedented. Unfortunately whatever immediate hope the victims had must have centered on Karla Bernardo. In this respect she totally failed, which brings us here today.
>
> (R. v. K. Bernardo 1993, 68)

Segal's statement that this case is an example of "an entire breakdown in the basic moral code by which society operates," removes Homolka as a legitimate member of society. By this process, she becomes a non-citizen, inhuman and a non-woman, incapable of morality and appropriate feminine behaviour, a common discursive characterization of women who commit acts of violence (Naylor 1995). Moreover, Homolka is painted as her victims' only possible salvation; given that Bernardo was seen as a normal man despite his violence, the real failure is fashioned as Homolka's for breaking the bonds of sisterhood by not freeing the girls and by participating in sexual assaults against them. This discursive production unevenly places responsibility for the crimes on Homolka and contributes to the sedimentation of our gaze on her as the more monstrous of the two. This is the first marker of the effects of taboo on the social, media, and legal constructions of Homolka as monstrous and dangerous, and is at the root of our cultural fixation on her. Segal's narrative is saturated with disgust, demonstrating the emotional response Canadians have had to Homolka's role in this case. While Bernardo is written off as another violent, even sadistic man, he (and unfortunately men's violence against women) is not atypical; it is Homolka who elicits our disgust for failing to be a nurturing and chaste woman who would attempt to save the girls.

Disgust is one of the most powerful emotions we experience; Miller (1997, 194–5) argues that it is essential to building a moral and social community because it allows us to create boundaries. Segal's question "What sort of person would agree to placing her sibling's life at risk?" paints Homolka as the antithesis of the nurturing woman and sister we culturally essentialize as natural for women. In fact, it is her role in her sister's death that elicits the most disgust and may therefore be interpreted as the greatest taboo Homolka violated. If disgust helps us to determine boundaries, it is Homolka's personal disgust threshold that we are questioning here. What made Homolka capable of violating this taboo by crossing the boundary from nurturing big sister to accomplice in said sister's sexual assault? Emphasizing her obvious moral failure, George Walker made the following submission about his client at her arraignment:

> She played a somewhat lesser role in the assaultive behaviour. Yet at the same time, she bears full responsibility. Indeed, in her capacity as Tammy's sister she will bear the continuing shame of violating all the trust that anyone, especially a younger sister, would have assumed.
>
> (R. v. K. Bernardo 1993, 63)

By accepting qualities such as nurturance and protection as the fundamental characteristics of femininity, womanhood and sisterhood, Homolka is not only constructed as a non-woman, but the disgust her actions elicit also causes the audience to understand her as inherently and indelibly without humanity. Paul Bernardo is lost in this interpretation, a side note that is irrelevant to the cultural disgust we feel toward Homolka. Morrissey (2003) goes so far as to claim that Homolka "*deliberately* pervert[ed] classically feminine values, like nurturance and care, as she described how she anaesthetized some of her victims with a cloth doused in Halothane, and then watched over them like a nurse while her male partner raped them" [our emphasis] (145). We question the deliberateness of this perversion; to say it was deliberate insinuates Homolka exhibited the cunning forethought to perform the role of caregiver in order to pre-emptively lay the groundwork for her self-narrative as a terrified victim that felt compassion for her quarry.

Homolka's perversion of traditionally feminine values extends to her role in helping to abduct Kristen French. With respect to this role, Paul Bernardo's defence counsel, John Rosen, described Homolka as a "Venus flytrap" – implying that she was more dangerous than Bernardo because she used her non-threatening femininity to ensnare young victims for her abusive husband. Rosen questioned Homolka extensively about this particular incident during her cross-examination at Paul Bernardo's trial. For example, he stated:

> As far as this poor girl knows, when she approaches that car, that's what she's greeted with, a honey voice asking innocently for directions behind a smiling face and blond hair, right?"
>
> (R. v. P. Bernardo 1995, 1996).

Rosen's description of Homolka as having a "honey voice," "smiling face," and "blond hair" emphasizes her attractiveness and non-threatening appearance in order to accentuate the stark contrast between this appearance and her actions.[1] He is suggesting that she used her hegemonic/pariah femininity to lure an innocent, implying that she is manipulative but also that she has the ability to blend into the community and move undetected throughout the social body. This portrayal alludes to the division between one's internal character and the shallowness and superficiality of the outside shell (Miller 1997). Homolka's beauty and youth are presented as alluring but also as a false front that masked the flaws in her internal character, namely the lack of emotional, moral and compassionate depth that allowed her to bypass normative socio-cultural disgust thresholds.

With this line of questioning, Rosen effectively transmogrifies the presentation of Homolka's character from sweet to cloying to threatening, which Miller (1997, 87) notes is a way to elicit disgust. Sweetness of character is typically seen as a virtue, but pushed too far it becomes saccharine, signifying shallowness and in this case *dangerousness*. Homolka's cloying sweetness was mentioned repeatedly throughout her testimony and cross-examination at Bernardo's trial. Bernardo's defence counsel reconstructed every kind gesture Homolka identified that she made toward her victims to be evidence of her duplicitousness; for example, giving Leslie Mahaffy a stuffed animal to help comfort her when she was upset or sharing her makeup and perfume with Kristen French. Given the gravity of the situation, these are obviously diminutive examples of kindness that were unconvincing in the courtroom and to the reporters and journalists covering the trials. Clearly, ending her relationship with Bernardo when he disclosed his plan to rape Tammy, going to the police instead of to work the morning after Mahaffy was abducted and letting French go or helping her to escape when she was alone in the house with her would have been decisive demonstrations of sisterhood. However, rather than reading these contextually trivial acts of kindness as intentionally manipulative perversions of femininity, we suggest that they demonstrate just how deeply entrenched cultural expectations of hegemonic femininity are given that they were performed in such a stressful and violent environment.

Contributing to the cultural view that Homolka violated the bonds of sisterhood, and in the same vein as her assistance in abducting Kristen French, Homolka participated in drugging and sexually assaulting a young woman known only as Jane Doe. Crown prosecutor Raymond Houlahan asked Homolka why she would befriend a young woman and then bring her to Bernardo, knowing that he would sexually assault her. Homolka's response demonstrated how her survival instinct superseded her disgust threshold:

> Because I was afraid of him, and because this would make him happy. And I was a lot better off with him being happy than him being angry with me. . . . Basically, I wanted to [sic] him to find somebody else and to leave me alone, to let me go.
>
> (R. v. P. Bernardo 1995, 463–4)

Homolka's response elicits disgust because she is openly acknowledging that she was willing to sacrifice other young women in order to escape Bernardo – a moral failure in a culture that values and glorifies personal sacrifice as heroic. This is especially the case for women who are expected to demonstrate the feminine and motherhood ideal of self-sacrifice (Kilty and Dej 2012). Our disgust at this breach of the bonds of sisterhood may be contrasted with comments made by two of the victims, which show them as having interpreted Homolka to be different from and less dangerous than Bernardo. At the request of Paul Bernardo's defence counsel, Homolka described a scene from one of the videotapes that was presented in court:

> He told me to bring him a Kleenex, and when I brought him one that wasn't enough so he called me a "fucking idiot." And Kristen said: "I don't know how your wife can stand being around you." And he told her "shut up," and she said "okay" and did. And then he told me to turn the camera off.
>
> (R. v. P. Bernardo 1995, 824)

Similarly, in his investigation into the validity of her plea bargain, Justice Galligan refers to conversations with Jane Doe, who stated that she did not want further charges to be laid against Karla Homolka:

> The first was that, in her heart, she knew that Paul Bernardo was the bad person. She told us that Karla Homolka was her friend and then said, "she had to do what she did, not because she wanted to, but because he made her do it." Her second reason was that now she just wants to be left alone.
>
> (Galligan 1996, 211)

These quotes intimate that the victims differentiated Homolka from Bernardo with respect to who they viewed as the more dangerous individual, recognizing her participation as being forced or coerced rather than wholly voluntary. This demonstrates that Homolka's violation of the bonds of sisterhood may be less pronounced, or at least more complex, than they appear at first glance, yet our cultural view of her remains fixated on the monstrous. A final example of Homolka's violation of the taboo surrounding the bonds of sisterhood that elicited the public's disgust and thus contributed to our sedimented view of her, centred on her seeming ability to "feel happy" in spite of her participation in the crimes:

Rosen: Well, as soon as you left them, you were so happy you couldn't believe how happy you were, isn't that right?

Homolka: That's how part of me felt yes.

Rosen: You told the police and I quote your words: "As soon as I left him I was in the hospital. I was so happy I couldn't believe how happy I was. I felt like I was 17-years old again, and I locked everything I had with Paul away to a corner of my mind. I forgot about Tammy, I forgot about Leslie and Kristen, I forgot everything, and like I made myself forget and I went out and I had a great time." Did you say that under oath to the police who were interviewing you?

Homolka: Yes, I said that. But there's more to it than that.

(R. v. P. Bernardo 1995, 1022–3)

Here Homolka is presented as failing to feel the necessary emotional weight of her crimes, something that she was accused of throughout her incarceration and upon her release (which we discuss further in the next chapter). Given the severity of her crimes, any reference to her experiencing joy makes her appear callous, which fits the monsterization discourse (Morrissey 2003) that suggests she lacks those sisterly and motherly qualities that are essentialized as natural for women. Homolka's ability to carry on with her daily life and routine despite the horrors that surrounded her (for example hosting Father's day dinner while Mahaffy's body lay in the root cellar of their home, blow-drying her hair after Bernardo strangled French so they could attend Easter dinner at her parents' house or "feeling happy" after she left Bernardo) was repeatedly cited as evidence of her cruelty and was used to narrate her as indifferent to her victims, which counteracts her glib examples of showing her victims kindness. Homolka's ability to perform normalcy is uncanny and shocking to our moral sensibilities; her abjectness disturbs social reason and order and provokes a collective feeling of disgust.

Scholars have rightly asserted that Homolka is an enigma who perplexes us because she does not fit neatly into the category of victimized woman that was created by second wave feminism (Comack 2014; Comack and Brickey 2007; McGillivray 1998; Morrissey 2003; Pearson 1998). More specifically, we contend that her elusiveness is linked to her debasement of the bonds of sisterhood by harming women while maintaining that, like them, she too was a victim. Such a taboo violation casts a different light on Homolka's victim narrative, which then performs as a thinly veiled attempt to minimize her responsibility and is what caused disbelief in the degree of impact her victimization had on her agency – many going so far as to contend that she was not a "true" victim despite forensic evidence to the contrary. Breaking the bonds of sisterhood is a taboo that helps cement the view of Homolka as an always already dangerous woman regardless of the amount of time that passes. Next we discuss how the sexual violence in this case reflects the violation of different sex taboos, which when combined with her gender further aggravated the cultural fascination with Homolka.

Sex Taboos: S/M, Bisexuality, and Incest

Taboos concerning sex appear at once alive and well, and at the same time waning or even dying. On one hand, western culture is saturated by images of and references to sex. On the other hand, we continue to witness tightly regulated morals about sex including, hetero-normativity, gendered and sexed sexual power relations, and discussions of acceptable sexual practices. Foucault (1980) outlines this schism about sexual mores in his explanation of the repressive hypothesis in the *History of Sexuality Volume 1*. He suggests that discourses, while constraining, are also productive and that while many believe we have become more repressed, discourses about sex abound. As discourses are multi-layered they carry historical significance such that the ways in which we discursively constitute certain characters remain over time. Since the Enlightenment, and to an even greater extent since the debut of industrialized capitalism, western cultures have witnessed both a growing prohibition of the sexual and an exponential growth in discussing, studying, analysing and categorizing all things sexual – proclivities, language, and fetishes, among others (Foucault 1980; Smart 2002). Smart (2002, 98) argues that, "sex became not merely another object of knowledge, but the privileged locus or secret of our being – our truth. Henceforth, in modern societies there has been a pursuit of the 'truth of sex' and of 'truth in sex'."

If we start with Foucault's premise that our personal confessions about sex are often thought to reveal the secret of our being, we may understand how Homolka's participation in procuring virgins for and raping virgins with Bernardo produced a juridico-discursive truth about her character and personhood, namely that she is sexually deviant and equally as culpable and dangerous as Bernardo. Yet Foucault's (1980) discussion of the emergence of carceral networks and the formation of the human sciences also teaches us that confessions are contextually bound. Given that the visual is the central format through which Homolka's confessional tale as an abused woman who was coerced and forced to participate in the crimes is questioned, we must return to the premise that the visual can horrify and elicit disgust because it, more than other mediums, contributes to the production of a sedimented gaze. In this case, the visual imagery is a secondary confession that threatens the believability of Homolka's self-narrative of victimism. These visual images were introduced in court as evidence and were subject to much scrutiny and analysis by a number of different actors – the police, Crown prosecution and defence lawyers, reporters and journalists, the public, and a series of experts – psy and legal alike. As such, the visual in this case became one of the primary analytics through which legal, media, and lay constructions of Homolka were produced and where Homolka's testimony and actions provide a paradoxical discursive caption to those visual images.

Part of the growing analytic of sex has been the increasing administration, management and government of sex. Regulation is made manifest in the form of cultural taboos and the criminalization of certain behaviours, both of which are evident in this case. Traditional western cultural sex taboos include the importance of maintaining sexual purity amongst women and girls until marriage, purity taboos surrounding menstruation, childbirth, monogamy, hetero-normativity, incest, and miscegenation, and taboos associated with age (for example debates about the age of consent) (Douglas 1966; Miller 1997; Webster 1973). For example, we see the lasting impact of the cultural taboos that constitute women as unclean due to menstruation (Webster 1973, 129) in John Rosen's (Bernardo's defence attorney) aggressive postulation that contrary to Homolka's claims that she did not want to participate in the assault on her sister, that her disgust was actually due to the fact that Tammy was in the middle of her menstrual cycle:

Rosen: Okay. But if it turns out, as we analyze the video, that the real reason that the kinky sex that you and he were into soured because your sister had either the beginning or the end of her period, and you didn't want to taste her vaginal blood, that's a different complexion, isn't it?

Homolka: That's not the truth.

(R. v. P. Bernardo 1995, 1448–9)

Rosen dismisses Homolka's claims of victimization and forced participation by invoking age-old cultural taboos about the dirt and impurity of menstruation that enable him to cast doubt on Homolka's testimony and to remake her as a pitiless predator.

When considering those sexual behaviours that are subject to criminal sanction, it is clear in the criminological literature that conceptualizations of the sexually violent stranger make up one of the most feared characters in western culture, despite the fact that the actual risk of this form of sexual victimization is low (Brennan and Taylor-Butts 2008). Fear of sexual victimization is rooted in the fear of a loss of purity; especially considering that purity is seen as counterbalancing danger (Douglas 1966, 2001). As Miller (1997, 129–30) writes:

> It is about doing dirt to someone who still is deemed to have some kind of innocence or purity (youth, beauty, and vulnerability) that can be polluted, but who possesses an inferior ethical disposition that sees no point in not making herself available for such pollution; that is, her inferior ethical nature makes her sensual.

Paul Bernardo fetishized young girls because he considered them to be pure (R. v. P. Bernardo 1995), which is a symbolic cultural value attributed to virginity. While a boy's virginity may be cast as embarrassing and perhaps even subject to ridicule, a girl's virginity is said to denote her purity, innocence, and integrity. Bernardo repeatedly expressed his desire to take the virginity of young girls (R. v. P. Bernardo 1995) – a desire that demonstrates a yearning to express sexual power by being the agent that ends sexual innocence. Given the cultural memorialization of the loss of virginity, Bernardo effectively wished to mark himself in the mind and memory of his victims, which can be read as a way to sadistically possess the individual. In this way, Bernardo, and Homolka by proxy as his dutiful aid, maintained the masculine subject gaze on their victims as object. The assaults may be read as a way to taint the pure by possessing them; to dominate, degrade, and humiliate through sexual intercourse confirms the already low ranking of the victim in the eyes of the perpetrator (Miller 1997, 129). In a reflection of the normative acceptance of male violence against women, while Bernardo's sexual sadism and virgin fetish was the root of the couple's victim selection "the betrayal was Homolka's" (Blatchford 1995) and it was she who was described as violating sex taboos. Homolka's inability to convincingly empathize with her victims combined with her ability to transgress cultural disgust thresholds (Miller 1997) led her, not Bernardo, to remain at the centre of our gaze.

Virginity was central to Bernardo's sexual cravings and played a key role in his selection of potential victims. One particular videotaped scene depicted the couple discussing the apprehension of girls as young as 13 so as to ensure their virginity for Bernardo who styled himself and wished to be referred to as "the King" by Homolka and their victims, both of whom he fashioned "sex slaves" (R. v. P. Bernardo 1995). Homolka described her relationship with Bernardo as one of master and slave, stating during her testimony at his trial:

Homolka: He made me call myself – um, specifically what he would say, or what he wanted me to say was: My name is Karla. I'm 17-years old. I'm your little cocksucker. I'm your little cunt. I'm your little slut, and I would have to repeat that until he told me to stop (R. v. Bernardo 1995, 31).

The disgust this point elicits is tied to our increasing cultural fear of sexual predators, particularly those who offend against children, the group assessed to be the most pure and innocent in any culture (Webster 1973; Miller 1997). Here we see that the ways Bernardo groomed Homolka were similar to the ways in which he expected his victims to act and to address him. The combination of sexual assault with a target victim group of virginal girls reflects but one of a number of features of this case that may be considered sexually taboo.

In the above exchange Homolka characterizes her relationship with Bernardo as one of master and slave and she also identified herself as having been Bernardo's "property." This pronouncement must be considered in contrast to the overarching production of Homolka as a hyper-sexual and sexually aggressive woman – especially in light of the cultural valuing of female sexual passivity, submissiveness, and innocence (Gilbert 2002; Seal 2009; Sjoberg and Gentry 2008; Smart 1992). Both legal and media narratives repeatedly referenced the fact that Bernardo and Homolka engaged in sexual intercourse on the night they met as evidence of her, albeit not his, sexual promiscuity, immorality, and dangerousness (see Pron 1995; R. v. P. Bernardo 1995; Williams 2004). This discourse also worked to reproduce every salacious detail of the couple's sex life so as to paint a picture of their sexual deviancy. The detailed accounts of the couple's personal sex life emphasized what appears on the videotapes and in Homolka's numerous letters and cards to Bernardo to be Homolka's willing participation in kinky sexual practices; this emphasis was used to suggest that because she partook in these acts with her boyfriend and later husband that she must also have willingly participated in the sexual assaults and homicides. In these discussions, Homolka, rather than Bernardo, remains at the centre of the gaze largely because,

> The permitted transgressor aids and abets the authorizer in a violation of the authorizer's most strongly held, disgust-manned defenses. But the true offender against the all-powerful rules of disgust is the permission giver. It is that person who authorizes the violation of the disgust rules by redefining the violation of him or herself in a disgust-transfiguring experience.
> (Miller 1997, 138)

If Homolka willingly engaged in what the textual data referred to as kinky and sado-masochistic (S/M) sex involving bondage, dog collars, and gags, as well as bisexuality, sex with prostitutes, and three-way orgiastic sex, she becomes the figure of disgust that allowed Bernardo to tie her up, to gag her, and to sodomize her. In this configuration Homolka is the permission giver, she authorized Bernardo's violation of the disgust rules in such a way that insinuates a reversal of the couple's gendered power relations that situate her as the abused woman. This discursive wrinkle complicates Homolka's claims that she did not enjoy these sex acts and that she only engaged in them to appease the abusive and domineering Bernardo; it also underscores the legal and media narrative that she was the clever mastermind behind the crimes who was able to deceive the criminal justice system. The visual images of Homolka engaging in consensual kinky sex acts with Bernardo helped consolidate the widely reported view that she was a willing, promiscuous and sexually deviant (read dangerous) partner. One of the dominant narratives in the transcripts and mass news media coverage produced a very particular character – the hypersexual woman – and even more rare, the female sexual predator (Denov 2004) – in contrast to Bernardo's everdayness and thus insignificance as a sexually violent man. This focus on Homolka's sexual deviancy partially normalizes Bernardo's, which is sadly considered to be less repugnant, or at the very least more common in a hetero-normative and patriarchal society.

Author Stephen Williams has written two books about the case. In his second book, *Karla: A Pact with the Devil* (2004), he included glossy colour photographs Bernardo took of Homolka[2] prior to their commission of the sexual assaults and murders. These photographs depict a nude Homolka gagged and bound with handcuffs in different sexual positions, again with Bernardo acting as the photographer and holding the subject position of the gaze. Williams (2004) describes the visual images of Homolka as evidence of the historicity of Homolka's sexual perversions and of her enjoyment in participating in the series of sexual assaults. It is, however, problematic to decontextualize photographs taken in private between two consenting adults as evidence of her wilful participation in rape and murder. In fact, Homolka is clearly the submissive in these images and in her writing on the various cards, notes and letters she gave to Bernardo, which while sexually explicit were typically deferential to achieving Bernardo's deviant sexual pleasure rather than her own. The videotapes show Homolka taking precise instructions from Bernardo, the master or "King" from whom she must ask permission for all things. In one particular scene she is even found telling Kristen French that only Bernardo may grant her permission to see Homolka's dog:

> A few minutes later, shortly before they were filmed performing sex acts on one another, Ms Homolka tries to calm Kristen down. "Are you nervous?" she asks. "It's okay." "Am I shaking?" Kristen asks. "No," Ms Homolka replies. "Just try to feel at home. "Can I ask a favour?" Kristen says moments later. "Can I see your dog without it attacking me before I leave?" "It's up to him," Ms Homolka says, indicating Mr Bernardo. The two women then perform various sex acts on one another while Mr Bernardo films them and gives occasional instructions.
>
> (Makin 6 June 1995, A1)

A photographic paradox emerges when contrasting an image of the submissive woman who takes instruction and asks permission from Bernardo with the image of a seductive woman blowing kisses, smiling, and even licking her lips on camera during the sexual assaults. It is thus unsurprising that the audience continues to ask, "is she evil?" and "which characterization is *true*?" This visual, like those in the photos Williams included in his book, effectively exemplify the image we continue to preserve of Homolka as a dangerous sexual deviant. There is no way to determine which of these images reflects the truth of Homolka's character or personhood; as we argued in chapter 3, Homolka represents the embodiment of both sides of this binary – she is both a woman *in danger* and a *dangerous woman* (Kilty and Frigon 2006). Despite our efforts to pigeonhole her as one or the other, she is both, and it is this simultaneous embodiment of two seemingly opposed discursive productions that contributes to building and maintaining the cultural fascination with and enduring interpretation of her as monstrous. In the final section of this chapter we examine the role death taboos played in the manifestation of the cultural fixation on and social construction of Karla Homolka as a cunning femme fatale.

Death Taboos: Body Desecration and Disposal

While some authors advance that death remains a taboo subject (Aries 1981; Gorer 1965) there is much evidence to suggest otherwise (Foltyn 2008; Harper 2009; Kellehear 1984; Lee 2008; Walter 1991). In his seminal critique of the death taboo, Tony Walter (1991, 297) demonstrates that the existence of the death taboo in modern society is "overdrawn and lacking subtlety" and may be deconstructed by critically examining it according to race, class, gender, occupation, social framing and levels of adherence to individualism. Walter's critique is important, as it does not completely dismiss the lingering effects of historic discourses about death and taboo. Rather than claiming western cultures continue to maintain the death taboo at a macro social level, Walter contextualizes it as something that certain groups and individuals maintain in specific circumstances.

While the wider taboos about death may be waning, Gorer's (1965) claim that a society that fails to discuss death and dying creates a kind of pornography of death by becoming obsessed with horror comics, war movies and disasters holds some explanatory power. However, western cultures no longer fail to discuss death, in fact the media use death as a primary source of entertainment and infotainment (Doyle 2003; Foltyn 2008; Harper 2009; Jewkes 2011a,b; Surette 1994, 2007). Foltyn's work in particular demonstrates the extent to which western societies are bombarded with discussions of forensic scientific images of corpses, both real and imaginary, as countless television shows and movies feature legal dramas based on cases of abhorrent sexual assaults, murders, and crime scene investigation or medical dramas that feature regular autopsies (Doyle 2003; Foltyn 2008; Harper 2009). This case is no exception to such cultural manifestations. Not only have there been a series of non-fiction crime novels written about this case (see: Burnside and Cairns 1995; Crosbie 1997; DeAngelo 2011; Pron 1995; Todd 2012; Williams 1997, 2004), Homolka specifically was culturally immortalized in a comic book (*Killer Karla*) and even a Hollywood movie (*Karla*). What is evident in the content across the different mediums that have depicted details of this case is that they effectively concentrate the gaze on Homolka.[3]

Surrounded by all of these images and discussions of death, it is not a surprising argument that we are no longer a death denying society. Largely due to the advancements made in medicine and public health individuals in western societies are living longer than ever before, with the average life expectancy in most western nations now reaching the late seventies or early eighties depending on different social determinants. Death is now seen as the natural finish to a long life and as such is generally less traumatizing than in the past; while our grandparents may be missed it is not considered to be as tragic as losing a child or an otherwise healthy person in the prime of their life (Lee 2008). It is this last argument that we may use as a point of departure for the current discussion. Legal and media discourses about violence frequently reassert common stock narratives about criminality and fear of crime (Jewkes 2011a,b; Surette 1994, 2007). At the same time that western societies are becoming more open to and comfortable with discussing death, we are also increasingly fearful of sexual and violent victimization (Hale 1996; Semmens et al. 2002). The Bernardo-Homolka case is one of the most widely discussed murder cases in Canadian history, with much of the mass media coverage detailing aspects that may be conceptualized in terms of taboos surrounding death and mortality.

While death may no longer be a taboo subject, certain death-related actions remain taboo. In fact, features of the death taboo are many and varied, but typically centre on spiritual or religious concerns about the afterlife and on fears about decay and the impurity of the corpse (Douglas 1966; Lee 2008; Webster 1971). Walter (1991, 296) claims that the taboo thesis is actually a theory about culture:

> Aries, like Gorer, argues that death is inevitably problematic; along with sex, it is one of the major ways in which "nature" threatens "culture". Death must therefore be "tamed", which societies traditionally do through religion and through ritual. But over the past few centuries, individualism, romanticism, and secularism have undermined the rituals, and the modern individual is left naked before death's obscenity.

The culmination of a number of different trends including a waning emphasis on death and mourning rituals (Walter 1991), the emergence of the risk society (Douglas 1966, 2001) and a growing fear of crime in spite of declining violent crime rates (Semmens et al. 2002), has created a perfect storm ripe for the criminological re-imagination of the death taboo. While late-modern individuals in western societies may not fear the pollution potential of the dead in the same way pre-modern societies once did, fear of death, dying and the dead remain – albeit they are now rooted in our fears about uncertainty, disorder, pollution, and of course – risk. The growing trend to more openly discuss death partially emerges from the risk society's drive to order, classify, name, manage, avoid, and negate risk (Foucault 1977, 1980). To regulate and govern risk, we must name it, identify it in all its forms and understand how it operates so as to try to predict when it might strike.

Risk, however, is largely unpredictable and irrational (Douglas 1966; Gardner 2008). The social anxiety and fear of death via violent victimization is stimulated by the incessant coverage of criminal cases in the news media and through fictional representations of violence as entertainment (Doyle 2003; Foltyn 2008; Gardner 2008; Jewkes 2011a,b; Surette 1994, 2007). With the advent of the 24-hour-a-day news cycle and coverage of crime, war, and disaster, the late-modern individual has little time to cleanse or purify post-exposure to risk, death or victimization, which may increase anxiety about the continued failure to tame risk. In this context, the graphic details of this case elicited a cultural fear of premature death via violent victimization or "stranger-danger", which may be conceptualized as a contemporary death taboo. First, Bernardo and Homolka treated the corpses of their victims as abject objects. The ways the couple disposed of their victims violates longstanding western death rituals, such as the careful and professional treatment of the body, including the mortician's "making up the dead" for public viewing. Disposing the dead in callous, disrespectful and taboo ways incited disgust – especially in light of the fact that the girls were ideal victims whose youth, purity, and innocence elicited cultural fears about risk and premature death. While it is important to note that many individuals who are guilty of murder violate death taboos by desecrating and disposing of the bodies of their victims in callous ways, we suggest that it is the constellation of taboos Homolka violated in conjunction with her gender and femininity that set her apart in terms of the concentrated and lingering cultural focus on and heightened levels of collectively felt disgust expressed toward her.

Homolka participated in the taboo desecration of her victim's bodies; for example, she tried to eliminate any forensic evidence of Kristen French having been in their home. Homolka washed and douched French's corpse, cut her fingernails and shorn her lengthy hair. The details are even more gruesome regarding Leslie Mahaffy's death. While Bernardo was found guilty of strangling both girls to death, his methods of body disposal were different for each victim. Kristen French's naked body was thrown over the side of a rural road into a steep ditch, while Bernardo dismembered Leslie Mahaffy's body and encased the parts into several large concrete blocks that the couple then threw into Lake Gibson. Like Homolka's participation in the sexual assaults, touching the dead outside of the duties associated with the professional realm (for example medical examination, autopsy and embalming, and other mortician preparations) and mutilating a corpse break normative disgust thresholds. Actions become taboo largely because they cross disgust thresholds; as Miller (1997, 82) writes:

> Some sights simply evoke disgust: gore and mutilation, the effects of violence on the body, especially when these are inflicted cruelly without justification. Something pre-social seems to link us to a strong sense of disgust and horror at the prospect of a body that doesn't quite look like one, either grotesquely deformed by accident of disorganized by mayhem.

The intersection of Miller's discussion of mutilated bodies evoking disgust and Foltyn's discussion of "the rise of the corpse" as an infotainment commodity is exemplified by the crime scene photographs Williams (2004) included in his second book about this case; namely, the image of Tammy Homolka's Halothane bruised face on the gurney in the morgue and a black and white photograph of Leslie Mahaffy's body parts encased in the concrete slabs that had split open on the shore of Lake Gibson. The dead are typically memorialized and honoured through different funeral and burial rituals; for example, public attendance at Kristen French's funeral in St Catharines was so heavy that attendees flowed out of the church and lined the city streets several persons deep. The corpses of French and Mahaffy evoked not only sadness at the tragedy, but also fear of violent victimization by a stranger and disgust as the bodies were so disorderly disposed of in unacceptable contexts. The couple's breach of the normative cultural boundaries surrounding the preservation and treatment of the dead reconfigured the bodies as culturally polluting in their violation of death and mortality taboo and pollution rules (Douglas 1966).

There is one final point to make about the manifestation of the death taboo in this case. Following the conclusion of Paul Bernardo's 1995 trial, the home the couple rented in Port Dalhousie, Ontario, where the crimes took place and which had since been defaced with graffiti, was torn down. While a new house was built on the site it has a different address than the former dwelling, akin to eliminating the number 13 sometimes seen in elevators. These acts symbolize an attempt to purify the site by ridding it of Karla Homolka and Paul Bernardo's presence and is similar to historical purification ceremonies and activities that involved using fire to purify a site tainted and tabooed by death (Webster 1973). Such a dramatic action reflects the lingering effects of death taboos and illustrates the collective disgust the public continues to feel toward this case.

Conclusion

While the news, television, and film mediums pornographize violence it is "death at a remove, death abstracted, intellectualised, professionalised, and depersonalised" (Gorer 1955; Foltyn 2008; Walter 1991, 295). Stories about the murder of young, attractive, white women often celebritize what Christie (1986) conceptualized as the ideal victim (Foltyn 2008) and media coverage is heightened when the case also involves a perpetrator that is similarly young, attractive, white, and female (Kilty 2010). Throughout this chapter we have attempted to demonstrate how the disgust the audience felt in response to the violence found in this case is linked to a series of taboos related to sisterhood and feminism, sex and death, and mortality. Once again, it is worth quoting Miller (1997, 195–6) at length:

> Cruelty generates a double disgust in the impartial spectator, that is, once we recover from the shock it can give. First, the perpetrator is looked on with fear and loathing, with the most intense kind of disgust and horror. Then a second disgust focuses on the degraded victim, whether bloody and disfigured or morally annihilated in the disgrace of having been so abused. Our pity and desire to relieve the suffering of the victim are inhibited by the same emotion that compels us to execrate the person responsible for the plight.

The public's loathing of Karla Homolka is rooted in the collectively felt emotion of disgust, which, as a threat to our purity, leaves *us* feeling polluted. We are certainly disgusted with the violence she participated in, but feeling disgust does not explain the cultural obsession with Homolka and the lesser focus on Bernardo. Of course the perceived injustice of the plea bargain adds to the concentrated gaze we maintain on Homolka, but it is also her transgression of the hetero-normative and patriarchal boundaries of hegemonic femininity and womanhood that demand sexual passivity and nurturance that mark her as *dangerous* and as Other. While steps were taken to purify post-Homolka (for example the high public attendance at Kristen French's funeral and the demolition of the house where the murders were committed) the fact that she garnered a plea bargain and reduced sentence continues to needle the public, especially given the visual evidence of her participation in the sexual assaults. Take for example, a sample of newspaper headlines describing the plea bargain: "Homolka plea bargain called a 'whitewash'" (Brown 1996, C12); "Tape caught Homolka in a lie: Crown could have revoked plea bargain for lying about fourth victim, Bernardo's lawyer testifies" (Stepan 2000, A5); "Odor lingers over Homolka case: Is plea bargaining being offered to compensate for lazy police work?" (*The Ottawa Citizen* 1996, A12); "Homolka deal stirs cries for public inquiry: Plea-bargaining system questioned in wake of revelations in murder trial" (Legall 1995, A4); "Crown really got suckered by Homolka's plea bargain" (*Times Colonist* 1995, 1); "Deals with the devil?: People hate plea bargains like Karla Homolka's; courts depend on them" (Dolik 1995, A10); "Karla Homolka's plea bargain still disputed many years later" (*Guardian* 2005, A5). As discussed in chapter 3, even veteran Canadian legal scholar and practicing lawyer Alan Young wrote a letter to the Attorney General imploring him to appeal Homolka's sentence and plea bargain in light of the visual evidence in the videotapes. As Morrissey (2003, 146) writes:

> Needless to say, Karla quickly became an enigma for the media, the girl the court artists couldn't draw; the girl the psychiatrists couldn't pin down to a diagnosis, a list of symptoms (Duncanson and Rankin 3.9.95); the girl who blithely crossed every boundary in the pursuit of her pleasure and that of her lover.

To be clear, we do not suggest that the public should forget Homolka's participation in these vicious crimes or that she should be excused for her behaviour. Ultimately, our goal has been to move beyond the public and institutional view of Karla Homolka that may be discontinuous with the present (Frosh 2001) in order to problematize the cultural fascination with her by examining the taboos she violated and the disgust these violations elicited. This cultural fascination is clearly demonstrated by a recent e-book published by Canadian journalist Paula Todd (2012), who ventured to Guadeloupe to "track down" Karla Homolka. The title of Todd's book perfectly illustrates how visual images can sediment a particular interpretation of someone's character and personhood in ways that may be discontinuous with the present: *Finding Karla: How I Tracked Down an Elusive Serial Child Killer and Discovered a Mother of Three.* Despite the fact that Karla Homolka was released from prison a decade ago after serving a 12-year sentence to warrant expiry, there is a public and journalistic expectation that she is only (and can only ever be) what was captured on the videotapes and in her courtroom testimonies. This perspective runs counter to one of the core values of our criminal justice system – that of rehabilitation – and exemplifies the long-lasting effects of stigmatization to which all criminalized persons are subject (Goffman 1963). Understandably, the collectively felt disgust toward Homolka's participation in these crimes runs deep; but characterizing Homolka as always already dangerous only contributes to her ongoing memorialization as the femme fatale of our criminological imagination and denies that she has changed or could ever change, is no longer a threat or is remorseful for her actions. In the next chapter, we examine the notion of remorse and the ways in which it was discursively constituted in relation to Homolka's 2005 release from prison.

Notes

1 Karlene Faith (1993) conceptualizes media constructions of women who use their femininity to lure their victims into harm's way as "super bitch killer beauties."
2 The book, originally published only in French, included these photographs in only the first print run – they were removed from successive print runs and from the English version of the book that was published a year later.
3 Lynn Crosbie's book *Paul's Case* is the one example where the focus was on Bernardo rather than Homolka.

5 Apologies and Iced Cappuccinos

Examining Media and Juridical Interpretations of Karla Homolka's Remorse Performative

When Karla Homolka was released from Joliette Institution, the federal prison for women in the province of Quebec, on 4 July 2005 after serving a 12-year sentence to warrant expiry, it reignited the furious media frenzy surrounding this case. For weeks prior to her release, reporters camped outside the prison with the hope of capturing a singular, present-day image of Homolka while in the prison yard. Some reporters sat atop neighbouring buildings for days and weeks on end in order to try to get a better aerial view of the prison yard with their telephoto lenses. This media circus was exacerbated by the fact that the Ontario Office of the Attorney General, supported by Timothy Danson, the lawyer for the Mahaffy and French families, attempted to secure the application of a series of strict parole conditions under s.810[1] of the *Criminal Code of Canada* that Homolka would have to obey upon her release. Homolka contested the s.810 application request, leading to a series of court appearances that created an opportune time for television and print journalists to rekindle the public's voracious interest in the caricature of Homolka that was established and had captivated the public 12 years earlier.

The discussions set out in the preceding chapters outlined the ways in which the gendered nature of the newsprint media coverage of Homolka relied on stock narratives about women's violence that are rooted in normative cultural expectations about femininity and womanhood. These stock narratives cast Homolka as simultaneously *in danger* and *dangerous*, monstrous and hypersexual, characterizations that are similarly reflected in media and judicial accounts of Homolka's seeming lack of remorse for her role in the sexual assaults and homicides. Although never clinically diagnosed as such, articulations of Homolka's failed expressions of remorse were also aggravated by journalists' suggestions that she is psychopathic and thus inherently psychologically remorseless, a pronouncement that discursively set the stage for the Attorney General's 2005 request for the s.810 application.

Building on the previous chapter's discussion of the public's collective feeling of disgust as a result of Homolka's violation of a number of different sex and death taboos, in this chapter we examine Homolka's perceived lack of shame and remorse for having transgressed those socio-cultural boundaries. Feeling shame and showing remorse for one's inappropriate behaviour demonstrates that despite having committed socially condemned actions the individual adheres to communal values and social norms and recognizes her failure to measure up to those standards (Bazemore 1998; Presser 2003; Weisman 2009, 2014). To be without remorse separates the individual from the broader moral community, marking them as distinct and apart from "the rest of us." Such a distinction reifies and further entrenches the archetype of the "evil" offender, the monsterized killer of our cultural imaginary. This chapter analyses media and juridical interpretations of Homolka's expressions of remorse by situating it as both a materially felt emotion and an identity performative that is expressed through a moral performance bound by the confines and contextual setting of the courtroom.

Remorse as a Materially Felt Emotion and Identity Performative

There is a growing body of thought-provoking literature on the concept of remorse and its connection to other related moral emotions such as shame. In fact, discussions and interpretations of remorse are a common trope in the judicial context and in media coverage of crime and justice stories. Problematically, however, remorse is affected by the "speedy assembly line" style of the contemporary criminal justice system and as such is often simply attributed to apologies following the submission of a guilty plea in exchange for a reduced sentence or other plea agreement (Bibas and Bierschbach 2004, 88). Exhibitions of remorse are exceedingly important in those American states that maintain the practice of capital punishment and where a successful moral performance of remorse can mean the difference between life and death. Given that the sincerity of the remorseful performance is challenging to ascertain and every accused person has a strong self-interest in trying to reduce their sentence, it is unsurprising that the courts frequently challenge or question allegations of remorse as having "no tangible exertion or demonstrable behavioural change (apart from the saddened expression, and perhaps the occasional tear or two), and being purely subjective it is almost impossible to rebut" (Bagaric et al. 2001, 365; Presser 2003).

This interpretation suggests that because of the difficulty in measuring the authenticity of an expression of remorse it is largely impossible to accept any such claim as genuine, which instead reinforces the notion that "the justice system may reward well-executed fakery and the 'acquired skill' of expressing 'appropriate' attitudes in the courtroom" (Bibas and Bierschbach 2004, 104–5); a position that essentializes the criminalized subject as always-already dishonest and untrustworthy. By emphasizing an offender's potentiality for hoodwinking the court, this explanation fails to recognize that expressions of remorse for criminal wrongdoing are bound by and constituted in and through the intimidating and coercive judicial context of the courtroom. It also leaves little room for the relational aspect of "doing" or performing remorse that many scholars claim requires interaction with the wronged party and or community in order to be unaffected and effective (Bazemore 1998; Bibas and Bierschbach 2004; Weisman 2009).

The extant literature is consistent in its description of the ways in which genuine remorse for having criminally wronged or harmed another may be evidenced. Most of these considerations centre on criminal justice demands for cooperation, such as an admission of guilt and entering a guilty plea, cooperating with, and providing evidence to the police, identifying co-offenders, making reparation, participating actively in correctional rehabilitation programming and voluntarily going into treatment (Bagaric et al. 2001; Martel 2010; Proeve et al. 1999; Proeve and Howells 2006; Wood and MacMartin 2007). The courts largely depend on these practices in order to move the congested criminal justice system forward more quickly, but judges also wish to convey that if "an offender is not 'lost,' that he has some self-transformative capacity that justifies (or requires) a lesser punishment" (Bibas and Bierschbach 2004, 94). For cases involving serious violent crime, such as Homolka's, reparation is arduous because there can be no equity found in her suffering and feelings of remorse; there is no working off the dollar value of the harm done such as may be possible for crimes involving stolen or vandalized property. For cases involving violence, remorse is typically exhibited through procedural cooperation by admitting guilt, taking responsibility for one's actions, and demonstrating the desire to learn, change, and grow as a person so as to prevent similar harms in the future[2]. Remorse, therefore, "is thought to denote greater responsiveness to rehabilitative interventions" (Martel 2010, 423), the result of which reifies and expands the state's role in managing the offender (Weisman 2009, 59).

Contrition is thus seen as an indicator that the individual continues to affiliate with and a signifier that she wishes to remain a member of the broader moral community. To be considered remorseful in the judicial context, it is not enough to offer the words "I am sorry"; rather, the individual must demonstrate that they are remorseful through taking actions that are accepted as indicators of sincere remorse (Weisman 2004, 125). It is in this sense that remorse is both a materially felt emotion and a performative (Presser 2003) that Martel (2010, 427) describes as a "discursive transaction," the evaluation of which Weisman contends "takes place in a context of suspicion" (2009, 50). Genuine expressions of remorse serve an impression management function (Goffman 1971) that the offender must engage in to distance themselves from the harmful actions they committed and to publically realign themselves with the normative moral order (Bibas and Bierschbach 2004; Martel 2010; Weisman 2004, 2009, 2014). Communicating and demonstrating remorse is an attempt to shed the stigma associated with criminalization but it also contributes to the creation of a divisive conceptualization of identity that posts the criminalized wrongdoer who harmed another against the "true self" that understands this behaviour to be unacceptable (Kilty 2010, 2011; Weisman 2009):

> The offender virtually splits herself or himself between the self that committed the offense and the self that joins with the aggrieved in agreeing that the offending act was morally unacceptable. The work of expressions of remorse or the offering of apology – if believed – is to

> represent the wrongdoer as other than the act for which she or he has been condemned. If the moral performance is successful, then it may be inferred that the self that condemns the act is more real than the self that committed the act. Contrariwise, for the unapologetic or unremorseful, the act becomes their essence. If they do not separate themselves from the act or if their apology or show of remorse is not believed, then the transgression comes to define who they are – the self that committed the offending act is the true self.
>
> (Weisman 2009, 50)

Not only do expressions of remorse affect socio-cultural impressions of the individual (Goffman 1971), they also contribute to the negotiation and even remaking of individual self-identity. The separation or social distancing between selves or identities is similarly reflected in the correctional zeal for prisoners to make themselves subject to a project of self-transformation that is facilitated through rehabilitative programming, which positions remorse as a marker of correctional potential or success, depending on its temporal expression.

Weisman (2009) outlines a series of criteria that are required in order for a moral performance of remorse to be validated. He argues that the performance of remorse must begin with a full admission of guilt and taking complete responsibility for one's actions. For the admission of guilt to be considered sincere, it cannot be situational or identify the offending behaviour as having been outside the individual's control. Therefore, the offender cannot be seen to be making excuses or justifications for perpetrating the act; those who do are seen as engaging techniques of neutralization (Sykes and Matza 1957) that attempt to deflect responsibility onto others and thus as unremorseful. Martel (2010) argues that because the criminalized subject must accept without modification, question or contextual alteration the state version of events in order for their expressions of remorse to be considered honest and unaffected, these moral performances are in effect "productions of Truth" that coercively silence counter-narratives. For a subject like Homolka, this point proved difficult and complicated her attempts for the courts, the media and the public to accept her exhibitions of remorse as genuine, as her entire crime narrative hinged on the relationship between her actions and the psychological, sexual and physical abuse she experienced at the hands of Paul Bernardo.

In addition to the verbal admission of guilt, the individual must also express remorse's associated paralinguistic cues and affects, namely those that show suffering, such as crying, facial and bodily gestures that illustrate shame (for example head bowing), feelings of sickness, the inability to sleep well and even pervasive or intruding negative thoughts about one's participation in the crime. These symptoms are often supported by reports from social workers, counsellors, psy-experts and other state officials that document and validate the individual's claims of distress. If accepted as truthful, these signifiers of distress are thought to show the individual's "true" feelings about their harmful actions and, most importantly, the rejection of their criminal self:

> The offender's "hauntedness", self-loathing, or depressive demeanor can be valorized in law as moral condemnation of the self that betrayed community even if pathologized in psychology as symptoms of mental disorder. The avowal of responsibility for the act coupled with the offender's demonstration of self-condemnation enacts the tension between doing and being – the offender has chosen to act in a manner that betrays community but they have shown on their body that they are loyal to community.
>
> (Weisman 2009, 58–9)

In this way, judicial appraisals of remorse attempt to accurately read the emotional and psychological mind of the accused by reading and interpreting their body. The remorseful subject must demonstrate their transformative potential by situating the criminal act as a point of rupture in their biographical past (Foucault 1972, 1994) that has led to significant and "deep characterological transformations" (Weisman 2009, 59). Homolka made one particular statement, from which the title of this chapter was taken, during her post-release interview with Radio-Canada that was picked up and referenced repeatedly in the media and was taken as evidence of her lack of remorse and continued shallowness and insincerity:

Napier: What is the first thing you would like to do with your family?
Homolka: I know it sounds stupid, but I would like to have an iced cappuccino from Tim Horton's. That is what I would like to do.

Media reporters and journalists characterized this response as insensitive and trite, largely because in order to exhibit the requisite shame for one's transgressions the wrongdoer must evidence a lowered self-esteem resulting from their criminal actions and the desire to shed that identity and return to their true moral self. To be able to speak of such a simple pleasure diverts attention from her self-presentation as a remorseful subject. In this sense, to be remorseful means to permanently maintain low self-esteem and to refrain from experiencing any type of happiness.

In the next section, we analyse the ways in which these criteria for determining the authenticity of remorse are gendered and how this affected media and juridical constructions of Homolka's remorse/remorselessness. Specifically, we question how the pervasiveness of constructions of hegemonic femininity/masculinity and victimism complicated judicial and media interpretations of Homolka's remorse performatives. In the section that follows, we consider how suggestions that Homolka suffers from symptoms of psychopathy negatively affected interpretations of the legitimacy of her expressions of remorse.

Victimism and Remorse: Little Girl Lost or Remorseless Woman?

Remorse is a type of juridical currency through which the criminalized subject may attempt to secure leniency from the courts and the correctional and parole release systems, although doing so also tautologically moderates judicial interpretations of the remorse as less than heartfelt. This fact explains why an apology, while reaffirming that the act was in fact transgressive and that the wrongdoer did perpetrate it, is not enough to warrant state acceptance of or public belief that the individual is truly remorseful. Homolka evidenced a number of traditional signifiers of remorse, which, in addition to the Crown needing her testimony in order to convict Bernardo, qualified the Court to offer her the plea agreement. For example: identifying her co-offender to the police, cooperating with the police so as to provide physical forensic evidence that would be used to convict both she and Bernardo, disclosing the details of her involvement in the accidental death of her sister Tammy – a crime the police were not aware of or investigating – and offering an apology for her participation in the crimes during her sentencing hearing and again upon her release from prison.

The severities of Homolka's crimes, however, act as a barrier to accepting her remorse as authentic. We contend that gender complicates remorse performatives, especially in those rare cases involving women convicted of violence and sexual violence. For example, while Presser (2003) found that men convicted of sexual violence express an inadequate sense of responsibility, Gaarder and Belknap (2002) found that women, in an attempt to embody an ethic of care that is a formative component of hegemonic femininity, maximize responsibility for their violent crimes despite having histories of victimization. The men in Presser's study actually rejected remorse by focusing on the negative consequences that the crime had for them, namely incarceration, instead "they felt victimized by the criminal justice system, and this experience preoccupied their talk with me as few other topics did" (2003, 814).

This finding led Presser (2003, 820) to contend that we must examine "the social grounds for remorse or its absence". However, understanding the social grounds for remorse (or lack thereof) requires consideration of the contextual concerns that Weisman (2009) found to threaten the veracity of remorse claims. Unlike the women in Gaarder and Belknap's study, Homolka situated her responsibility firmly within a narrative that emphasized the physical, psychological and sexual abuse she experienced at the hands of Paul Bernardo. This victim narrative was ever-present throughout her involvement with the criminal justice system and was one of the largest impediments to media and public acceptance of her as a truly remorseful subject. As far back as her sentencing hearing, we have evidence of Homolka's efforts to quell social condemnation of her actions through the production of a remorseful performance that situates her actions within the context of her victimization. The following is a statement read in court during her 1993 sentencing hearing by her then lawyer, George Walker:

> She would have been the fourth victim. It's a classic case of wife beating. It starts with the verbal abuse, the demeaning, taking away your self respect, isolating from – isolating you from those persons who may have been able to exercise some degree of control over her – over her, other than Mr Bernardo. Then it moves on to the occasional violent, physical assault, the

> promises of not doing it again and it continues on a gradual scale, and ultimately it, in my submission, it would have followed that my client would not have escaped Mr Bernardo. It was only a matter of time. Again, I do not make these submissions to deter from the horrific nature of the offences, but I point out to this Court, that given my client's psychological make up in the beginning, she was exactly what he needed. She was the conduit, she was the vehicle. She does not seek to minimize her involvement, it's right there. Mr Segal has read the facts in. She does not take exception to the facts. She was there. She was there when both Kristen French and Leslie Mahaffy died and she was there when her own sister died. But, once the sister died, Paul Bernardo had her. But from that point on, as the doctor said, indicated, there was very little that she could do in her own mind.
>
> (R. v. K. Bernardo 1993, 78–9)

Mr Walker's statement situates Homolka's involvement in the sexual assaults and homicides as secondary to Bernardo's and as the result of his ongoing physical and emotional violence toward her. In an effort to lend greater credibility to this claim, Walker cites official psychiatric and medical reports that support his presentation of Homolka as understanding the magnitude of her offences and as distressed by her role in them. Clearly drawing on Lenore Walker's (1979) classic description of the battered woman syndrome, Mr Walker's narrative positions Homolka as a victim akin to her own, an identity performative that aims to suggest that she is more like Leslie Mahaffy, Kristen French, and Tammy Homolka than she is Paul Bernardo. In terms of the self-transformation that is required to successfully demonstrate remorse (Kilty 2010; Martel 2010; Weisman 2009), this discursive move was problematic in that it expected the audience to sympathize and empathize with a woman who participated in gravely harming other young women so as to save her own skin.

Consequently, despite Walker's statements that Homolka "does not seek to minimize her involvement" and "does not take exception to the facts," by positioning her participation in these crimes as a result of her victimization, reporters, journalists and the Canadian public understood her as doing exactly that. Homolka's refusal to dismiss the effects of her victimization as the cause of her criminality remained a point of contention for the courts, the federal correctional system as well as for journalists and reporters, all maintaining that this demonstrated a failure to show a fully developed and internalized sense of remorse. Take, for example, how Patricia Pearson (1998, 52) described Homolka's testimony at Paul Bernardo's 1995 trial as a complete deflection of responsibility:

> The effect, in the case of Karla Homolka, was startlingly clear in the courtroom. Encouraged to attribute every move, every want, every look on her fiercely intelligent face to the machinations of Paul Bernardo, Homolka renounced her claim to be an adult. She infantilized herself, relinquishing her spirit, will, passion, pride, resourcefulness, and rage. Her wheat-blond

> hair fell across her wan like face like a curtain as she sat on the stand for three weeks, and divested herself of a soul.

Pearson's characterization clearly positions Homolka as a remorseless subject who was looking to foster sympathy in what she has also described as "the abuse excuse." For the remorse to be accepted the subject must not only show that they feel shame for perpetrating the transgression, they must also avoid situating their actions as the result of contextual issues that were beyond their control (Sundby 1998; Weisman 2009). As Martel (2010) contends, for an offender to be accepted as remorseful they must adopt the unadulterated state version of the facts of the case as "*the* production of Truth" [our emphasis]. Failure to do so is taken as indicator that the individual does not accept the appropriate level of responsibility for their crimes, which is taken to suggest that they have not fully engaged in the self-transformation that is required of the remorseful criminal subject. In effect, the subject must characterize their actions as those that they freely chose to commit.

Problematically, the juridical demand for the accused to confess responsibility without acknowledging mitigating factors inherently genders the judicial interpretation of remorse in cases involving women that were subject to intimate partner violence. This corresponds with the fact that very few women who raise the battered woman syndrome in court are acquitted (Frigon 2003; Sheehy 2014; Sheehy et al. 2012a,b). For example, Shaffer (1997) found that in the 5 years following the precedent setting Lavallée case in 1991 there were 35 cases in Canada where women raised this defence; 16 were charged with homicide and only 3 were successfully acquitted in court. Similarly Sheehy et al. (2012a) found that of the 36 cases between 2000–10 in which women raised the battered woman syndrome for having killed their abusive partners, only 12 (33 percent) were either successfully acquitted or saw charges dropped. While Homolka did not act violently toward her abuser, as is common for most battered women, to suggest that the violence that she suffered had no effect on her actions ignores the environment of torture within which she lived. Moreover, to think that remorse is only authentic if the transgression is constructed as an act of unremitting free will is a stark and unhelpful dichotomy that ignores any number of intersecting mitigating factors, such as addiction, poverty, mental illness and, yes, victimization that influence an individual's decision-making and actions.

While her victim narrative remained central to critics' refusals to accept her remorse as genuine, it is not simply because of Homolka's insistence that she participated in these acts of sexual violence out of fear for her life that the public questioned and rejected her claims of remorse. Rather, it is also due to the categorical heinousness of the facts and details of the case – namely, the taboos that were broken and the disgust they elicited amongst the collective moral public. Take for example the words of journalist Catherine Ford (17 Nov 2002, A15) of the *Calgary Herald*:

> It's comforting for Canadians to think there are some crimes so heinous as to place the killer and his accomplices beyond the pale of society forever. The

> psychopathic Paul Bernardo and his willing wife earned that questionable honour. In their kidnapping, sexual torture and slaying of two teenagers, after "practicing" on Homolka's own sister until she died, and their videotaping of these young girls being brutalized, they earned the moral revulsion of Canadians. Even bleeding hearts turn to stone when faced with the enormity of what these two did. Nonetheless, Homolka's real sentence starts on that summer day in 2005 when she is released, an ostensibly free woman. Whether she exhibits any remorse for her actions, or continues to believe herself just another victim of a dominating, abusive man will make no difference.

Ford argues that Homolka's moral performance is inconsistent with her claims of remorse, which she links to the public's "moral revulsion" toward her. More than that, however, Ford identifies that it was "the enormity" of Homolka's actions and the crimes themselves that stimulated the public's – even the most progressive and liberal amongst us, whom she describes as "bleeding hearts" – resolute vitriol toward her and which coloured any self-assertions of remorse as tainted and highly questionable. Ford's position reflects Australian feminist Belinda Morrissey's (2003) description of Homolka as presenting a limit case for feminist scholars – she is the enigma that we cannot explain. She may have been battered, but she is too far from the archetype of "the battered woman" to be understood therein. This viewpoint suggests that there are some crimes that for many citizens there is no hope for an offender to be sincerely remorseful and which place the offending party, in Ford's words, "beyond the pale of society forever." Alas, this is a static and absolutist position that sees no space for authentic apology and remorse because the offender is understood to be stanchly dishonest and disloyal to the moral order.

This fact did not dissuade Homolka from continuing to express remorse as contextually situated within her narrative of victimhood. Perhaps believing that consistency in this narrative was central to her acceptance as truthful, Homolka was steadfast over the 12 years of her incarceration that she only participated in these criminal acts out of fear for her own safety as well as that of her loved ones. To exemplify this fact it is worth quoting at length from the interview Homolka gave with Radio-Canada on the day of her release from Joliette Institution:

Napier: You said you still live with what you did. Do you feel remorse?

Homolka: I cry often. I am unable to forgive myself. I think about what I did, and often I think I don't deserve to be happy because of that.

Napier: Everyone judges what you did. How do you judge what you did?

Homolka: The acts were terrible. I was in a situation where I could not see clearly, or I was not able to ask for help, or I was completely overwhelmed in my life. I regret it enormously, because now I know that I had the power to stop all that, but when it was happening, I didn't think I had any power.

Napier: You didn't even have the power to stop what you were doing?
Homolka: I did not initiate the offences. I followed. Yes, I did what I did, but . . .
Napier: When you think about it today, do you *still* see yourself as a victim at the time of the crimes?
Homolka: All the people who say my role was equal to his [Bernardo's] do not know the case. Secondly, yes, I was under his control.

When journalist Joyce Napier begins this exchange by asking whether or not she felt remorse, Homolka responds in the affirmative explaining that she suffers from the associated affects of crying, intrusive thoughts and a lowered self-worth that causes her to feel as though she does not deserve happiness. Homolka was then asked to comment on the ways in which she judges her actions, in other words, how she morally understands her participation in the crimes. Here, Homolka tempers her acceptance of responsibility for the crimes by referring to the fact that she did not act alone and her participation was conditioned by her history of victimization – going so far as to say that she was "under his [Bernardo's] control". In this narrative Homolka relinquishes much of her agency and reveals a kind of dissonance between what may be sincere materially felt remorse for her actions and inactions that led to the tragic deaths of her victims and the juridical demand for taking complete and unfettered responsibility. We support Presser's (2003) argument that it is important to consider the social grounds for remorse because it problematizes the normative juridical characterization of remorse as an unadulterated expression that can be easily read from interpreting the body of the accused within the coercive confines of the courtroom. Contextualizing remorse requires assessing a materially felt emotion that may vary from person to person depending on their socio-cultural experiences, which adds a layer of scepticism to the already difficult if not impossible task of teasing out authentic performatives from manipulative and inauthentic ones.

Homolka's failure to abandon this victim narrative also provides an important segue to the next theme, where we turn our attention to the concept of psychopathy, a fledgling characterological representation of Homolka that was raised in the media coverage and symptoms of which were referenced during her cross-examination at Bernardo's trial. Given that individuals that are clinically diagnosed with psychopathy are seen as innately remorseless and incapable of self-transformation or change, the portrayal is especially relevant to the current discussion.

Moral Vacuity, Psychopathic Tendencies, and Remorse

> But it is through remorse that the world of transgressors is divided not just into those who transgress but into those whose misconduct will come to define their character and those whose character will lead us to redefine their misconduct. The result is an ever expanding narrative of what makes a claim to remorse credible or not and what expressions of character are perceived by the court as separating the offender from the act or aligning the offender with the act.
>
> (Weisman 2009, 51)

In this quote, Weisman explains how the heinousness and gruesomeness of the criminal act can come to define and even socially constitute the internal character of the individual wrongdoer. While a perceived lack of remorse during the criminal trial, which Kadri aptly describes as a "theatre of contrition" (2005, 213), is typically associated with a guilty verdict, it may also come to be viewed as "a symptom of an underlying pathology that marks the wrongdoer as variously diseased, impaired, or otherwise incapable of feeling what a normal member of the community would feel under similar circumstances" (Weisman 2007, 189). This interpretation marks the violent criminal transgressor as intrinsically different from the collective moral public, constituting the individual who is understood to be psychopathic as an evil and even inhuman caricature. This narrative process lays the groundwork for the socio-political calls for the individual's permanent incapacitation and even capitally sanctioned death.

Prototypical symptoms of antisocial personality disorder and psychopathology include a lack of remorse, guilt, and shame for harm done to others due to an innate moral and emotional block that leads to a lack of compassion for and empathy with others. Without a connection to the broader moral community the individual is said to commit the harmful act with full cognitive awareness that it is wrong and will bring about social disapproval and moral condemnation (Cleckley 1976; Hare 1996; Weisman 2007). In this way, psychopathy is best understood as an affective disorder that prevents the individual from being able to experience emotions and affects in normative socio-cultural ways that are essential for the development of positive interpersonal relationships. The psychopath is thought to have an underdeveloped set of emotions that only permits them to experience feelings in a shallow or superficial way, which means that they are able to mimic emotional responses without materially feeling them (Cleckley 1976; Hare 1996; Weisman 2007). This is especially true for what have been described as moral emotions – such as feelings of empathy, compassion and remorse. Without the materiality of moral emotions, the individual may find it difficult to subscribe to the codes of behaviour set out by the normative moral order and that are required of participation in community life.

Weisman's consideration of what the perceived absence of remorse has come to symbolize – namely psychopathology in the form of antisocial personality disorder or psychopathy – provides a much-needed discussion of the problematic linkages made between someone's actions and their core identity. He demonstrates that characterizing certain convicted persons as without remorse works to create a divide between the individual and the community, first by way of their transgressions and second by way of the dangerous personality characteristics that their transgressions are seen to signify. In this sense, the failure to demonstrate customary expressions of remorse becomes an indicator of a psychobiological incurable illness that is said to signal the individual's innate and ever-present potentiality for future dangerousness. As Weisman (2007, 199) argues, "for the psychopath, action is a reflection of being." Interpretations of psychopathy as an incurable illness not only solidifies the dichotomy of normal versus the pathological, it also creates a kind of "therapeutic pessimism" (Weisman 2007) that suggests that the individual is largely unresponsive to rehabilitative interventions. While the individual is thought to understand the difference between right and wrong, they are not exempt from criminal responsibility and are thus more likely to be subject to extraordinary periods of incapacitation (Hare 1996).

This contemporary conceptualization sees the psychopathic subject as an exceptional performer, capable of mimicking the affective emotions required to build trust with others in order to take advantage of them. Characterizing the psychopath as an actor who uses superficial charm (Cleckley 1976) to engage in impression management (Hare 1996) positions her[3] as the charismatic stranger lurking among us. Embracing this framing of her character, Homolka's critics stressed that during her testimony at Paul Bernardo's 1995 trial she only mimicked affective displays of real victimhood, empathy for her victims and remorse for her actions in order to garner sympathy from the court. Newsprint data were rife with references to Homolka's lack of emotion while on the stand, her "dead blue eyes," and to her quiet sobs which were described as being for show rather than sincere expressions of remorse, guilt and sadness. This characterization did not wane at all with the passage of her 12 years inside prison. Take for comparative example, the following two quotes from articles written about Homolka during her 1993 trial and the June 2005 s. 810 hearing prior to her release from federal prison:

> Karla Homolka invariably looked immaculate: different outfits every day, her cheeks rouged, her hair elegantly coiffured. But in her round blue eyes, there seemed to be something dead, as if something was missing. Trapped by the awful circumstances, besieged by all the attention, she projected anger more than remorse in her gaze, as though she still could not quite grasp why she was on trial.
>
> (Appleby 7 July 1993, A1)

> Her head bowing ever lower at a court hearing here yesterday, Homolka began repeatedly dabbing her eyes with a Kleenex and didn't stop until several moments later. The episode of apparent sorrow – punctuating a day in which she betrayed little emotion of any kind – was prompted by a witness's description of how she and Paul Bernardo, her ex-husband, raped and inadvertently killed her sister, Tammy. One skeptical spectator actually scanned Homolka's face with opera glasses for evidence of real tears. The verdict among onlookers was divided. "She showed what I would call contrived emotion," said Mr Danson, who looked on from a front-row seat. "As soon as those facts [about the crimes] were over, it was like snapping your fingers. She was right back without a scintilla of emotion. . . . That has a lot of the hallmarks of psychopathy," Mr Danson said.
>
> (Blackwell 3 June 2005, A1)

Both Appleby and Blackwell demonstrate how common it is for the courts, reporters and journalists, jurors and the public to connect details about the accused's demeanour, attire, and facial expressions to interpretations of their guilt and remorse (Sundby 1997). As we have shown in the preceding chapters of this book, reporters, journalists, and the public relentlessly scrutinized Homolka's narrative, appearance, and her paralinguistic and affective cues throughout the course of her testimony and cross-examination at Paul Bernardo's 1995 trial. As Blackwell describes, "one skeptical spectator actually scanned Homolka's face with opera glasses for evidence of real tears" and the public was divided on whether or not they were sincere. This intense degree of scrutiny of Homolka's facial expressions and affective cues was typically described as a search for humanity within a figure of evil that was incomprehensible to the public. Homolka was cast as an enigma with a Teflon veneer and shallow emotional quality; journalists described her attire and courtroom performance on a daily basis, dissecting every movement, tear or lack thereof as evidence of her desire to dupe the Court and the public into believing her victim narrative.

As Sundby (1997) found, what struck Canadian journalists and the courts most was what they perceived to be Homolka's lack of emotion while discussing the horrific details of the crimes. The subject who fails to convincingly display that they have suffered as a result of their criminal actions and who is able "to maintain a calm demeanour, [and] [] avoid flooding out" is more likely to draw the ire of the court, the media, and the public. Weisman cites R. v. D.B.B. (2004, 148), where the accused was described as failing to show "a scintilla of remorse" (2009, 58), which is ironically the exact phrase Tim Danson, lawyer for the French and Mahaffy families, uses to describe Homolka's emotional display in the above quote. While tearing up at the mention of her sister, she is said to resort back to a cold and icy demeanour that is the "tell" that denotes her psychopathy. Just as Appleby suggests she lacks the emotional depth to understand the gravity of her offences or "why she was on trial" given that she understood herself primarily as a victim, submitting that she is psychopathic is a sure way to solidify the characterization of her true self as a remorseless subject.

There were a number of times over the years where Homolka made a comment to the effect that due to the gravity of the crimes she committed no expression of remorse could ever be proportionate and would thus appear to be false or condescending. During her courtroom testimony in 1995, Homolka stated "I find it very difficult to put my feelings into words, because putting them into words trivializes the whole thing" (R. v. P. Bernardo 1995, 471). In fact, it is not uncommon for offenders to be advised by their legal counsel to avoid any elaborate emotional displays, which can be seen as a sign of guilt that would negatively affect the individual's defence or as the skilled fakery of a remorseless subject (Bibas and Bierschbach 2004). However, given that courtroom performatives "operate on the assumption that what is not shown is also not felt" any silences or reserved composure are likely to be read as remorselessness (Weisman 2007, 195). There is no doubt that Homolka's involvement in the crimes in addition to her questionable victim discourse harmed her status as a credible and remorseful witness.

Also discrediting was that during her cross-examination defence counsel John Rosen repeatedly cited the inequity between the harm she caused, her short sentence, and her lack of emotional distress, which allowed him to perform the role of an exasperated and indignant moral authority – all the while defending the man who murdered Leslie Mahaffy and Kristen French. Countless exchanges between the two showcased Rosen's use of sarcasm to mock Homolka's claims of victimization as exaggerated excuse making. What was particularly damning to her remorse performative were journalist reports of her ability "to hold her own" with an experienced lawyer while on the witness stand that marked her as distinctly different from the passive and remorseful victim who participated out of fear for her life that she claimed to be. *Toronto Star* columnist Rosie DiManno wrote about this disjuncture several times:

> Over the course of the day, she became more emboldened with Rosen, more combative, more hostile to his suggestions. One might suggest that, in fact, Homolka held her own quite nicely with this wily attorney. Homolka is one tough cookie. She is nobody's fool, not even in confrontation with a razor-edged defence attorney. Her innate intelligence – and Rosen revealed yesterday that psychological testing had placed Homolka in the top 2 percentile of the population – cuts through the construct of her oftentimes clumsy narrative. She did not submit meekly to Rosen. She did not crack. She just wasn't a pushover. Not at all like the girl she claims to have been as Mrs Paul Bernardo.
>
> Homolka had made her court debut in a prim white blouse, hair limp, face unpainted, stepping almost daintily into the witness stand as the textbook battered spouse of a sexual sadist, psychologically injured, and emotionally vulnerable. So slight and wraith-like, so . . . un-threatening. But by the end of her testimony, Homolka's assertive personality had emerged. Just as her attire had become less demure, her make-up more pronounced, her hair coquettishly curled, so did her natural intelligence rise to the surface, self-assuredness replacing hesitancy, the instinctive shoving aside the rehearsed, and her controlling tendencies usurping the thrust-and-lunge of hostile questioning. The girl can't help it. She is simply nobody's victim. And she knows how to do this.
>
> (5 July 1995, A8)

DiManno's narrative situates Homolka as a highly intelligent and cunning manipulator whose courtroom performance cracked her victim façade to show the "real" Karla, whose "true" self was emotionally invulnerable, strong-willed, independent-minded – the antithesis of a submissive and beaten woman. By emphasizing Homolka's ability to stand up to a skilled and aggressive defence attorney, DiManno showcases not only Homolka's cleverness, but also her ability to be defiant toward hostile men. This colouring contributes to monsterizing

Homolka as a deviant and dangerous Other – "an essentialist portrait" of her identity as "something apart from the human" (Weisman 2007, 205), namely, the clever psychopath popularized by primetime legal dramas.[4]

DiManno details Homolka's beauty and appearance, using the obvious contrast between her dangerousness and the hegemonic femininity she used to mask that dangerousness to encourage the reader to see Homolka as a willing participant and thus as remorseless. Women, being the family's primary caregiver, are innately expected to be more emotional, compassionate and nurturing than are men, a cultural paradigm that genders the construct of psychopathy. As a result, juridical interpretations of remorse are thus invariably complicated by the gendered characterological expectations of hegemonic masculinity and femininity. As we discussed in greater detail in previous chapters, newsprint media coverage was rampant with descriptions of Homolka's beauty; here, DiManno's references to her appearance are used to signal her inherent and dangerous narcissism – a common personality symptom for individuals clinically diagnosed with psychopathy (Hare 1996).

Allegations of Homolka's narcissism peaked with the revelations that after watching Bernardo strangle Kristen French to death, she left the room to blow dry her hair (Makin 2 Sept 1995, D1) and calling her parents selfish for requesting that she opt for a less extravagant wedding following the death of her sister Tammy (Duncanson and Rankin 8 July 1995, A1). Such shocking disclosures contributed to further discredit Homolka's assertions of sympathizing with her victims as they seemed to show that she was not haunted by her actions and was able to carry on with her daily life, even obsessively planning her wedding to Bernardo. This disjuncture with her claims of remorse led journalists to reframe her self-professed gestures of compassion with her victims, such as offering Leslie Mahaffy her favourite stuffed bear for comfort, as wholly contrived and shallow attempts to show herself as remorseful. As with her acts of sexual violence, Homolka situated her ethic of care as being tempered by the violence to which she was subject. The cognitive dissonance between her experiences of personal victimization and her ability to victimize innocent young women created an emotional schism that perverts the audience's interpretation of her attempts to show compassion and lent weight to the idea that she had psychopathic tendencies.

To bolster their uncredentialed allegations that Homolka is psychopathic, journalists reached out to Robert Hare, a leading scholar in psychopathy research, Canadian researcher and creator of the clinical forensic assessment tool known as the Psychopathy Checklist, for expert commentary:

> "What bothers me about him, and her, too, is the casual way these horrific things are described on the witness stand," said psychologist Robert Hare of the University of British Columbia, one of the world's leading experts on psychopaths. "When a psychopath commits a violent act, they're not doing it because they're malicious or malevolent or evil. They're doing it because they don't give a damn." Two psychologists called by the Crown suggested

> Homolka suffered from battered woman syndrome. Rendered helpless and hopeless by repeated beatings, someone in her shoes could feel obliged to take part in the most heinous crimes, they said. Hare is skeptical. "We look for very simple explanations for complex behaviour," he said. "To me, battered woman syndrome does not explain what she did." Even a psychiatrist retained by the prosecution – but not called as a witness at Bernardo's trial – said Homolka's role in the horrific crimes can't be fully explained by the abuse she suffered. "Karla Homolka remains something of a diagnostic mystery," Dr Angus McDonald wrote in his report, which the Bernardo jury never saw. "Despite her ability to present herself very well, there is a moral vacuity in her which is difficult, if not impossible, to explain."
>
> (Blackwell 2 Sept. 1995, A3)

The aforementioned references to Homolka's narcissism were used to evidence the notion that she was morally vacuous, a common signifier used to denote psychopathy and remorselessness. In this passage, Homolka is portrayed as an enigma whose actions and narrative explanations exist in an inexplicable paradox. She is constituted as a clinical conundrum, a woman who eludes diagnostic classification, a likely psychopath who is able to present herself well enough to "pass," in the Goffmanian sense, as "normal." While she never received a clinical diagnosis of psychopathy and Dr Hare never met let alone observed or clinically analysed her, to say that a person is morally vacuous is to describe them as emotionally hollow, as being without the emotional depth required to materially experience those moral emotions like shame and remorse that help us to keep our behaviour in check according to socio-cultural norms and boundaries. Depicting Homolka as without an internal moral compass discursively facilitates her narration as at the very least theoretically psychopathic and certainly as unremorseful.

In the final section of this chapter, we examine the self-transformation project that is an essential part of the production of a remorseful moral performance. We consider how the "therapeutic pessimism" (Weisman 2007) associated with psychopathy complicated juridical, media, and public acceptance of Homolka as a transformed and remorseful moral subject as told through the state's attempt to apply post-carceral sanctions on a warrant expiry offender. We also analyse Homolka's s own narrative of self-transformation as presented in her interview with Joyce Napier of Radio-Canada on the day of her release from Joliette prison.

Therapeutic Pessimism and the Transformed Moral Subject

Clinically, psychopaths are essentialized as morally vacant and are thus said to be extraordinarily resistant to rehabilitative interventions, engendering what Weisman (2007) describes as "therapeutic pessimism." If said persons are thought to be clinically impervious to correctional and psychiatric treatments and intervention strategies they will be at pains to demonstrate that they have engaged in a sincere and authentic self-transformation process or that they are truly remorseful moral subjects. The therapeutic pessimism of psychopathy is that it positions the individual as a static subject who remains emotionally untouched by time and experience. Not surprisingly, individuals convicted of violent offences who are thought to display psychopathic tendencies may be more likely to be incapacitated for longer than average periods of time (Hare 1996). Under Canadian criminal law the vast majority of criminalized persons serve two-thirds of their sentence in prison before being released to the community with mandatory parole conditions they must abide by for the duration of the length of their sentence. Should an offender serve their sentence in prison to warrant expiry, they are released without parole conditions. For exceptional cases, a successful application made under s.810 of the *Criminal Code of Canada* (CCC) is the only way to ensure that the individual is subject to parole conditions and community supervision; legally speaking this is quite rare and is typically reserved for repeat violent and paedophilic offenders.

Karla Homolka was never granted parole release or temporary escorted day passes, serving the duration of her 12-year sentence in federal prison. In June 2005 a 2-day hearing was held before Quebec Judge Jean R. Beaulieu who ruled that upon her release on 4 July 2005, Homolka would still pose a risk to the public-at-large, despite her completion of the treatment and programming assigned to her in her correctional rehabilitation plan. As a result, using section 810.2 of the *Criminal Code*, certain restrictions were placed upon Homolka as a condition of her impending release:

- She was to tell police her home address, work address, and with whom she lives.
- She was required to notify police as soon as any of the above changed.
- She was likewise required to notify police of any change to her name.
- If she planned to be away from her home for more than 48 hours, she had to give 72 hours' notice.
- She could not contact Paul Bernardo, the families of Leslie Mahaffy and Kristen French, Jane Doe or anyone convicted of a violent criminal offence.
- She was forbidden to be with people under the age of 16.
- She was forbidden from consuming drugs other than prescription medicine.
- She was required to continue therapy and counselling.
- She was required to provide police with a DNA sample.

While some of these conditions might seem obvious and innocuous, it is important to recognize that this application was an additional measure of surveillance applied to an individual that had already served her sentence. Homolka appealed the decision and the Supreme Court of Quebec overturned it in November 2005, meaning she has been at liberty without incident and without any form of community supervision since that time.

The stark nature of juridical interpretations of remorse would fashion Homolka's appeal as a legal manoeuvre that signifies remorselessness, as law's truly remorseful subject would not question a penal sanction because they understand themselves as deserving whatever punishments are meted out by the legal authorities (Weisman 2007). To be accepted as sincerely remorseful, the individual must abandon mobilizing legal energy for a kind of legal passiveness that ensures that they unquestioningly accept the state's production of the Truth of the events, their motivations and their character (Martel 2010). By appealing Judge Beaulieu's decision, Homolka instead constituted herself as a victim – this time of an unfair criminal justice system that was taking extraordinary measures to subject her to an exceptional form of correctional surveillance. This move, as in her combative testimony while testifying at Bernardo's trial, demonstrated her strength, resolve, and ability to challenge repressive actions taken against her, which her detractors argue is discursively at odds with her self-narrative as a submissive woman and victim. This position fails to acknowledge that the transformed subject would have to demonstrate the requisite emotional strength and moral character not only to abide by society's rules but also to identify injustice. Once again, the sensational nature of her crimes precludes Homolka from possible victim status.

Upon release, Homolka unequivocally declared that she had reformed while incarcerated; for this proclamation to be juridically successful, she would have to demonstrate a degree of psychological growth and maturity that would facilitate the transformation of her identity as a submissive and beaten victim to that of a remorseful moral subject. Homolka spoke about her process of self-transformation during her interview with Radio-Canada's Joyce Napier; the exchange began with a discussion of whether or not she believed she has paid her debt to society:

Napier: You have been out for a couple of hours. Karla Homolka is free now. Do you feel that you have paid your debt to society?

Homolka: That's a tough question. Legally, yes. Emotionally and socially, no.

Napier: What do you do to pay your debt emotionally and socially to a society that is clearly still judging you?

Homolka: I think socially I need to do as much as possible to help people. Emotionally, I live constantly with what I did, and that will never end.

At the start of this exchange, Homolka expresses an important aspect of any successful remorse performative in that she demonstrates her understanding and acceptance of the fact that she deserved the punishment she received. More than that, however, she recognizes that her debt to society is ongoing because of the severity of her crimes. By identifying her emotional suffering as constant and permanent, Homolka asserts that in order to continue her lifelong project of self-transformation into a moral subject, she will have to continue to give back to society both "emotionally and socially" as reparation for her transgressions. Differentiating her legal debt from her emotional and social debt also demonstrates her awareness that the carceral sentence was but one aspect of the debt she owed and that to be truly remorseful she must indefinitely continue to evidence her transformation and identity as a person committed to upholding the moral values of the community. This aspect of the interview bodes well for Homolka's desire to show herself as a reformed and transformed moral subject; in the following quote, Homolka describes the measures she took to facilitate this process:

Homolka: In prison I was part of a peer-support group. It is a group of women who help other inmates. I did many things like that in prison, and I want to continue outside.
Napier: If you are here today it is to tell people that you are no longer a threat to society, because that is a fear? Who are you, the exemplary prisoner or a criminal?
Homolka: I was an exemplary prisoner. I have no doubt about that. I did all my programs, even some that were not part of my correctional plan. I did volunteer work. I helped other women. I never got an internal [disciplinary] report. I did a lot of things. I went to school. I got my degree. I improved my French.

Here, Homolka strives to point out the different things she did to recreate herself as a moral subject who will follow the normative codes of conduct set out by the courts and the broader moral community. Homolka describes herself as a model prisoner; she participated in correctional programming, attended university and earned a Bachelor of Arts degree, volunteered as a peer support counsellor and learned French so as to become bilingual. By obeying prison rules and practices, she occupies the rare position of having never earned a disciplinary infraction during her period of incarceration. Homolka's narrative emphasizes her transformation from a woman capable of committing sexual violence into a woman others in distress lean on for emotional support. Being a peer-counsellor requires that your peers trust you and your counsel; it also evinces that correctional authorities believed she was not a danger and could in fact be a source of support to other prisoners. Homolka initiated this segment of the interview by stating that she would like to transfer the peer-support skills she learned in prison to her future work in the community as part of her continued efforts to display and prove that she is remorseful. This point stands in stark contrast to characterizations of her as a manipulative and unrepentant woman. Picking up on this, Napier questions Homolka about whether or not she remains a danger:

Napier: Are you still a danger today?
Homolka: Not at all. Not at all.
Napier: You are not likely to follow again?
Homolka: No.
Napier: Why won't you follow now like you did in the past?

Homolka: I am an adult. In the past I was 17. There were a lot of things I didn't know. I was afraid of being abandoned. I absolutely wanted a relationship. I had no confidence in myself. I know a lot of things about myself I didn't know then.

Both age and the passage of time are important components in an individual's ability to successfully convey their remorse as genuine (Kilty 2010) and to separate their "true" identity from the self that willingly broke the moral boundaries of the community (Kilty 2011), which this particular excerpt highlights well. In an effort to situate her transformative shift from a dangerous woman to a remorseful and harmless woman, Homolka reminds the audience that she is no longer an adolescent trapped in a violent relationship without the emotional skills, maturity, or strength to either leave or seek help. In her response to Napier's question about her likelihood of following and assisting another violent man, Homolka reports that she has matured emotionally, that she understands herself better and that this knowledge will enable her to make better decisions in the future. In effect, Homolka identifies the passage of time while incarcerated as aiding her to become more self-actualized and to replace her simultaneously at risk and risky criminal identity with a "self that is committed to the moral community" (Weisman 2009, 60). Distancing herself from the notoriety of her criminal acts was an important part in the process of re-imagining her identity. At the same time, Homolka explained that despite her moral transformation, and as any truly remorseful person would and should be, she remains haunted by her transgressions:

Napier: So you are today, Karla Homolka, really a free woman?
Homolka: No I don't think I will ever be free. There are different kinds of prisons. There are prisons made of concrete and there are interior prisons. I think I will always be in an interior prison.
Napier: Why?
Homolka: Because of what I did. I would like to go back and do things differently, but I can't.
Napier: So these are things you will never forget?
Homolka: Never. Never. I think about it every birthday, every Christmas, all the time.

In this exchange, Homolka attempts to showcase her remorse by situating the suffering she experiences as a result of her actions as omnipresent and eternally incomplete, which is the only morally acceptable response given the severity and horror of her crimes. Despite longing to change the past, she must show that she loathes herself for the egregious harms she committed and the pain she caused her victims, their families and the broader community and that she lives with those awful memories each day. Homolka performs as the remorseful and repentant wrongdoer, who is forever caught in the emotional prison of her own making. This particular comment received widespread attention in the Canadian news media, with disbelievers fashioning the interview as an attempt to manipulate the public into seeing her as remorseful. While many journalists suggested that her remorse was insincere and that she was instead a residual attention seeker for heading straight to the television news media upon her release from prison, scholars argue that "offenders determined to express remorse and to apologize may have to resort to the news media to circumvent criminal procedure's barrier of silence" (Bibas and Bierschbach 2004, 100). As her lawyer, Sylvie Bordelais stated:

> First of all it seemed important to sensitize the population that my client has two choices – either to live like a hunted animal until someone uncovers her, and we don't know what would happen next, or she can take the time to come and meet the people, give them her point of view, explain to them who she is and what she wants to do. She chose to take this second solution and come meet a medium we consider serious, and that is why we are here, so she can take the time to talk and introduce herself to the public. We have heard a lot of talk about her, from all sorts of people who said they knew her, and had different motivations to talk about her. Now she is here. She will be able to explain herself and what her objectives are.

Contextualizing the justification for speaking with the very media that Homolka has publically called out as sensational and hounding, Bordelais invites the audience to meet her client again for the first time. This interview was a way for Homolka to publically apologize for her actions and to try to quell public condemnation of her release by reaffirming that she is not only remorseful, but that she is also a changed person. Bordelais' turn of phrase "so she can take the time to talk and introduce herself to the public" suggests that any preconceived notions the public may have of her client are likely to be both false and sensational. To introduce yourself implies that the audience does not already know you; in this case, the public knows Homolka only as the woman who helped Bernardo abduct, rape, and kill young girls. If she wants the public to see her as a different person, as no longer a danger, whose primary identity is distinct and apart from the identity conjured as a result of her former transgressions she must convince us that she is remorseful. This interview is the only communication Homolka has had with the media since her release in 2005, thus disconfirming accusations that she seeks media attention. Homolka relocated to Guadeloupe with her new husband, has given birth to three children, and has largely remained invisible to the public's eye until CTV journalist Paula Todd tracked her down and appeared at her door looking to report on the state of her life abroad. As it has always been with this case, it is the public's fascination and even obsession with Homolka that keeps her in the headlines.

Conclusion

Fascination with Karla Homolka has only recently desisted, although it took moving to another country for "Homolka sightings" to abate, but her name still captures headlines, such as when it was invoked in the federal government's decision to change Canada's rules regarding pardon application requirements. In this chapter, we have tried to identify some of the most common narratives and counter-narratives that speak to Homolka's remorse. We agree with Weisman who argues that no matter how convincing the narrative of remorse, suffering, and self-transformation may be, there are simultaneous counter-narratives that positioned Homolka as "ruled less by conscience than by self-interest" (2009, 64; 2014). As Ruth Jamieson suggests: "the discursive operation of blaming produces evasions and attributions of guilt" and a kind of "moral authority of the victim" (2012, 115). Critics argue that Karla Homolka's claims to victimhood and remorse were demonstrative of an attempt to assign blame to her ex-husband in order to position herself as less blameworthy and to evade the same degree of condemnation and punishment. The difficult aspect of determining whether or not an individual is truly remorseful is that there are always multiple narratives that exist at the same time, which in addition to the "flexible criteria for identifying remorse" foster ambiguity in media, public and judicial assessments of it (Weisman 2009, 64). For Homolka, the "tension between being and doing" remorse (Weisman 2009, 58) was complicated by gendered expectations of emotion and behaviour especially in light of accusations that she suffered from psychopathic tendencies that rendered her morally vacuous.

Homolka's unwavering reliance on an explanatory narrative that situated her immoral criminal actions within the context of her personal victimhood signified to many that her claims of remorse were partial, disingenuous, and hypocritical. How can one claim to be a victim and that that victimization led to the ability to participate in victimizing others? Bonnycastle (2012) addresses this question in her research on men convicted of sexual offences, arguing that correctional rehabilitative programming for such offenders refuses to allow them to acknowledge their own sexual victimization, focusing exclusively on their responsibility for having sexually violated others. The treatment requires that the individual repeatedly write and rewrite their autobiography, each time ensuring that it reflects the state version of events, making no allowance for considering personal victimization as a potential mitigating or explanatory factor. There were media reports that Homolka initially refused to participate in sex offender programming because she refused to see herself as a sexual offender and was not convicted of a sexual offence. It is worth noting that given the length of her sentence and the fact that much correctional programming remains inaccessible to the prisoner until they are nearing their release, these reports might not be wholly accurate. However, Homolka's refusal to relinquish a victim discourse problematized her successful performance as a transformed moral subject, which was only aggravated by the gendered assumptions that female victims are passive and submissive, a characterization that her courtroom performatives countered.

Weisman (2009, 65) contends that our interpretations of remorse are more than reactive and are in fact constitutive in that they create a kind of "moral economy of suffering" that determines what each individual must do in order to be understood as truly remorseful. For cases involving extreme violence and sexual assault, the complex intersection of race, class, gender, sexuality, among other structural and embodied oppressions makes determinations of remorse much more complicated than listening for the apology and watching the individual's affective cues. That said, given the gravity of her offences and the vast sensationalism she generates, we must question whether it is at all possible for Homolka to be accepted as genuinely remorseful. Speaking of a moral economy of suffering is exceptionally difficult in this case, for what would a self-transformation look like for Homolka to be able to establish herself as a committed member of the broader moral community? Beyond admitting guilt, identifying her co-offender, assisting the police to secure damning evidence to be used against her, admitting her guilt in a crime the police were unaware of, offering an apology, following her correctional plan, earning a university degree, becoming a peer-support counsellor, learning a second language, and remaining completely out of the public eye since her release, what more must she do?

We submit that it is extraordinarily difficult, if not impossible, to ascertain the veracity of an individual's claims of materially feeling a moral emotion like remorse. There will always be disbelievers who claim that Homolka's remorse was superficial and that the tears she shed in court were crocodile tears. However, as time is the most telling feature in terms of evidencing sincere remorse, we may remember that Homolka has been walking among us for 10 years without incident. Even sceptical CTV journalist Paula Todd was shocked to see that she appears to be a well-adjusted and nurturing mother of three. Perhaps the question is not whether or not she is truly remorseful that is the hallmark of her self-transformation, but whether or not we as the audience of this crime drama in the real are able to accept her as a woman who made the most grievous mistakes one can make and who caused life-changing and life-ending harm, but who is also unlikely to harm anyone in future. As Weisman so eloquently writes:

> One of the ironies of this process is that, if it achieves its purpose, the jurors will come to divest themselves of the very same qualities of empathy, suffering over the harm wrought on another, and identification with the victim that they found so conspicuously absent in the remorseless offender. The degradation process not only transforms the offender but also those who will decide the offender's fate. Ultimately, the remorseless offender who has been reconstituted as no longer belonging in human society is someone towards whom the juror has had to learn to overcome his or her own feelings of remorse in order to vote for death.
>
> (Weisman 2007, 211)

While Weisman is speaking specifically about cases of capital punishment, which was abolished in Canada in 1976, his point when applied more broadly captures one of the major impetuses for our having written this book. Drawing on Garfinkel's classic concept of status degradation, Weisman contends that the public as audience is transformed from a moral community into a collective that overlooks the very moral standards used to condemn the actions of the transgressor in order to vote in favour of death. While most Canadians may have wished for Homolka to remain in prison as long as Bernardo, there were some that took moral vengeance to the extreme. Over the years, countless man-on-the-street interviews that alluded to the interviewee's desire for Homolka to die or to be killed were cited in the newsprint coverage. More dramatic is that at the height of media reporting during the mid- to late-1990s, a website entitled the "Karla Homolka Death Pool" was created so that members of the public could place bets on when she would be murdered, noting that "when the game is over, we all win." The website, which has since been taken down, denounced taking matters into your own hands, sarcastically writing that "that would be cheating." Homolka did receive death threats by mail while in prison and her family received similar threats at their home in St Catharines. There is no question that Homolka's actions and inactions were vile and loathsome, but we must rethink how our cultural response to her has not only been emotionally visceral, but also affected by the hetero-normative and gendered expectations of femininity. Of course, it is our hope that Homolka's remorse is sincere and that she has undergone the self-transformation required to develop the moral strength and resolve to never fall prey to such depraved behaviour again. Given the extreme nature of her crimes, it is very likely that Homolka will remain shunned from Canadian society for the rest of her days and we suggest that our collective social remembrance of the innocence of the victims lost does not mean we have to continue to drown in the anger and inexplicableness of it all.

Notes

1 For further reference, see section 810 of the Criminal Code here: http://laws-lois.justice.gc.ca/eng/acts/C-46/section-810.html

2 Restorative justice programs do exist in Canada, however they are sparse, underfunded and difficult to access. While beyond the scope of this chapter, it is important to note that there is much debated literature on the value of engaging restorative practices in cases of violence. For examples, see: Bazemore 1998; Daly 2006; Kilty 2010; and Zehr 2005.

3 There is a dearth of literature that examines psychopathy in women, although it is thought to be more rare than amongst men (Verona and Vitale 2006). It is of note that to our knowledge, Homolka never received an official clinical diagnosis of psychopathy; rather we are basing this discussion around the judicial and media constructions of her as such and the counter-narratives she herself has offered on the few occasions in which she spoke publically. As recently as November 2014, the CBC's investigative documentary program *Doc Zone* reported that Homolka scored a mere 5/40 when assessed using Hare's Psychopathy Checklist while Bernardo scored 35/40.

4 It is of note that the American television show *Law and Order* did model a "ripped from the headlines" episode after the details of this case, with the female character initially posed as a victim only later to be revealed as the psychopathic woman that got away with murder while her less intelligent male partner was incarcerated for life (Atherton 21 Feb. 2000, B10).

6 Conclusion

We have followed this case as it has unfolded for 25 years. First as concerned citizens who were captivated and horrified by the facts of the case as they were presented in the media and as they were revealed throughout the trials, then increasingly as interested feminist academics perplexed by the highly sensationalized juridical and media narratives that seemed to twist and remake its "stars" according to shifting legal necessity. This book examines how Karla Homolka was constructed in the corpus of textual data we assembled that was composed of the trial transcripts from Karla Homolka's 1993 plea and sentencing hearing, Paul Bernardo's 1995 criminal trial, the Galligan Report, Karla Homolka's 2005 prison release interview with Radio-Canada, and all of the newsprint media coverage referencing Karla Homolka in some capacity that was available on the Canadian Newsstand database. Guided by a series of key theoretical constructs we identified the central themes in the textual data and uncovered important temporal sequences across and connections between those themes, which allowed us to trace the evolution of the narratives constructed about our unique case subject. Briefly, we may highlight that the original juridical and media narratives about Karla Homolka situated her as the beautiful and youthful but victimized wife of a sexual sadist who unwillingly assisted her husband in committing these crimes because she was afraid for her life. This narrative eventually imploded as the video footage of the couple's joint sexual assaults against their victims surfaced and showed her to be a much more willing participant than she had led the authorities to believe. This fact does not negate Homolka's experiences of victimization, just as her experiences of victimization cannot erase her role in the crimes; the tragedy of this case and Homolka's culpability in creating that tragedy are certainly not in question.

We also utilized the theoretical concepts to generate alternative readings of the case with the aim of problematizing the ongoing cultural fixation with Karla Homolka, for she is, undoubtedly, the most notorious criminalized woman in Canadian history. While Homolka is certainly the most infamous, she is, as Elizabeth Comack (2014, 48) stated, quite different demographically from most women who come into conflict with the law:

> Although Homolka may be the most notorious, she is by no means the most representative of the women who come into conflict with the law. Indeed,

> Homolka is very much an anomaly or exception in terms of women most likely to be criminalized. Women are most often charged with property offences such as theft and fraud rather than with serious violent crimes such as murder and sexual assault. When women are charged with a violent offence, it is most likely to be for level one or common assault. In addition, what distinguishes Karla Homolka from most criminalized women is her class position. Homolka grew up in a suburban middle-class family home, while the majority of women who find themselves in conflict with the law come from marginalized economic situations. Race is another factor: Homolka's "whiteness" contrasts with the overrepresentation of Aboriginal women and women of colour in Canada's prisons.

Given her exceptional status, our goal was to provide a more sophisticated reading, not simply of Homolka, but also of the media fascination with her. We took Comack's (2014) argument to heart as we embarked upon a research project that tried to make sense of how the intersection of race (whiteness), class, gender, norms of femininity, and broken taboos coalesced to consecrate Homolka as a figure of evil who committed acts of enigmatic violence. Ultimately, this book attempts to identify some of the different features of this case that contributed to the cultural preoccupation with Karla Homolka more so than any other criminal subject in Canadian history.

We engage in two final discussions by way of concluding this book: (1) Karla Homolka's relevance as a case study amidst the broader feminist project of critically analysing women who commit acts of violence; and (2) The value of conceptualizing Karla Homolka as an enigmatic subject who perpetrated acts of enigmatic violence and what this theoretical construct might contribute to the small but growing literature on "the concept of enigmatic experience for the analysis of violent experiences" (Ronsbo 2006, 147).

Situating Homolka as a Case Study in the Broader Analysis of Women and Violence

While there are limitations inherent to any study, conducting intensive and interpretive case research is most commonly critiqued for its lack for generalizability. Rather than accepting a positivist evaluation as our "received view" (Lincoln and Guba 2003), we are reminded of the importance and value of the "thick rich description" Geertz (1973) called upon us to generate when conducting interpretive and hermeneutic work. We make no claims that the theoretical arguments (or "findings") we make in this research can easily be (or should be) extrapolated and generalized to other cases of women that have committed acts of violence either alone or with a partner. However, by using Karla Homolka as an object lesson for this theoretically guided interpretive qualitative case inquiry, it is our hope that this book will be able to shed light on some of the ways in which certain criminal cases come to occupy such prominent spaces in the mainstream media and broader cultural imaginary and how one-dimensional and often sensational character tropes come to dominate our interpretations of women who commit acts of violence. One concern we should note with respect to using Homolka as a comparative case is her rareness as a woman convicted of manslaughter, perpetrator of sexual assault, and in having served her sentence until warrant expiry, factors that make it easy to mark her as an outlier case amongst criminalized women more generally. While it is a limitation of this book, due to the sheer volume of data we accumulated for but one case it was beyond the scope of this project to conduct substantive and in-depth comparative case analyses between Karla Homolka and other distinctive cases of women that have committed similar acts of sexual violence to assist a male lover or spouse, although this would certainly be a worthwhile endeavour for a future research project. Notable cases include Myra Hindley in the UK, Michelle Martin in Belgium and Catherine Birnie and Valmae Beck in Australia.

Despite the authorial capital that long-term coverage of this case afforded many journalists, many of whom went on to write true crime books about the case, it is impossible to empirically ascertain whether or not Karla Homolka engaged in these acts of sexual violence because she was afraid, because she was narcissistically desirous of a misguided and even delusional fairy-tale romance with her abuser, or because she was sexually aroused by the violence and was actually just as willing a participant as Paul Bernardo. Different authors have made all of these diverse claims. What is evident is that as Homolka's motives and narrative of abuse were increasingly questioned (by the police, the courts, legal scholars, feminists, mainstream media, and the public), her plea agreement came to be described as having been borne out of sheer necessity, with the police and the Crown, at the time, requiring her testimony and cooperation in order to secure a conviction against Bernardo. After the videotaped evidence was uncovered and Justice Galligan (1996) was called upon to investigate the veracity of the plea agreement, Karla Homolka, who had long become the titular character in this crime drama, became the "one who got away" in the minds of most Canadians.

While she was initially narrated as a victim and coerced participant, following the discovery of the videotaped evidence of the sexual assaults, juridical and media discourses shifted to construct Homolka more as a manipulative victimizer than an unwitting victim. Throughout this book we have argued that this dichotomous identity construction led to a collective cultural and socio-political malaise about Karla Homolka, which was commonly expressed in the form of hateful backlash toward her. Public and political backlash toward Karla Homolka's plea agreement and 12-year sentence was vitriolic and continues to resurface every time she is mentioned in the media. In a similar vein, politicians evoke her name to garner greater public and cross-partisan support when proposing stricter criminal justice initiatives, such as when, in 2010, the federal government hurried to pass new legislation in order to prevent Homolka from being able to apply for a pardon, which she was eligible to do the following month[1]. Furthermore, the backlash toward her plea agreement led her to be recast once again, but this time as the doubly dangerous brilliant and beautiful mastermind behind the crimes. This particular construction was undoubtedly helped along by the defence approach taken by Paul Bernardo's legal counsel, which situated Homolka not only as a willing participant but also as a criminal strategist that aided Bernardo in planning the crimes and evading the police, and even as the real killer. References to Homolka's intellect and even IQ started to emerge in the media coverage during the early years of her incarceration, with stories often describing her as more intelligent than Paul Bernardo, who was characterized as a failed accountant and "wannabe" rapper.

These characterizations certainly award Homolka greater agency in terms of her role and participation in the crimes than she has ever suggested she possessed or expressed herself. This explanatory rupture led many journalists to question how such an intelligent woman could be the pawn in someone else's crimes, especially when she was thought to be more intelligent than him. It also led news reporters to question whether she lied about the extent of the abuse she suffered in order to garner sympathy and to manipulate criminal justice authorities. If she did lie about the extent of her victimization and she was a willing participant, how can we believe anything she says? If she can "fool" the police and the courts, what else is she capable of? Homolka is difficult to comprehend, precisely because she does not fit neatly into a victim versus perpetrator typological dichotomy. How does one woman embody two dialectically opposed extremes? Is it possible to accept her narrative of victimhood while also realizing her potential dangerousness?

However, these types of questions also disturbingly demarcate our collective inability to come to grips with women's violence while tacitly accepting men's violence as normative and thus less shocking and even less threatening to our cultural and criminological imaginary as well as the misogynist cultural fear that intelligent women can deceive men in positions of power. Such questions also problematically insinuate that intelligent women with a network of supportive family members and friends do not become victims of intimate partner violence. Allusions that Homolka's victimization was, at best, less severe and/or less frequent than she suggested, or, at worst, that she was deserving of some form of abuse given her participation in these heinous crimes, does a disservice to all victims of intimate partner violence by obscuring the complicated and multivaried legacies of interpersonal emotional, sexual, and physical trauma.

Questions of agency were central to Belinda Morrissey's (2003) efforts to problematize what she sees as a growing reliance on victim discourses to explain women's violence at the expense of retaining a sense of agency for women who act violently. While Morrissey did not deny that Homolka experienced abuse, she questioned the duration and extent to which Bernardo beat her and minimized the effects of the violence Homolka endured with little evidence to support her skepticism. Morrissey's thesis effectively cast doubt on Homolka's claims of diminished agency and responsibility; however, her analysis of agency is at times too extreme in that it posts agency and victimism as polar opposites, essentially creating a dichotomy between those individuals who act with full agency and control and those whose actions are without agency. While

Homolka participated in harming innocent victims rather than her violent abuser, to deny that her experiences of victimization influenced her actions is the same flawed logic that questions why women who kill their abusers failed to leave them, just as erasing her agency in light of her victimization positions her as a hapless automaton. Instead, we have argued that agency exists along a continuum and may have multiple sites of both constraint and enablement that are context dependent for each individual. In this sense, we situated Homolka's actions as constrained by her violent and volatile relationship with Paul Bernardo and thus not as freely chosen or completely voluntary.

Following Sandra Harding (1993, 2004), we adopted a standpoint feminist position to frame this research and guide our analyses. Standpoint feminism privileges women's voices and the perspectives of marginalized individuals more generally. Given that standpoint feminism posits that knowledge is situated and subjective, this framework allowed us to lend weight to Homolka's voice amidst the dominant institutional narratives constructed about her. Critics may contend that using Homolka's own words as part of our data set trivializes the suffering of her victims; her victim narrative and attempt to relate her victimization to that of her sister, Leslie Mahaffy, and Kristen French certainly elicited disgust given that she, unlike her young victims, was able to escape Paul Bernardo with her life. While we recognize that her experiences of victimization influenced her participation in these crimes, it is important to remember that there are degrees of victimization that are not comparable. Juxtaposing Homolka's courtroom testimony and post-release interview as "captions" to the images of her smiling for the camera while she participates in sexually assaulting her victims readily demonstrates their diametrically opposed nature. Reflecting Homolka's dual status as both a woman *in danger* and a *dangerous* woman, the inconsistency between her self-narrative and the videotaped evidence significantly contributed to the public backlash, collectively felt disgust and general cultural malaise expressed toward her.

Morrissey (2003) specifically described Homolka as a "limit case" for feminist scholars who, with a few notable exceptions, avoid writing about her because of the nature of her crimes and because the harm she participated in causing was perpetrated against innocent young female victims, including her own sister, rather than her abuser. Comack (2014: 36) similarly describes Homolka's involvement in these crimes as a "decisive event" that contributed to shifting interpretations of women's violence toward explanations that proclaimed that not only are women violent, but that "women's violence is quantitatively and qualitatively equal to that of men's" (37). This pivotal shift in how women's acts of violence are interpreted is problematically echoed in how few women are able to successfully raise the battered woman syndrome as expert evidence to support their claims of self-defence (Frigon 2003; Sheehy 2014; Sheehy et al. 2012a,b).

The public's collective disgust at Homolka's taboo violations also contributed to her constitution as an enigmatic subject; her enigma lay in our inability to reconcile her material experiences of battery, constrained choice, self-preservation, and violence. To better situate this discussion, we highlight some of the theoretical contours of the terms enigma and enigmatic violence, their pertinence to the

Karla Homolka case and their potential to contribute to theoretical discussions and debates about women's violence.

Enigmatic Violence, Enigmatic Subject

As Helen Boritch (1997, 2) rightly pointed out, ". . . there was little that was unusual or mysterious about Bernardo." Conversely, and as Elizabeth Comack (2014, 36) elucidated, "Homolka, however, was the central enigma of the drama that unfolded." The Oxford dictionary defines the noun "enigma" as *a person, thing or situation that is mysterious or difficult to understand.* As an adjective the term "enigmatic" is similarly defined as *difficult to interpret or understand; mysterious.* The term "enigmatic violence" has primarily been used to analyse acts of political violence and to date is most often taken up (although the literature is sparse and in its infancy) by scholars working in the fields of anthropology and conflict studies. For example, both Pappe (2014) and Naaman (2007) use the examples of the Israeli news coverage and cinema content that represents Palestinian terrorism – especially that committed by women suicide bombers – as inexplicable and lacking a "proper" motive to explain how certain acts of violence come to be described as enigmatic. Anthropologist Henrik Ronsbo was the first to conceptualize how violence is "experienced as enigmatic" through an ethnographic case study of "the post-conflict subjectivities in the Peruvian Sierra" (2006, 148). In this work, Ronsbo demonstrates how situating violence as an enigmatic experience can help to showcase and hopefully disrupt the gendered hegemonic power relations that silence women's experiences of violence at the same time that it sustains narratives that emphasize men's agency. In our efforts to examine how violence was experienced as enigmatic in this particular case, we found that as journalists, reporters, criminal justice authorities, politicians, and the public questioned and even ridiculed Homolka's narrative of victimization, they *also* heavily emphasized her agency, which contributed to creating a discursive split between the two. In his description of how violence comes to be experienced as enigmatic, Ronsbo (2006) argues that:

> The concept of [the] enigmatic experience implies that a signifier is recognized by interlocutors, [e.g., victims, witnesses], but they are unable to create a relation to a signified. This is so because the perpetrator of violence has no access to meaning beyond the simple instrumentality of the act of violence, and for this reason the victim has no access to meaning beyond the feelings of pain and suffering. Thus, the experience of violence erupts in the grey zone, in the zone of the enigmatic, and while I recognize that violence is instrumental from the perpetrators point of view, such instrumentalism is never exhaustive of meaning in terms of particular relationships of signification.
> (149)

By situating the eruption of violence within a grey zone, Ronsbo is not only able to problematize the one-dimensional characterization of perpetrators of violence that rely on aged tropes, such as those that resurrect and reinforce dominant stereotypes about women's "natural" social roles and femininity, but also the simplistic portrayal of victimhood that is typically absent in discussions of agency, race, ethnicity, indigeneity, sexuality, gender, poverty, and social exclusion and that are most commonly found in mainstream media coverage of incidences of violent crime. By conceptualizing experiences of violence as instrumental primarily (and perhaps only) to the perpetrators of those acts, but also as "never exhaustive of meaning in terms of particular relationships of signification," Ronsbo's work enables us to see that there are multi-varied and complex meanings and interpretations of violence that are dependent on how the interpreter signifies the particular acts. Therefore, to try to render seemingly inexplicable acts of needless violence, such as those committed by Bernardo and Homolka, intelligible with superficial explanatory discourses that monsterize Homolka and the way she was said to engage her femininity (like a "Venus-fly trap") reflects but one relationship of signification. This particular relationship of signification, however, reinforces hierarchical gendered power relations that contribute to the narration of women's acts of violence as inherently more shocking, disturbing, problematic, and dangerous than when the same acts of violence are perpetrated by men. This relationship of signification is observable in both the volume of media coverage that focused almost exclusively on Homolka and in the discursive content of the media and courtroom proceedings we analysed.

While one of the central reasons for the mainstream media's sustained coverage of Homolka was linked to the fact that she received a plea agreement and lesser sentence than Paul Bernardo, which subsequently galled the Canadian public and fermented the longstanding social and political backlash discussed above, we may only hypothesize about whether or not media coverage would have differed substantively had the videotapes been recovered sooner so that the Crown was able to try and convict her alongside Bernardo. Would journalists have employed different relationships of signification to explain these senseless acts of enigmatic violence? This is of course impossible to know, but we suspect that narratives that denied her victimhood and monsterized her character are likely to have been present regardless, given the longstanding cultural imperative to uphold normative gender role ideals that dichotomize female passivity and male aggression. It is helpful to return to Ronsbo (2006, 150), who proposes that:

> Even as the notion of enigma entails the absence of signification, it still recognizes the experience as a signifier, that beyond the enigmatic experience there may lie a space of language, yet as Veena Das reminds us, their [sic] also lies a space of silence and it is exactly because the enigmatic experience points both to the exterior and interior of language that it can be reduced to neither of the two. . . . Enigmas become displaced either to silence or language, they either become signified, entextualized and recognized as meaningful within a larger discursive community and are thereby experienced and circulated in various materials such as narratives and

performances or they become embodied as ineffable and silenced forms of poisonous knowledge.

The patriarchal division of gendered power relations in contemporary western cultures contributes to how Karla Homolka, and the violent woman more generally, as an enigma in the criminological imagination, became "signified, entextualized and recognized as meaningful" in juridical and mainstream newsprint media discourses. Her enigmatic status was not displaced to silence, but rather to language "within a larger discursive community" that was "experienced and circulated in various materials" including, television and film, news reporting, fiction and non-fiction books, academic texts, a comic book, online blogs and websites, as well as more formal juridical and criminal justice narratives. Homolka was signified as the most notorious female criminal in Canadian history – entextualized by the juridical and media narratives that at once recognized her uniqueness as a criminalized woman (that is, via her whiteness, middle-class status and participation in sexually violent crimes) yet simultaneously signified her as indicative of the emerging new breed of violent woman to be feared (Comack and Brickey 2007; Kilty and Frigon 2006; Pearson 1997). Our research demonstrates how Karla Homolka came to be identified legally, culturally, and politically as the violent woman *sui generis*. Problematically, her uniqueness, which should signal that her case is a special one that is confined to its own facts and thus may not engender broader application, continues to be politically referenced in order to pass more conservative criminal justice legislation.

What is important to consider here is that while Homolka was signified, entextualized and widely recognized as a dangerous Other, she was *also* embodied as ineffable largely because she resolutely maintained an expository victim narrative. By discursively constituting her subjectivity first and foremost as a victim of longstanding and severe intimate partner violence, Homolka attempted to signify and entextualize herself as more alike to her victims than to her abusive husband Paul Bernardo. In her own words via courtroom testimonies and her post-release interview, Homolka actively rooted her acts of violence within her experiences of victimization – situating them as a kind of perverse battery prevention technique. One of the most frequent criticisms we uncovered in the corpus of data was with respect to this aspect of Homolka's ineffability and was embedded in questions about the sincerity of both her victim narrative and her claims of remorse. If she were legitimately a battered woman, why would she help her abuser sexually assault innocent teenagers, including her own sister, instead of leaving him or harming him in order to escape? Given the reduced sentence Homolka received for testifying against Bernardo, if she were genuinely remorseful would she have appealed the court's decision to use s.810.2 of the *Criminal Code* to place specific restrictions on her as a condition of her release? If she were "truly" remorseful, would she have given a television interview post-release? Employing the concept of enigmatic violence allowed us to contextualize Homolka's subjectivity as both *dangerous* and *in danger*, rather than either or, and thus to better understand both the "enabling and paralyzing" effects (Ronsbo 2006, 149) her experiences of violence and victimization had on her as well as on the juridical and media attempts to make sense of her actions.

Homolka's victim narrative was overwhelming and even unspeakable to many who claimed that she did not behave as a "real" victim would, a position that problematically creates a narrowed categorization of what "true" victimhood looks like. Subsequently, Homolka's use of a victim narrative to explain her actions came to be signified and entextualized in juridical and media discourses as a form of "poisonous knowledge" (Ronsbo 2006) – as though her breath that carried those words time and again was infectious and by proximal association likewise had the potential to poison, or, at the very least, taint the victim narratives presented by other criminalized women. The discursive effect of this proximal knowledge poisoning came in the form of backlash to what critics have called "the abuse excuse," which suggests that violent women are treated leniently in the criminal justice system (Pearson 1997). One major consequence of this backlash is that the media generated a moral panic about women's violence and "the nasty girl" (Barron and Lacombe 2005; Comack 2014), which in effect "poisoned" and worked to silence the important and longstanding feminist position that many criminalized women do experience victimization and that that victimization is intersectionally manifested and linked to their experiences of criminalization.

Women's violence is often signified as enigmatic whether it takes place in the social and/or familial realm or in the most explicit expressions of state or political violence (for example female soldiers, suicide bombers). The similarity across these diverse experiences of violence is that the origin and meaning of the violence is frequently located in the woman's monstrous body in an effort to maintain the signification of normative femininities. As Naaman (2007, 933) found, the representations of Palestinian female suicide bombers as monsters or mythic martyrs in Israeli and Western media reflect "the ideological crises that women's bodies cause when they enact violence." Women who intentionally and visibly undertake acts of violence are bound up in a social phenomenon that highlights the instability of meanings around the "perceived roles of women in armed struggles, religion and traditional gendered settings" (Naaman, 2007, 933). Naaman (2007) found that when women commit terrorist acts, their crimes, unlike those committed by men, are rarely explained as demonstrations of political violence with a specific and identifiable motive, but rather as a woman's illogical response to a personal circumstance such as a broken romantic relationship, mental instability and infertility. Whether it is an explicit signifier of political violence, as in the case of female Palestinian suicide bombers, or the more "senseless" violence committed by Bernardo and Homolka, women's acts of violence are often signified, entextualized and represented as enigmatic because they transgress the boundaries of conventional gender norms.

Final Thoughts

Karla Homolka embodies many normative cultural standards; she is white, upwardly mobile within the middle class, heteronormative and physically attractive according to western aesthetic ideals. As such, she represents some of the most dominant segments of Canadian society. Her victims were similarly socially situated and as such their "worthiness" was reinforced in the media by the unnamed and silent contrast to "unworthy" victims that are predominantly women of colour (Gilchrist 2010; Jiwani 2006; Razack 2000). Homolka's similarity to her victims and to dominant segments of the Canadian public was frequently referenced in the newsprint media coverage, highlighting that she was, or at least appeared to be, "just like us," and making it all the more shocking and inexplicable that she transgressed those standards by sexually harming her "sisters" – both literally and figuratively. Homolka's seeming normality enabled the initial acceptance of her victim narrative; but when the videotapes of the sexual assaults were finally uncovered and she was recast as enjoying her participation in the crimes, and thus failing to act like a "true" victim, the media capitalized on the discursive schism between her identity as both *in danger* and *dangerous* and her sensational remaking as Canada's most dangerous woman intensified. In this way, Homolka's signification as an enigma was a "decisive event" (Comack 2014) that denotes a shift in how women's violence was discursively constituted in the media. The decade of the 1990s was especially characterized by the media-driven socio-political fear that women were becoming just as violent as men, which critical and feminist scholars have aptly described as a moral panic (Barron and Lacombe 2005). As such, there was an abundance of sensational coverage of stories involving violent women and/or girls that captivated public attention and the media's thirst for a provocative "newsworthy" story (Jewkes 2004).

While the narratives about Karla Homolka mutated over time, intensifying the mystery shrouding the different interpretations of her character and agency, Paul Bernardo was never an enigma; his violence being more typical in that he sought to dominate and humiliate his female victims both sexually and in death – a common feature of narratives about men who commit acts of sexual violence and homicide against women. Our detailed analyses of court transcripts and newsprint media coverage and our use of critical and feminist literatures and diverse theoretical constructs found both within (that is dangerousness, victimization, intersectionality, and remorse) and outside (that is taboo, disgust, the gaze, and enigmatic violence) of traditional criminology helps to demystify our cultural preoccupation with Karla Homolka. Following Ronsbo's (2006, 149) argument that violence erupts in a grey zone and is experienced as enigmatic because we are "unable to create a relation to the signified" (that is the woman who appeared to be an upstanding member of dominant society, yet whose taboo violations elicited a profound and collectively felt disgust at her transgressions of the boundaries of womanhood, femininity, and even feminism), we moved our analysis away from trying to explain Homolka towards examining how she became the object of our gaze and what about her role in this case led to such a sustained cultural fascination with her. While Karla Homolka is an elusive character and her participation in these acts of sexual violence remain unfathomable, even to some critical and feminist criminologists, without examining our cultural reaction and connection to the signified, we problematically contribute to her mythicized construction as an enigmatic subject.

Note

1 This legislation extended the time period, which must be crime-free, that a person convicted of a serious personal injury offence has to wait before they are allowed to apply for a pardon from 5 to 10 years. The National Parole Board is now also expected to deny a pardon if it could be considered to throw the reputation of the criminal justice system into disrepute. To make this determination the NPB must consider the nature, gravity and duration of the offence; the circumstances surrounding the commission of the offence; and information relating to the applicant's criminal history. These changes effectively make it impossible to grant Homolka a pardon, no matter how much crime-free time passes from the commission of the offences.

Appendix

Methodology

Case Study

This book reflects our efforts to conduct an in-depth case study analysis of Karla Homolka. While different researchers have examined her in individual articles or have made reference to her in book chapters (Denov 2004; Kilty and Frigon 2006; McGillivray 1998; Morrissey 2003) and journalists have written a series of true crime novels about the case more broadly (Burnside and Cairns 1995; Crosbie 1997; DeAngelo 2011; Pron 1995; Williams 1997, 2004; Todd 2012), to date, no one has conducted the level or depth of scholarly analysis presented herein. In short, this book proposes an alternative reading of the juridical, media and public narratives about Karla Homolka. We offer a research-generated re-telling or re-storying of Homolka's discursive and narrated characterizations, which called upon us to examine the diverse elements of her story, including her self-narratives and performatives and the juridical and media discourses and narratives generated about her character. This process allowed us to identify key themes and to uncover important sequences and connections within those themes so as to retell how she was narrated in potentially new ways. We want to reiterate that we do not question her culpability and complicity in these crimes nor their horrible and tragic nature.

Thomas contends "the case that is the *subject* of the inquiry will be an instance of a class of phenomena that provides an analytical frame – an *object* – within which the study is conducted and which the case illuminates and explicates" (Thomas 2011a, 513). While Karla Homolka is the primary subject and lens of this case study, the object is the analytic frame and theoretical focus (Thomas 2011a,b). Our theoretical focus was quite diverse and included references to conceptual development in the areas of intersectionality, dangerousness, victimization, disgust and taboo and remorse as they were tempered by theorization pertaining to gender and femininity. The analyses presented in this book reflect the results of an exploratory and descriptive outlier case study, which are examinations of deviant or atypical cases that might be extreme in nature, however they are often said to reveal more information than representative cases (Thomas 2011a,b; Yin 2009, 2011). Given Homolka's uniqueness as a woman convicted of manslaughter and as a perpetrator of sexual assault, she generated unprecedented media coverage and sensationalism that reconstituted her as an infamous celebrity of sorts. These facts in conjunction with the legal rareness of having served her sentence until warrant expiry makes it easy to mark this case as an outlier amongst those criminal cases involving women. Our goal was to generate an analysis that is full of thick, rich description and narrative detail in order to tell a particular story that encourages us to look at an old "problem" in new ways (Yin 2009, 2011). This analytic process required that we also "look [ ] at what is not said or [ ] at silences and gaps, dismantle [ ] dichotomies, and analyze [ ] disruptions" within and across the textual materials that made up the data sample (Feldman 1995, 51). Given that in-depth exploratory and descriptive case studies typically include different types of data that are collected over a lengthy period of time (Creswell 2009), which Thomas (2011a,b) refers to as a diachronic case study, we included textual materials (juridical and media) dating from 1993 (the year of Homolka's arrest, plea, and sentencing hearing) to the present day in our data sample.

Foucault's (1975) case study, *I Pierre Rivière, having slaughtered my mother, my sister and my brother*, and Farran's (1987) case study of Ruth Ellis, the last woman to be hanged in Britain, provide methodological support for the case approach adopted herein. To investigate the link between psychiatry and criminal justice, Foucault analysed exhibit evidence, expert evaluation and testimony, trial transcripts, newspaper accounts, as well as Rivière's personal memoir penned while in prison; Farran similarly examined newspaper accounts, police reports, and the transcripts from Ellis' trial and appeal. Taking Foucault's and Farran's work as a methodological point of entry, we aimed to excavate and chronicle the shifting narratives about Homolka as they relate to broader theoretical foci. As Farran (1987, 1) writes on the Ellis case:

> The three books that have been published have all concentrated on her "life, murder and trial", with great emphasis being paid to excavating her "life" and what kind of woman she was, as a sufficient as well as a necessary explanation for the murder and trial. In one sense this is completely to be expected, for this is usual practice carried out by a wide range of people involved in or with such cases (for example, the police, lawyers, journalists, etc.) in trying to account for such activities as murder. However, in another sense the form such biographies have taken is unexpected, for they are actually primarily concerned with her "sexual life"; and this seems dependent in their constructions of events on the "fact" that she was a woman of a particular "type".

This project similarly proceeded with an exhaustive examination of the trial transcripts and newspaper coverage in order to elucidate the ways in which Karla Homolka was constituted and narrated by different legal actors, media commentators and journalists and expert witnesses. Foucault (1975) found that conflicting psychiatric evaluations of Rivière created a "battle among [expert] discourses" related to the subject's treatability and punishment suitability, while Farran (1987) found Ellis was constituted as an unreasonable, totally blameworthy, ruthless, sexually deviant and immoral woman. At times these imaginings constituted both Ellis and Rivière in contradictory or dichotomous ways, similar to Homolka's characterizations over time.

Textual Data Sample

Our data sample consisted of both juridical and news media texts. To examine how particular aspects of this case and of Karla Homolka's persona were constituted and (re)presented over the years within juridical, mass media and contemporary cultural discourses, we examined a number of different data sources, including: the transcripts from Karla Homolka's 1993 plea and sentencing hearing (120 pages); Homolka's 2005 post-incarceration interview with Radio-Canada; Karla Homolka's testimony and cross examination at Paul Bernardo's 1995 trial (2242 pages); the *Report to the Attorney General on Certain Matters Relating to Karla Homolka* (herein referred to as the *Galligan Report*) (342 pages); and a massive review of the entire body of Canadian newspaper press coverage referencing "Karla Homolka" (which generated 9,229 results in a general search).

We secured the two sets of trial transcripts and a copy of the Galligan Report in order to examine Homolka's characterization in the juridical context, which is a unique aspect of this research. Notably, it was important to use materials that would showcase Homolka's own voice rather than only the voices of journalists that wrote about her. While her voice was certainly confined by the boundaries of the courtroom and the official legal processes to which she was both subject and object (Smart 1976, 1989), using the transcripts did engender a (bounded) sense of her self-narrative and construction of events. Without the ability to properly observe and interview her, using the court transcripts was the only way we were able to provide space in the text for an examination of Homolka's personal discourse, without having to conduct a secondary analysis of her narratives as presented in and through other commentator's interpretations. The Galligan Report was also an essential component of our data sample. As a formal government inquiry into the judiciousness and legality of her plea agreement it carefully considers a number of criticisms offered about Homolka's character and personhood (for example that she is a compulsive liar, that she manipulated the Ministry of the Attorney General, that she was not a "real" victim and that she was the mastermind behind the crimes) as described throughout the news media and trial transcript data.

In addition to the trial transcripts and the Galligan Report, our sample consisted of a vast amount of newspaper data. The Canadian Newsstand Major Dailies database contains newspaper archives from 21 English-language major national and regional Canadian newspapers, 18 of which are available in full text (ProQuest 2011). For the media analysis, all the full-text newspaper articles and items published between 1 January 1993 and 31 January 2014 that included the name "Karla Homolka" in either the citation or the document text were downloaded. This amounted to 9,229 documents for analysis, including: news articles, columns, editorials and letters to the editor and summary news items. Of note, the photographic images that originally accompanied the news stories (for example photographs of Bernardo, Homolka and their victims and courtroom sketches) were not available for formal analysis as these items are not included in the database. However, in our efforts to trace the developments in this case over the years we kept physical copies of select front-page news stories featuring some of the most commonly published photographs, which are also easily retrievable online, such as the hospital photograph of Homolka's bruised and battered face, the photograph of Homolka leaving her parents' home for court and the school photographs of the three victims. As such, while we consider some of these photos in our analysis the book does not concentrate its analytic focus on them.

While this sample size is much larger than what is used for most qualitative media analyses, the results should not be considered generalizable beyond the case in question due to its unique nature, the unprecedented volume of coverage and voracious public interest that this case generated over the years (Fleming 2007). The sheer volume of articles in the database speaks to the unusual nature of the case, the horrific details and to the enduring fascination with Karla Homolka; indeed, one of the only other names with more newspaper coverage hits in the realm of Canadian criminal justice is Paul Bernardo (12,456 hits). Other notable names from the case also generated many hits, including Kristen

Table A.1 News coverage of Karla Homolka

News Source and Location	*Full-Text Hits*	*Coverage Share*
Calgary Herald; Calgary	507	5%
Daily News; Halifax	557	6%
Edmonton Journal; Edmonton	475	5%
Financial Post; Toronto	60	>1%
The Gazette; Montreal	728	8%
The Globe and Mail; Toronto	1,136	12%
Guardian; Charlottetown	165	2%
Kingston Whig Standard; Kingston	508	5%
Leader-Post; Regina	96	1%
National Post; Don Mills	575	6%
The Ottawa Citizen; Ottawa	758	8%
The Province; Vancouver	211	2%
StarPhoenix; Saskatoon	175	2%
Sudbury Star; Sudbury	244	3%
Telegram; St John's	123	1%
Telegraph-Journal; Saint John	104	1%
Times Colonist; Victoria	342	4%
Toronto Star; Toronto	1,458	16%
The Vancouver Sun; Vancouver	468	5%
The Windsor Star; Windsor	463	5%
Winnipeg Free Press; Winnipeg	41	>1%
Total	**9,194**	**100%**

Source: Canadian Newsstand major dailies' database.

French (9,415), Leslie Mahaffy (7,282) and Tammy Homolka (1,853).[1] The following table shows the number of full-text articles on Karla Homolka in the Canadian Newsstand database by source.

All of the major Toronto newspapers assigned specific reporters to cover the trials in their entirety. Together, three of the major Toronto daily newspapers – *The Globe and Mail*, *National Post*[2] and *Toronto Star* – accounted for 34 percent of the news articles in the database. Of note, Toronto's other major daily paper, the *Toronto Sun*, is not included in the analyses as its archives are not available from the Canadian Newsstand Major Dailies database. The *Sun* did offer comprehensive coverage of the case and was often the first source to publish photographs of Homolka (for example, *The Sun* published Bernardo and Homolka's wedding pictures, images of Homolka in prison, exclusive interviews with Homolka's friends and former lovers and so on). This degree of media attention not only resulted in significant coverage in Toronto newspapers, but also in several books about the case written by Toronto-based journalists (Burnside and Cairns 1995; Crosbie 1997; Pron 1995; Williams 1997, 2004).

When broken down by year, coverage was heaviest in the years with major developments in the case. In particular, the database includes 1,987 stories written in 1995, representing 22 percent of all stories, and 1,850 stories (20 percent of the total) written in 2005; these years represent Bernardo's trial and Homolka's release, respectively. On 5 July 2005, the day after Homolka's release from prison, 58 news stories were printed about her in the major dailies. Seven of these news items appeared in *The Globe and Mail*, including contributions from five reporters (Timothy Appleby, Marion Dorosh, Tu Thanh Ha, Ingrid Peritz and Katie Rook) and one columnist (Christie Blatchford).

Newspapers were chosen as the primary site for the media analysis because there are competing publications that published daily and had the opportunity

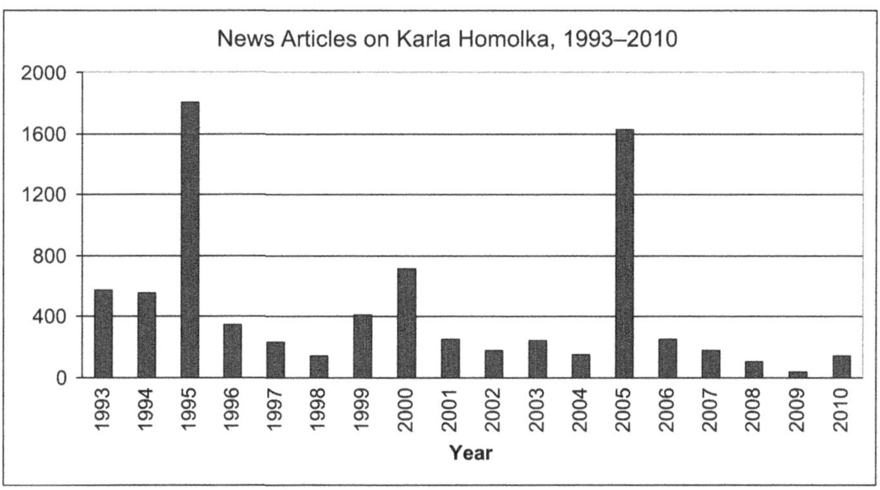

Figure A.1 Canadian Newsstand major dailies' articles referencing "Karla Homolka"

to provide different points of view. Newspapers are also widely distributed and well archived; databases, such as the one we used, Canadian Newsstand, include the full text of the stories dating back several years, which allowed us to search for and retrieve relevant articles easily. As newspapers devote a disproportionate amount of textual and visual space to crime and justice stories – especially those that are most sensational – they are frequently used for discourse and content analyses of major crime cases (Barnett 2006; Jewkes 2011a,b; Surette 1994, 2007; Wardle 2003, 2007; Wilczynski 1997). Another benefit of printed news stories is that they are generally longer and more detailed than television and radio news items, and thus provide more information for analysis. In the Homolka case, the large number of newspapers reporting on the trial, often including teams of journalists and columnists from major newspapers, allowed for different opinions to be included. For example, on 30 June 1995, during Paul Bernardo's trial, the *Toronto Star* alone published four stories on the case, including the accounts and viewpoints of three journalists (John Duncanson, Nick Pron and Jim Rankin) and one columnist (Rosie DiManno), plus accompanying illustrations provided by a courtroom artist hired by the paper (Paul McCusker).

Television and radio news broadcasts and magazine articles that also provided coverage of the case and trial were not included in the sample, as these are not archived in the same comprehensive and easily accessible manner. While more recent cases are now being examined through newer media forms (for example, Internet news articles, blogs and so on), these sources were not considered for this project because the investigation and trials all occurred before the Internet became a primary means of distributing information. For more recent stories, certain types of online media have the disadvantage of lacking peer review (for example, blogs, self-publishing), sometimes having ambiguous origins in both time and space, being too numerous to quantify or sort in a meaningful way, being easily revised (stories can be, and often are, modified from the original versions after their initial publication), all of which make it difficult to collect a sample that accurately reflects events and public perceptions at a given point in time (Li and Walejko 2008; Weare and Lin 2000). Although Internet newsgroups were decidedly important in terms of publishing and distributing information on the case when the publication ban was in effect (Dorland and Walton 1996; Shade 1994), their access was far from universal and was largely limited to those privileged with both the financial and technological resources to access the web. As the stories from non-newspaper media sources are more difficult to obtain and their availability will be limited in comparison, creating a comprehensive and representative sample of news coverage from these sources would have been extremely difficult.

General Coding Process and Analytic Category Development

In order to organize the sheer volume of textual material, we read and coded the data into broad themes. Coding began with the basic open-ended research question, "how is Karla Homolka described, presented, understood, characterized, and/or narrated?" From this question, we relied on an open coding technique that highlighted key themes and trends in Homolka's textual presentation over time so as to account for temporality in any shifts in her characterizations (Strauss and Corbin 1998; Yin 2009, 2011). While we did not force the data into predetermined analytic categories, we did read the texts with some broad narrative figurations in mind, notably with an eye for discussions about her: ordinariness, similarity to her victims, dangerousness, victimization, sexualization, capacity to manipulate, psychopathy, narcissism, beauty/aesthetics, femininity, and remorse. That said, we also aimed to allow the data to speak for itself (Strauss and Corbin 1998) so as to permit categories to emerge organically and to become populated based on trends in the data rather than only through a unidirectional application of the preconceived notions and narrative figurations we brought to the analytic table. The coding frame we developed through this process enabled us to highlight patterns within and between different data sources and to showcase narratives that were either recurring or noticeably absent (Jewkes 2011a,b; Strauss and Corbin 1998; Surette 1994, 2007; Yin 2009, 2011).

While some authors (Bird and Dardenne 1988; Chibnall 1981) argue that news stories about particular issues or cases are largely similar and simply recount the same facts in the same order thus generating what amounts to a "triumph of formulaic narrative construction" (Bird and Dardenne 1988, 67), the accounts in the data sample are not without individual influence. As with academic writing, the different legal actors, reporters, journalists, and columnists "read" the case as a text and interpreted and communicated that reading through the lens of their own experiences and biases; while impartiality may be the goal, it is an ideal and not a reality (Reinharz 1992; Stanley and Wise 1993). For this case, the selection of "newsworthy" topics, the presentation of the various actors and the nuances in the authors' accounts often betray the sentiments of the differing sides of legal counsel (that is, Crown versus defence), individual journalists, as well as newspaper editors. After the data were coded into broad categories, we re-examined those categories in greater analytic depth and detail to begin to refine them into a manageable number, to develop a more sophisticated understanding of the connectedness across categories, and to explore changes in those narratives over time.

The data were initially coded into 17 categories. While a more nuanced reading would easily have generated many additional subcategories, the themes and categories were intentionally restricted to a high-level analysis due to the sheer volume of data in the sample. The general and temporal coding categories used included: the investigation; the publication ban; the trials of both Homolka and Bernardo; the plea bargain; her application for release and eventual release; various personal/aesthetic attributes; and public and media perceptions. These categories are largely straightforward and were used to capture the development of different narrations over time, Homolka's role in the events and to chronicle the main events of the case as they occurred.

The categories pertaining to Homolka specifically were more nuanced in order to identify how she was differently constituted and represented within and between different data sources. The first major thematic category related to Homolka's dual construction as both dangerous and in danger; for which analytic categories included: the level of danger she presented to the public (whether she was thought to pose a danger to others, including to her victims and their families, Bernardo and other individuals); her status as a victim and the degree of her victimization (whether she was *in danger* – from Bernardo, from fellow prisoners while incarcerated, or from the general public upon her release); or whether her potential for danger was presented as being ambiguous. Of note, newspapers did not present Homolka in only one way; often, articles written by different journalists and columnists in the same paper – sometimes appearing on the same day – would narrate Homolka in drastically different ways.

Homolka's physical appearance and sexuality also figured prominently in the data. Using the general theme of "sexuality," the data were coded to include: general discussions of Homolka's appearance and attractiveness (including numerous descriptions of her eyes, hair, clothing, makeup, and fitness and body shape), reports of the nature of her different sexual relationships (with Bernardo, with other men before and after Bernardo, with women in prison and with one man while in prison) and commentary on her pregnancies and new role as a mother. Two subcategories were created to address Homolka's representations as both a sexual victim and sexual predator. The first contained commentary that constituted or commented upon Homolka's identity as Bernardo's sexual victim and the potential risk of her sexual victimization following her release from prison. By contrast, the second subcategory included text that presented her as a sexual aggressor in the sexual assaults and murders as well as in her pursuit of other relationships.

Several coding categories were generated to map the juridical, media, and public reactions both to Homolka and to the case. A high-level, broad category entitled "famous/infamous" included Homolka's treatment as a notorious celebrity in all its forms. This expansive category contains commentary about the "fans" and trial-watchers that followed the case; the plethora of creative works stemming from the case (including fiction and non-fiction books, plays, artwork, a comic book, primetime television legal dramas, infotainment television shows and a feature length Hollywood movie); and ironically, coverage of and commentary on the volume of media coverage that the case received.

We generated another category to capture public sentiments on the case in order to compile the public's sense of moral outrage that was directed toward the crimes, Homolka's plea bargain and sentence, her living conditions in prison and towards Homolka as an individual. Specific examples include discussions of Homolka's "sweetheart deal," her university correspondence courses and characterizations of her "club fed" lifestyle in prison and of her life after release. These sentiments were largely captured through reporters' interviews with key individuals in the cases, including the victims' families and lawyer, commentaries in the major newspapers from regular columnists who followed the case, newspaper editorials and featured op-eds and direct public sentiment from letters to the editor and quoted man on the street interviews.

In the later years of the case, a category entitled "retribution" was added to capture negative sentiments regarding Homolka's release and the general threats that were directed at her. This category included news items such as the Ontario government's highly-publicized warnings that Homolka was not welcome in the province, online death pools predicting the length of time between her release and her death (presumably by unnatural causes) and reactions from the individuals in the Montreal neighbourhoods that Homolka was rumoured to be considering as potential residential destinations upon her release. This category also contained any discussions of Homolka as a remorseful or remorseless subject, the different interpretations of her self-narratives as a victim, as less responsible, as reformed, as apologetic/remorseful and the affective cues (or lack thereof) related to remorse that she was said to exhibit while in court.

The "just like us" category explored the collective public discomfort that Bernardo and Homolka generated as a result of appearing so seemingly "normal" – that is, youthful, attractive, white, heterosexual and belonging to the upwardly- mobile middle class, with some commentators naming them the Barbie and Ken of serial killers. These stories often mention the quiet, middle-class neighbourhood where the couple lived, Homolka's love of animals, her idealization and anticipation of marriage and family life, her teenage years, the couple's physical attractiveness and the normative, albeit idealized, outward public image that the couple worked so diligently to present.

The "race, whiteness and 'good girls'" category further explored the "us" versus "them" divide noted in the "just like us" code and included discussions of these matters as they pertained to Homolka and Bernardo as well as to the victims and their families. The category included representations (or lack thereof) of race, class, space and gendered expectations of "respectable behaviour." In our readings of these concepts of respectable behaviour and whiteness, we focused on instances where different legal actors and journalists interrogated the victims' actions (both before and after encountering Homolka and Bernardo) and their ultimate "worthiness" as victims. The category also included any references to the dissonance between Homolka's (and Bernardo's) behaviour and the gendered, raced and classed norms against which her actions were juxtaposed.

A category entitled "minutiae" was created to capture the breadth of news coverage on Homolka, especially in the later years of the case. This category included small events and news items that would not normally be considered newsworthy for anyone but the most famous celebrities; these items are outside of the realm of what is normally reported on for prisoners or ex-prisoners. The events include Homolka's transfers between prisons, her release plans, the conditions of her release, sightings of her after her release and reports on Homolka's prison relationships with Lynda Veronneau and Jean-Paul Gerbet, all of which serve to highlight her atypical celebrity status.

Of note, the majority of the news coverage during the early years of the case (before 1995) primarily discusses the legal facts of the case, the publication ban and the inability to report on the events of Homolka's trial. In the later years, Homolka's name is connected with many other high-profile court cases, ranging from O.J. Simpson to Robert Latimer to Robert Pickton. Her name was also linked to many important national criminal justice issues in Canada, including debates over the sex offender registry, statutory release, section 810.1 orders, and more recently, reform of the legislation regarding a convicted person's eligibility to receive a pardon.

Notes

1 Other infamous Canadian cases with significant numbers of hits in the database for all years up to 14 July 2014 include David Milgaard (5,139), Marc Lépine (4,662), Clifford Olson (4,703), Robert Pickton (8,067), Robert Latimer (4,616), Ripudaman Singh Malik (3,749), Inderjit Singh Reyat (3,101), Russell Williams (11,580), and Maurice Boucher (2,696).

2 Of note, the *National Post* has only been published since 1998. Therefore, it did not cover the early years of the case, including both trials.

References

Ahmed, S. "Embodying Strangers." In *Body Matters: Feminism, Textuality, Corporeality*, edited by A. Horner and A. Keane, 85–97. Manchester: Manchester University Press, 2000a.
Ahmed, S. *Strange Encounters: Embodied Others in Post-Coloniality*. London: Routledge, 2000b.
Ahmed, S. "Collective Feelings or, The Impressions Left by Others." *Theory, Culture and Society* 21 (2004a): 25–42.
Ahmed, S. *The Cultural Politics of Emotion*. New York: Routledge, 2004b.
Ahmed, S. *Promise of Happiness*. Durham: Duke University Press, 2010.
Alcoff, L.M. *Visible Identities: Race, Gender and the Self (Studies in Feminist Philosophy)*. Oxford: Oxford University Press, 2005.
Allen, H. "Rendering Them Harmless: The Professional Portrayal of Women Charged with Serious Violent Crimes." In *Criminology at the Crossroads*, edited by K. Daly and L. Maher, 54–68. New York: Oxford University Press, 1987.
American Psychiatric Association. *Diagnostic and Statistical Manual of Mental Disorders 5th Ed.* Arlington: American Psychiatric Association, 2013.
Appleby, T. "Mask Lifts as Curtain Falls TRAGIC END: Homolka Finally Couldn't Hide Her Emotions." *The Globe and Mail* A.1, 7 July 1993.
Appleby, T. and G. Abbate. "Press Ban Sought in Trial Homolka Not Innocent Victim of Mate, Court Hears." *The Globe and Mail* A.1, 29 June 1993.
Aries, P. *The Hour of Our Death*. New York: Vintage Books, 1981.
Atherton, T. "TV Series Explores Real Life Legal, Moral Dilemmas: Canadian Writer for Law and Order Draws on Homolka Case to Highlight What Happens When Lawyers Plea Bargain with Criminals." *The Ottawa Citizen* B.10 / FRONT, 21 Feb 2000.
Bagaric, M. and K. Amarasekara. "Feeling Sorry? – Tell Someone Who Cares: The Irrelevance of Remorse in Sentencing." *The Howard Journal* 40 (2001): 364–76.
Balfour, G. and E. Comack. *Criminalizing Women: Gender and (In)Justice in Neo-Liberal Times*. Halifax: Fernwood Publishing, 2006.
Banks, M. "Spaces of (In)Security: Media and Fear of Crime in a Local Context." *Crime, Media and Culture* 1 (2005): 169–87.
Barnett, B. "Medea in the Media: Narrative and Myth in Newspaper Coverage of Women Who Kill Their Children." *Journalism* 7 (2006): 411–32.
Barron, C. and D. Lacombe. "Moral Panic and the Nasty Girl." *Canadian Review of Sociology and Anthropology* 42 (2005): 51–69.
Bazemore, G. "Restorative Justice and Earned Redemption." *American Behavioral Scientist* 41 (1998): 768–813.
Berlant, L. *Cruel Optimism*. Durham: Duke University Press, 2011.
Bertrand, M.A. *La Femme et le Crime*. Montreal: L'Aurore, 1979.

Bibas, S. and R.A. Bierschbach. "Integrating Remorse and Apology into Criminal Procedure." *The Yale Law Journal* 114 (2004): 85–148.

Bird, E. and R. Dardenne. "Myth, Chronicle, and Story: Exploring the Narrative Qualities of News." In *Media, Myths and Narratives: Television and the Press*, edited by J. Carey, 67–86. Newbury Park: Sage Publications, 1988.

Blackwell, T. "Psychologists Suggest Bernardo and Homolka are Psychopaths." *The Ottawa Citizen* A.3, 2 September 1995.

Blackwell, T. "A Little Older, but Still in Command." *National Post* A.1, 3 June 2005.

Blatchford, C. "Teen Victim the Conscience of This Trial." *The Toronto Sun* 8 July 1995.

Blatchford, C. "In Her Best Little-Girl Voice." *The Globe and Mail* A.1, 3 June 2005.

Bonnycastle, K. *Stranger Rape: Rapists, Masculinity, and Penal Governance.* Toronto: University of Toronto Press, 2012.

Bordo, S. *Unbearable Weight: Feminism, Western Culture and the Body*. Oakland: University of California Press, 1993.

Boritch, H. *Fallen Women.* Scarborough: Thompson, 1997.

Boyd, S.C. *Mothers and Illicit Drugs: Transcending the Myths.* Toronto: University of Toronto Press, 1999.

Boyd, S.C. *From Witches to Crack Moms: Women, Drug, Law and Policy*. Durham: Carolina Academic Press, 2004.

Boyd, S.C. "Representations of Women in the Drug Trade." In *Criminalizing Women: Gender and (In)Justice in Neo-Liberal Times*, edited by G. Balfour and E. Comack, 131–51. Halifax: Fernwood Publishing, 2006.

Boyd, S.C. *Hooked: Drug War Films in Britain, Canada, and the United States.* New York: Routledge, 2008.

Brazao, D. "Passionate Love Led to Storybook Wedding." *The Ottawa Citizen* B2, 20 February 1993.

Brennan, S. and A. Taylor-Butts. *Sexual Assault in Canada: 2004 and 2007*. Ottawa: Statistics Canada, 2008.

Brown, B. "Homolka Plea Bargain Report Called 'Whitewash'." *The Windsor Star* C.12, 19 March 1996.

Brown, M.K., M. Carnoy, E. Currie, T. Duster, D.B. Oppenheimer, M.M. Shultz and D. Wellman. *Whitewashing Race: The Myth of a Color-Blind Society*. Berkley: University of California Press, 2003.

Brown, S. "What's the Problem Girls? CCTV and the Gendering of Public Safety." In *Surveillance, Closed Circuit Television and Social Control*, edited by C. Norris, J. Moran and G. Armstrong, 207–20. Aldershot: Ashgate, 1998.

Burnside, S. and A. Cairns. *Deadly Innocence: The True Story of Paul Bernardo, Karla Homolka, and the Schoolgirl Murders*. New York: Warner Books, 1995.

Butler, J. *Gender Trouble: Feminism and the Subversion of Identity*. New York: Routledge, 1990.

Butler, J. *Bodies that Matter: On the Discursive Limits of 'Sex'*. New York: Routledge, 1993.

Butler, J. "Bodily Inscriptions, Performative Subversions." In *Feminist Theory and the Body: A Reader*, edited by J. Price and M. Schildrick, 416–22. Edinburgh: Edinburgh University Press, 1999.

Cain, M. "Realist Philosophy and Standpoint Epistemology." In *Feminist Perspectives in Criminology*, L. Gelsthorpe, and A. Morris, 124–40. Milton Keynes: Open University Press, 1990.

Campbell, Justice A. *Bernardo Investigation Review.* Ottawa: Ministry of the Solicitor General and Correctional Services, 1996.

Canadian Press Newswire. "Crown Really Got Suckered by Homolka's Plea Bargaining." *Times Colonist* 1, 7 Sept. 1995.

Chandler, C. "Feminists as Collaborators and Prostitutes as Autobiographers: Deconstructing an Inclusive yet Political Feminist Jurisprudence." *Hastings Women's Law Journal* 10 (1999): 135–48.

Chibnall, S. "The Production of Knowledge by Crime Reporters." In *The Manufacture of News: Social Problems, Deviance and the Mass Media*, edited by S. Cohen and J. Young, 75–98. London: Constable, 1981.

Christie, N. "The Ideal Victim." In *From Crime Policy to Victim Policy: Reorienting the Justice System,* edited by E.A. Fattah, 17–30. Basingstoke: Macmillan, 1986.

Cleckley, H.M. *The Mask of Sanity: An Attempt to Clarify Some Issues About the So-Called Psychopathic Personality*, 5th Edition. St. Louis: Mosby, 1976.

Collins, P.H. *Black Feminist Thought: Knowledge, Consciousness, and the Politics of Empowerment.* New York: Routledge, 2000.

Comack, E. *Feminist Engagement with the Law: The Legal Recognition of the Battered Woman Syndrome.* Ottawa: The CRIAW papers, 1993.

Comack, E. "The Feminist Engagement with Criminology." In *Criminalizing Women: Gender and (In)Justice in Neoliberal Times*, edited by E. Comack, and G. Balfour, 22–55. Halifax: Fernwood Publishing, 2014.

Comack, E., and G. Balfour. *The Power to Criminalize: Violence, Inequality and the Law.* Halifax: Fernwood Publishing, 2004.

Comack, E., and S. Brickey. "Constituting the Violence of Criminalized Women." *Canadian Journal of Criminology and Criminal Justice* 49 (2007): 1–36.

Connell, R.W. and J.W. Messerschmidt. "Hegemonic Masculinity: Rethinking the Concept." *Gender and Society* 19 (2005): 829–59.

Creswell, J. *Research Design; Qualitative and Quantitative and Mixed Methods Approaches.* London: Sage, 2005.

Crosbie, L. *Paul's Case: The Kingston Letters.* Toronto: Insomniac Press, 1997.

Daly, K. "Restorative Justice and Sexual Assault." *British Journal of Criminology* 46 (2006): 334–56.

Daly, K. and M. Chesney-Lind. "Feminism and Criminology." *Justice Quarterly* 5 (1988): 101–43.

Davey, F. *Karla's Web: A Cultural Investigation of the Mahaffy-French Murders.* New York: Viking Press, 1994.

DeAngelo, L. *The Twisted Relationship of Karla Homolka and Paul Bernardo: Serial Killers.* Baldwin City: Webster's Digital Services, 2011.

de Beauvoir, S. *The Second Sex.* New York: Knopf, 1953.

Dell, C.A. "The Pre-Meditated Creation of the Violent Female Offender in Canada." *Alternate Routes* 15 (1999): 83–116.

Dell, C.A. "The Criminalization of Aboriginal Women: Commentary by a Community Activist." In *Crimes of Color: Racialization and the Criminal Justice System in Canada*, edited by W. Chan and K. Mirchandani, 127–38. Peterborough: Broadview Press, 2002.

Denov, M. *Perspectives on Female Sexual Offending: A Culture of Denial.* Aldershot: Ashgate Publishing, 2004.

DiManno, R. "Homolka Testimony has Chilling Consistency." *Toronto Star* A.10, 23 June 1995.

DiManno, R. "A Breathtaking, Relentless Cross-Examination." *Toronto Star* A.8, 5 July 1995.

DiManno, R. "Karla a Blank Canvas for Courtroom Artists." *Toronto Star* A.9, 6 July 1995.

DiManno, R. "Will the Real Karla be in Court Today?" *Toronto Star* A.8, 2 June 2005.

Dolik, H. "Deals with the Devil?: People Hate Plea Bargains Like Karla Homolka's; Courts Depend on Them." *Calgary Herald* A.10, 3 Sept. 1995.

Doob, A.N. "The Blurring of the Role of the Victim: Bernardo Trial." *The Globe and Mail* A.21, 14 September 1995.

Doran, N. "'Making Sense' of Moral Panics: Excavating the Cultural Foundations of the 'Young, Black Muggers' in Crimes of Colour." In *Racialization and the Criminal Justice System in Canada*, edited by W. Chan, and K. Mirchandani, 157–75, Peterborough: Broadview Press, 2002.

Dorland, M. and P. Walton. "Untangling Karla's Web: Post-National Arguments, Cross-Border Crimes, and the Investigation of Canadian Culture." *American Review of Canadian Studies* 26 (1996): 31–48.

Douglas, M. *Purity and Danger: An Analysis of Concepts of Pollution and Taboo*. Harmondsworth: Penguin Books, 1966.

Douglas, M. "Dealing with Uncertainty." *Ethical Perspectives* 8 (2001): 145–55.

Dowler, K., T. Fleming and S.L. Muzzatti. "Constructing Crime: Crime, Media and Popular Culture." *Canadian Journal of Criminology and Criminal Justice* 48 (2006): 837–50.

Doyle, A. *Arresting Images: Crime and Policing in Front of the Television Camera*. Toronto: University of Toronto Press, 2003.

Duncanson, J., and J. Rankin. "Homolka Opposed Wedding Delay: Letter Slams Dad for 'Wallowing' in Grief Over Tammy." *Toronto Star* A.1, 8 July 1995.

Faith, L. *Unruly Women*. Vancouver: Press Gang Publishers, 1993.

Faith, K. "What About Feminism? Engendering Theory-Making in Criminology." In *Explaining Criminals and Crime*, edited by R. Paternoster, and R. Backman, 287–302. Los Angeles: Roxbury Press, 2001.

Faith, K. and Y. Jiwani. "The Social Construction of 'Dangerous' Girls and Women." In *Marginality and Condemnation: An Introduction to Critical Criminology*, edited by B. Schissel and C. Brooks, 83–107. Halifax: Fernwood Publishing, 2002.

Farran, D. *The Trial of Ruth Ellis: A Descriptive Analysis*. Master of Arts Thesis. Studies in Sexual Politics, Sociology Department, The University of Manchester, 1987.

Feldman, M. *Strategies for Interpreting Qualitative Data*. Thousand Oaks: Sage Publications, 1995.

Fleming, T. "The History of Violence: Mega Cases of Serial Murder, Self-Propelling Narratives, and Reader Engagement." *Journal of Criminal Justice and Popular Culture* 14 (2007): 277–91.

Fontaine, N. "Surviving Colonization: Anishinaabe Ikwe Gang Participation." In *Criminalizing Women*, edited by G. Balfour, and E. Comack, 113–30. Halifax: Fernwood Publishing, 2006.

Ford, C. "Killer Karla Can Run, but She Can't Hide." *Calgary Herald* A.15, 17 November 2002.

Foucault, M. *Archeology of Knowledge*. New York: Harper and Row, 1972.

Foucault, M. *I Pierre Riviere, Having Slaughtered My Mother, My Sister, and My Brother*. London: Random House Inc, 1975.

Foucault, M. *Discipline and Punish: The Birth of the Prison*. Translated by A. Sheridan. New York: Vintage, 1977.

Foucault, M. *Language, Counter-Memory, Practice: Selected Essays and Interviews*. Ithaca: Cornell University Press, 1980.

Foucault, M. *The History of Sexuality, Vol. I*. New York: Vintage, 1980.

Foucault, M. 'The Ethics of the Concern for Self as a Practice of Freedom." In *Ethics: Subjectivity and Truth*, edited by P. Rabinow and M. Foucault, 281–302. New York: The New Press, 1994.

Frankenberg, R. *White Women, Race Matters: The Social Construction of Whiteness*. Minneapolis: University of Minnesota Press, 1993.

Frankenberg, R. *Displaying Whiteness: Essays in Social and Cultural Criticism.* Durham: Duke University Press, 1997.

Frigon, S. "A Gallery of Portraits: Women and the Embodiment of Difference, Deviance and Resistance." In *Post Critical Criminology,* edited by T. O'Reilly Fleming, 78–110. Scarborough: Prentice Hall, 1996.

Frigon, S. "La Création de Choix Pour les Femmes Incarcérées: Sur les Traces du Groupe d'Étude sur les Femmes Purgeant une Peine Fédérale et de ses Consequences." *Criminologie* 35 (2002): 9–30.

Frigon, S. *L'Homicide Conjugal au Féminin: D'Hier à Aujourd'hui.* Montréal: Éditions Remue Ménage, 2003.

Frigon, S. "Mapping Scripts and Narratives of Women who Kill in Fiction (Cinema) and in Fact (Trials): Inscribing the Everyday." In *Killing Women: The Visual Culture of Gender and Violence,* edited by A. Burfoot and S. Lord, 3–20. Waterloo: Wilfrid Laurier University Press, 2006.

Foltyn, J.L. "Dead Famous and Dead Sexy: Popular Culture, Forensics, and the Rise of the Corpse." *Mortality* 13 (2008): 153–73.

Freud, S. trans., *Civilization and Its Discontents* New York: W.W. Norton and Company, 2010.

Frosh, P. "The Public Eye and the Citizen-Voyeur: Photography as a Performance of Power." *Social Semiotics* 11 (2001): 43–59.

Gaarder, E. and J. Belknap. "Tenuous Borders: Girls Transferred to Adult Court." *Criminology* 40 (2002): 481–517.

Galligan, P.T. *Report to the Attorney General on Certain Matters Relating to Karla Homolka.* Toronto: ADR Chambers, 1996.

Gardner, D. *Risk: The Science and Politics of Fear.* Toronto: McClelland and Stewart, 2008.

Garner, S. *Whiteness: An Introduction.* Abingdon: Routledge, 2007.

Garner, S. "A Moral Economy of Whiteness: Behaviours, Belonging and Britishness." *Ethnicities* 12 (2012): 445–64.

Geertz, C. "Thick Description: Toward an Interpretive Theory of Culture." In *The Interpretation of Cultures: Selected Essays,* edited by C. Geertz, 3–30. New York: Basic Books, 1973.

Giddens, A. *Modernity and Self-Identity: Self and Society in the Late Modern Age.* Cambridge: Polity Press, 1991.

Gilbert, P.R. "Discourses of Female Violence and Societal Gender Stereotypes." *Violence Against Women* 8 (2002): 1271–300.

Gilchrist, K. "Multiple Disadvantages: The Missing and Murdered Women of Vancouver." In *Gender Relations in Canada: Intersectionality and Beyond,* edited by A. Doucet and J. Siltanen, 174–5. New York: Oxford University Press, 2008.

Gilchrist, K. "'Newsworthy' Victims? Exploring Differences in Canadian Local Press Coverage of Missing/Murdered Aboriginal and White Women." *Feminist Media Studies* 10 (2010): 373–90.

Gillespie, K. and M. Shephard. "Karla's mother: 'Give her a chance'." *Toronto Star* 1, 4 November 1999.

Glaser, B. and A. Strauss. *The Discovery of Grounded Theory : Strategies for Qualitative Research.* New York: Aldine Transaction, 1967.

Goffman, E. *Stigma: Notes on the Management of Spoiled Identity.* New Jersey: Prentice-Hall, 1963.

Goffman, E. *Relations in Public: Microstudies of the Public Order.* New York: Basic Books, 1971.

Gorer, G. "The Pornography of Death." *Encounter* 5 (1955): 49–52.

Gorer, G. *Death, Grief and Mourning in Contemporary Britain.* London: Cresset Press, 1965.

Grosz, E. *Chaos, Territory, Art: Deleuze and the Framing of the Earth.* New York: Colombia University Press, 2008.

Hale, C. "Fear of Crime: A Review of the Literature." *International Review of Victimology* 4 (1996): 79–150.
Hall, J. "Affluent Appearance Hid Face of a Killer: AM Edition." *Toronto Star* A.18, 7 July 1993.
Hall, S. "The Narrative Construction of Reality: An Interview with Stuart Hall." *Southern Review* 17 (1984): 3–17.
Haraway, D. *Simians, Cyborgs and Women: The Reinvention of Nature.* New York: Routledge, 1991.
Harding, S. *The Science Question in Feminism.* Milton Keynes: Open University Press, 1986.
Harding, S. *The Feminist Standpoint Theory Reader: Intellectual and Political Controversies.* London: Routledge, 2004.
Harding, S. "Rethinking Standpoint Epistemology: What IS Standpoint Objectivity?" In *Feminist Epistemologies*, edited by L. Alcoff and E. Potter, 49–82. London: Routledge, 1993.
Hare, R. "Psychopathy: A Clinical Construct Whose Time has Come." *Criminal Justice and Behavior* 23 (1996): 25–54.
Harper, S. "Advertising *Six Feet Under.*" *Mortality* 14 (2009): 203–25.
Hatty, S., and J. Hatty. *The Disordered Body: Epidemic Disease and Cultural Transformation.* New York, NY: State University of New York Press, 1999.
Hazelwood, R., J. Warren and P. Dietz. "Compliant Victim of the Sexual Sadist." *Australian Family Physician 22* (1993): 474–9.
Headley, C. "Delegitimizing the Normativity of 'Whiteness': A Critical Africana Philosophical Study of the Metaphorcity of 'Whiteness'." In *What White Looks Like: African American Philosophers on the Whiteness Question*, edited by G. Yancy, 87–106. New York, Routledge, 2004.
Hewitt, R. *White Backlash and the Politics of Multiculturalism.* Cambridge: Cambridge University Press, 2005.
Howarth, J. "Executing White Masculinities: Learning from Karla Faye Tucker." *Oregon Law Review* 81 (2002): 186–219.
Jagger, G. *Judith Butler: Sexual Politics, Social Change and the Power of the Performative.* New York: Routledge, 2008.
Jamieson, R. "Punition, Blâme et Stigmate dans une Irlande du Nord Post-Conflit: L'expérience d'Anciens Prisonniers Politiques." *Criminologie* 45 (2012): 115–36.
Jeffords, S. *Hard Bodies: Hollywood Masculinity in the Reagan Era.* New Jersey: Rutgers University Press, 1994.
Jensen, R.E. "A Content Analysis of Youth Sexualized Language and Imagery in Adult Film Packaging 1995–2007." *Journal of Children and Media* 4 (2010): 371–86.
Jewkes, Y. *Media and Crime: Key Approaches to Criminology.* London: Sage Publications, 2011a.
Jewkes, Y. "The Media and Criminological Research." In *Doing Criminological Research* edited by P. Davies, P. Francis and V. Jupp, 245–61. London: Sage Publications, 2011b.
Jiwani, Y. *Discourses of Denial: Mediations of Race, Gender, and Violence.* Vancouver: University of British Columbia Press, 2006.
Jiwani, Y. "Doubling Discourses and the Veiled Other: Mediations of Race and Gender in Canadian Media." In *States of Race, Critical Race Feminism for the 21st Century,* edited by S. Razack, M. Smith, and S. Thobani, 59–86. Toronto: Between the Lines Press, 2010.
Jiwani, Y. and M.L. Young. "Missing and Murdered Women: Reproducing Marginality in News Discourse." *Canadian Journal of Communication* 31 (2006): 895–917.
Jordan, E. "Don't be Fooled by Karla Homolka's Acting Job." *The Province* A21, 21 December 2005.
Kadri, S. *The Trial: From Socrates to O.J. Simpson.* New York: Random House, 2005.
Kamir, O. *Framed: Women in Law and Film.* Durham: Duke University Press, 2006.

Kellehear, A. "Are we a 'Death-Denying' Society? A Sociological Review." *Social Science and Medicine* 18 (1984): 713–21.

Kennedy, J. "Unspeakable Evil Shows its Ordinary Face." *The Ottawa Citizen* B2, 11 July 1993.

Kershaw, A. and M. Lasovich. *Rock-a-bye Baby: A Death Behind Bars*. Toronto: McClelland and Stewart, 1991.

Kilty, J.M. "Gendering Violence, Remorse, and the Role of Restorative Justice: Deconstructing Public Perceptions of Kelly Ellard and Warren Glowatski." *Contemporary Justice Review: Issues in Criminal, Social, and Restorative Justice* 13 (2010): 155–72.

Kilty, J.M. "Tensions within Identity: Notes on how Criminalized Women Negotiate Identity Through Addiction." *Aporia* 3 (2011): 5–15.

Kilty, J.M. and E. Dej. "Anchoring Amongst the Waves: Discursive Constructions of Motherhood and Addiction." *Qualitative Sociology Review* 8 (2012): 6–23.

Kilty, J.M. and S.C. Fabian. "Deconstructing an Invisible Identity: The Reena Virk Case." In *Reena Virk: Critical Perspectives on a Canadian Murder*, edited by M. Rajiva and S. Bataharya, 122–55. Toronto: Canadian Scholars Press, 2010.

Kilty, J.M. and S. Frigon. "Karla Homolka – From a Woman in Danger to a Dangerous Woman: Chronicling the Shifts." *Women and Criminal Justice* 17 (2006): 37–61.

Kong, R., and K. AuCoin. "Female Offenders in Canada." *Jusristat: Canadian Centre for Justice Statistics* 28 (2008): 1–23.

Koskela, H. "The Gaze Without Eyes: Video-Surveillance and the Changing Nature of Urban Space." *Progress in Human Geography* 24 (2000): 243–65.

Lawton, V. "Villain or Victim? Homolka Still an Enigma After Testimony: [FINAL Edition]." *The Ottawa Citizen* A.4, 15 July 1995.

Lee, R.L.M. "Modernity, Morality, and Re-enchantment: The Death Taboo Revisited." *Sociology* 42 (2008): 745–59.

Legall, P. "Homolka Deal Stirs Cries for Public Inquiry: Plea-Bargaining System Questioned in Wake of Revelations in Murder Trial." *The Vancouver Sun* A.4, 1 Sept. 1995.

Li, D., and G. Walejko. "Splogs and Abandoned Blogs: The Perils of Sampling Bloggers and Their Blogs." *Information, Communication and Society* 11 (2008): 279–96.

Lincoln, Y.S., and E.G. Guba. "Paradigmatic Controversies, Contradictions, and Emerging Confluences." In *The Landscape of Qualitative Research: Theories and Issues*, 2nd Edition, edited by N.K. Denzin and Y.S. Lincoln, 253–91. London: Sage, 2003.

Low, S.M. "The Edge and the Center: Gated Communities and the Discourse of Urban Fear." *American Anthropologist* 103 (2001): 45–58.

Mahony, T.H. "Women and the Criminal Justice System." *A Gender-Based Statistical Report*. Ottawa: Statistics Canada, 2011.

Makin, K. "French Made to Smile During Rape, Tape Show Victims' Families Stay Away as Bernardo Jurors View Scenes of Violence, Degredation." *The Globe and Mail*, A.1, 6 June 1995.

Makin, K. "Killing Timed for Alibi, Homolka says Bernardo Wanted French Alive Longer as 'Sex Slave,' but Wife Persuaded Him Easter Dinner was Cover." *The Globe and Mail* A.4, 28 June 1995.

Makin, K. "The Bernardo Trial." *The Globe and Mail* D.1, 2 September 1995.

Makin, K. "K-Day is Here." *The Globe and Mail* F.1, 21 May 2005.

Martel, J. "Remorse and the Production of Truth." *Punishment and Society* 12 (2010): 414–37.

Martin, D.L. "Punishing Female Offenders and Perpetuating Gender Stereotypes." In *Making Sense of Sentencing,* edited by J.V. Roberts, and D.P. Cole, 186–99. Toronto: University of Toronto Press, 1999.

Massey, D. *Space, Place and Gender.* Cambridge: Polity Press, 1994.

Mathiesen, T. "The Viewer Society: Michel Foucault's 'Panopticon' Revisited." *Theoretical Criminology* 1 (1997): 215–34.

McGillivray, A. "A Moral Vacuity in her which is Difficult if not Impossible to Explain: Law, Psychiatry and the Remaking of Karla Homolka." *International Journal of the Legal Profession* 2 (1998): 255–88.

Mennie, J. "At Least we Know the Evil That is Karla Homolka." *The Gazette* A.7, 7 May 2005.

Millbank, J. "From Butch to Butcher's Knife: Film, Crime and Lesbian Sexuality." *Sidney Law Review* 18 (1996): 451–73.

Miller, D. "Capturing the Beauty of the Beast: Aileen Wuornos, Charlize Theron and *Monster.*" *Bright Lights Film Journal* (2004). Retrieved July 16, 2014, from http://brightlightsfilm.com/

Miller, W.I. *The Anatomy of Disgust.* Cambridge: Harvard University Press, 1997.

Morrissey, B. *When Women Kill: Questions of Agency and Subjectivity.* London: Routledge, 2003.

Mulvey, L. "Visual Pleasure and Narrative Cinema." *Screen* 16(3) (1975): 6–18.

Muzzio, D. and Halper, T. "Pleasantville? The suburb and its representation in American movies." *Urban Affairs Review* 37 (2002): 543–74.

N.A. "Bernardo saga to resume." *Leader-Post* A1, 25 March 2000.

N.A. "Karla Homolka's Plea Bargain Still Disputed Many Years Later." *Guardian* A.5, 20 June 2005.

Naaman, D. "In the Name of the Nation: Images of Palestinian and Israeli Women Fighters." In *Killing Women: The Visual Culture of Gender and Violence*, edited by A. Burfoot and S. Lord, 273–91. Waterloo: Wilfred Laurier Press, 2006.

Naaman, D. "Brides of Palestine/Angels of Death: Media, Gender, and Performance in the Case of the Palestinian Female Suicide Bombers." *Signs: Journal of Women in Culture and Society* 32 (2007): 934–55.

Naylor, B. "Women's Crime and Media Coverage: Making Explanations." In *Gender and Crime*, edited by R. Emerson Dobash, R.P. Dobash and L. Noaks, 77–95. Cardiff: University of Wales Press, 1995.

Neroni, H. *The Violent Woman: Femininity, Narrative and Violence in Contemporary American Cinema.* New York: SUNY Press, 2005.

Newmahr, S. *Playing on the Edge: Sadomasochism, Risk, and Intimacy.* Bloomington: Indiana University Press, 2011.

O'Shea, K. "Killing the Killers: Women on Death Row in the United States." In *Killing Women: The Visual Culture of Gender and Violence*, edited by A. Burfoot and S. Lord, 67–82. Waterloo: Wilfred Laurier Press, 2006.

Overall, C. "Homolka Case Suggests Some Women Can Choose to be Monsters." *Standard* 4, 12 June 1995.

Pain, R.H. "Social Geographies of Women's Fear of Crime." *Transactions of the Institute of British Geographers* 22 (1997): 231–44.

Pappe, I. *The Idea of Israel: A History Of Power And Knowledge.* London: Verso Books, 2014.

Pearson, P. *When She Was Bad: Violent Women and the Myth of Innocence.* Toronto: Vintage Canada, 1997.

Peffley, M., T. Shields and B. Williams. "The Intersection of Race and Crime in Television News Stories: An Experimental Study." *Political Communication* 13 (1996): 309–27.

Pollack, S. "Dependency Discourse as Social Control." In *An Ideal Prison?*, edited by K. Hannah-Moffat, and M. Shaw, 72–81. Halifax: Fernwood, 2000.

Pollack, S. "Therapeutic Programming as Regulatory Practice in Women's Prisons." In *Criminalizing Women*, edited by G. Balfour and E. Comack, 236–49. Winnipeg: Fernwood, 2006.

Pollack, S. and K. Kendall. "Taming the Shrew: Regulating Prisoners through 'Women-Centred' Mental Health Programming." *Critical Criminology* 13 (2005) 71–87.

Presser, L. "Remorse and Neutralization Among Violent Male Offenders." *Justice Quarterly* 20 (2003): 801–25.

Price, J. and Shildrick, M. *Feminist Theory and the Body: A Reader.* Edinburgh: Edinburgh University Press, 1999.

Proeve, M.J. and K. Howells. "Effects of Remorse and Shame and Criminal Justice Experience on Judgements About a Sex Offender." *Psychology, Crime and Law* 12 (2006): 145–61.

Proeve, M.J., D.I. Smith and D.M. Niblo. "Mitigation Without Definition: Remorse in the Criminal Justice System." *Australian and New Zealand Journal of Criminology* 32 (1999): 16–26.

Pron, N. *Lethal Marriage: The Unspeakable Crimes of Paul Bernardo and Karla Homolka.* Berkeley: Seal Books, 1995.

Pron, N. and J. Duncanson. "Homolka Press Ban 'Absurd' Trial Told." *Toronto Star* Sec. B, A.1, 30 June 1993.

Pron, N. and J. Rankin. "Homolka Describes Sex Role-Playing Pretended to be Slain Schoolgirls to Try to Please her Husband." *Toronto Star* A.11, 22 June 1995.

ProQuest. Canadian Newsstand. Retrieved 8 June 2011, from http://www.proquest.com/en-US/catalogs/databases/detail/canadian_newsstand.shtml

Rankin, J. "Pain Won't go Away Debbie Mahaffy, Mother of Leslie, says Going to the Courthouse was like Going for Surgery Every Day." *Toronto Star*, E.1, 29 October 1995.

Razack, S.H. "Gendered Racial Violence and Spacialized Justice: The Murder of Pamela George." *Canadian Journal of Law and Society* 15 (2000): 91–130.

Razack, S.H. "A Violent Culture or Culturalized Violence? Feminist Narratives of Sexual Violence Against South Asian Women." *Studies in Practical Philosophy* 3 (2003): 80–104.

Reinharz, S. *Feminist Methods in Social Research.* New York: Oxford University Press, 1992.

Robert, D., R. Belzile and S. Frigon. "Women, Embodiment of Health and Carceral Space." *The Journal of Prisoners' Health* 3 (2007): 176–88.

Robertson, C. "Representing Miss Lizzie: Cultural Convictions in the Trial of Lizzie Borden." *Yale Journal of Law and the Humanities* 8 (1996), Article 2 Retrieved 16 July 2014 from http://digitalcommons.law.yale.edu/yjlh/vol8/iss2/2

Ronsbo, H. "Displacing Enigma and Shaping Communal Hegemony – Towards the Analysis of Violent Experience as Social Process." *Dialectical Anthropology* 30 (2006): 147–67.

Rose, G. *Feminism and Geography: The Limits of Geographical Knowledge.* Minneapolis: University of Minnesota Press, 1993.

Sobchack, V. *Carnal Thoughts: Embodiment and Moving Image Culture.* Oakland: University of California Press, 2004.

Schildrick, M. *Embodying the Monster: Encounters with the Vulnerable Self.* Thousand Oaks: Sage Publications, 2002.

Schippers, M. "Recovering the Feminine Other: Masculinity, Femininity, and Gender Hegemony." *Theory and Society* 36 (2007): 85–102.

Schur, E. *Labelling Women Deviant.* Philadelphia: Temple University Press, 1983.

Seal, L. "Discourses of Single Women Accused of Murder: Mid-Twentieth Century Constructions of 'Lesbians' and 'Spinsters'." *Women Studies International Forum* 32 (2009): 209–18.

Semmens, N., J. Dillane and J. Ditton. "Preliminary Findings on Seasonality and the Fear of Crime: A Research Note." *British Journal of Criminology* 42 (2002): 798–806.

Shade, L. "Desperately Seeking Karla: The Case of Alt. Fan. Karla Homolka." Presented at the Canadian Association for Information Science Conference Proceedings, Montréal Québec: CAIS, 1994. Retrieved from http://www.cais-acsi.ca/proceedings/1994/Shade_1994.pdf

Shaffer, M. "The Battered Woman Syndrome Revisited: Some Complicating Thoughts on Five Years After R. v. Lavallée." *The University of Toronto Law Journal* 47 (1997): 1–33.

Shaw, M. "Women in Prison and Their Defenders." *British Journal of Criminology* 32 (1992): 438–53.

Shaw, M. "Conceptualizing Violence by Women." In *Gender and Crime*, edited by R. Emerson Dobash, R. Dobash and L. Noaks, 115–31. Cardiff: University of Wales Press, 1995a.

Shaw, M. *Understanding Violence by Women: A Review of the Literature.* Ottawa: Correctional Service of Canada. (http://www.csc-scc.gc.ca/text/prgrm/fsw/fsw23/toce_e.shtml), 1995b.

Sheehy, E.A. *Defending Battered Women on Trial: Lessons from Transcripts.* Vancouver: UBC Press, 2014.

Sheehy, E., J. Stubbs and J. Tolmie. "Defences to Homicide for Battered Women: A Comparative Analysis of Laws in Australia, Canada and New Zealand." *Sydney Law Review* 34 (2012a): 467–92.

Sheehy, E., J. Stubbs and J. Tolmie. "Battered Women Charged with Homicide in Australia, Canada and New Zealand: How do They Fare?" *Australian and New Zealand Journal of Criminology* 45 (2012b): 383–99.

Sisjord, M.K. and E. Kristiansen. "Elite Women Wrestlers' Muscles." *International Review for the Sociology of Sport* 44 (2009): 231–46.

Sjoberg, S., and C.E. Gentry. "Reduced to Bad Sex: Narratives of Violent Women from the Bible to the War on Terror." *International Relations* 22 (2008): 5–23.

Smart, B. *Michel Foucault, Revised Edition.* New York: Routledge, 2002.

Smart, C. *Women Crime and Criminology: A Feminist Critique.* London: Routledge and Kegan Ltd, 1976.

Smart, C. *Feminism and the Power of Law.* London: Routledge, 1989.

Smart, C. *Regulating Womanhood: Historical Essays on Marriage, Motherhood and Sexuality.* London, New York: Routledge, 1992.

Snider, L. "Female Punishment: From Patriarchy to Backlash?" In *The Blackwell Companion to Criminology*, edited by Colin Sumner, 228–51. Oxford: Blackwell, 2004.

Stanley, L. and S. Wise. *Breaking Out Again: Feminist Ontology and Epistemology.* London: Routledge, 1993.

Stepan, C. "Tape Caught Homolka in Lie: Lawyer: Crown Could Have Revoked Plea Bargain for Lying About a Fourth Victim, Bernardo's Lawyer Testifies." *The Ottawa Citizen* A5 19 April 2000.

Strauss, A. and J. Corbin. "Grounded Theory Research: Procedures, Canons, and Evaluative Criteria." *Qualitative Sociology* 13 (1990): 3–21.

Strauss, A. and J. Corbin. *Basics of Qualitative Research: Techniques and Procedures for Developing Grounded Theory*, 2nd Edition. Sage Publications, 1998.

Sundby, Scott. 'The Capital Jury and Absolution: The Intersection of Trial Strategy, Remorse, and Death Penalty', *Cornell Law Review* 83 (1998): 1557–98.

Surette, R. "Predator Criminals as Media Icons." In *Media, Process, and the Social Construction of Crime: Studies in Newsmaking Criminology*, edited by G. Barak, 131–58. New York: Garland Publications, 1994.

Surette, R. *Media, Crime, and Criminal Justice: Images, Realities, and Policies.* Belmont: Thomson Wadsworth, 2007.

Sykes, G.M. and D. Matza. "Techniques of Neutralization: A Theory of Delinquency." *American Sociological Review* 22 (1957): 664–70.

Taras, D. *Power and Betrayal in the Canadian Media.* Peterborough, ON: Broadview Press, 2001.

Task Force on Federally Sentenced Women. *Creating Choices.* Ottawa: Correctional Service of Canada, 1990.

The Ottawa Citizen. "Odor Lingers Over Homolka Case: Is Plea Bargaining Being Offered to Compensate for Lazy Police Work." *Calgary Herald* A.12, 20 March 1996.

Thomas, G. "A Typology for the Case Study in Social Science Following a Review of Definition, Discourse and Structure." *Qualitative Inquiry* 17 (2011): 511–21.

Thomas, G. *How to do your Case Study: A Guide for Students and Researchers*. Thousand Oaks: Sage, 2011.

Todd, P. *Finding Karla: How I Tracked Down An Elusive Serial Child Killer*. eBook: Canadian Writers Group/The Atavist, 2012.

Verdun-Jones, S. *Canadian Criminal Cases*. Toronto: Harcourt Brace and Comany Canada, 1999.

Verona, E. and J. Vitale. "Psychopathy in Women: Assessment, Manifestations, and Etiology." In *Handbook of Psychopathy*, edited by C.J. Patrick, 415–36. New York: Guildford Press, 2006.

Wallace, A. "Things Like That Don't Happen Here: Crime, Place and Real Estate in the News." *Crime, Media and Culture* 4 (2008): 395–409.

Walker, L. *The Battered Woman*. New York: Harper and Row, 1979.

Walter, T. "Modern Death: Taboo or Not Taboo?" *Sociology* 25 (1991): 293–310.

Wardle, C. "The 'Unabomber' vs. the 'Nail Bomber': A Cross-Cultural Comparison of Newspaper Coverage of Two Murder Trials." *Journalism Studies* 4 (2003): 239–51.

Wardle, C. "Monsters and Angels: Visual Press Coverage of Child Murders in the USA and UK, 1930–2000." *Journalism* 8 (2007): 263–84.

Weare, C. and W.-Y. Lin. "Content Analysis of the World Wide Web." *Social Science Computer Review* 18 (2000): 272–92.

Webster, H. *Taboo: A Sociological Study*. New York: Octagon Books, 1973.

Weisman, R. "Showing Remorse: Reflections on the Gap Between Expression and Attribution in Cases of Wrongful Conviction." *Canadian Journal of Criminology and Criminal Justice* 46 (2004): 121–38.

Weisman, R. "Remorse and Psychopathy at the Penalty Phase of the Capital Trial: How Psychiatry's View of 'Moral Insanity' Helps Build the Case For Death." *Studies in Law, Politics, and Society* 42 (2007): 187–217.

Weisman, R. "Being and Doing: The Judicial Use of Remorse to Construct Character and Community." *Social and Legal Studies* 18 (2009): 47–69.

Weisman, R. 2014. *Showing Remorse: Law and the Social Control of Emotion*. Farnham Surrey: Ashgate.

White, J.W. and Kowalski, R.M. "Deconstructing the Myth of the Nonaggressive Woman." *Psychology of Women Quarterly* 18 (1994): 487–508.

Wilczynski, A. "Child-Killing by Parents: Social, Legal and Gender Issues." In *Gender and Crime*, edited by R.E. Dobash, R.P. Dobash and L. Noaks, 167–80. Cardiff: University of Wales Press, 1995.

Wilczynski, A. "Mad or Bad? Child-Killers, Gender and the Courts." *British Journal of Criminology*, 37 (1997): 419–36.

Williams, S. *Invisible Darkness: The Horrifying Case of Paul Bernardo and Karla Homolka*. Toronto: Little, Brown and Co, 1997.

Williams, S. *Karla: A Pact with the Devil*. Berkeley: Seal Books, 2004.

Wood, L.A. and C. MacMartin. "Constructing Remorse: Judges' Sentencing Decisions in Child Sexual Assault Cases." *Journal of Language and Social Psychology* 26 (2007): 343–62.

Yancy, G. *What White Looks Like: African-American Philosophers on the whiteness Question*. New York: Routledge, 2004.

Yeager, M. "Ideology and Dangerousness: The Case of Lisa Colleen Neve." *Critical Criminology* 9 (2000): 9–21.

Yin, R.K. *Case Study Method: Design and Methods.* Thousand Oaks: Sage, 2009.
Yin, R.K. *Qualitative Research from Start to Finish.* New York: Guilford Press, 2011.
Young, I.S. *On Female Body Experience: 'Throwing Like a Girl' and Other Essays.* Oxford: Oxford University Press, 2005.
Zehr, H. "Evaluation and Restorative Justice Principles." In *New Directions in Restorative Justice: Issues, Practice, Evaluation*, edited by E. Elliott and R.M. Gordon, 296–303. Cullompton, UK: Willan Publishing, 2005.

Legal Cases and Statutes

R. v. K. Bernardo. (6 June 1993). (unreported) Ontario Court General Division, St. Catharines Registry No. 125.
R. v. P. Bernardo. (1995). O.J. No. 2249 Court No. 274/94, Ontario Court of Justice General Division, Toronto.

Index